WOMEN AS SUBJECTS
South Asian Histories

D1518976

Women as Subjects

South Asian Histories

Edited by

Nita Kumar

University Press of Virginia

Charlottesville and London

Also by Nita Kumar

The Artisans of Banaras: Popular Culture and Identity, 1880-1984 (1988)

Friends, Brothers, and Informants: Fieldwork Memoirs of Banaras (1992)

First published 1994 by Mandira Sen
for Stree, an imprint of Bhatkal & Sen
Calcutta

First published 1994 in the United States
of America by the University Press of Virginia
Box 3608 University Station
Charlottesville, VA 22903
© 1994 by Nita Kumar

Library of Congress Cataloging-in-Publication Data

Women as subjects : South Asian histories / edited by Nita Kumar.
    p.   cm. — (Feminist issues : practice, politics, theory)
   ISBN 0-8139-1521-X. — ISBN 0-8139-1522-8 (pbk.)
    1. Women—India—Social conditions.   2. Women—India—Economic
conditions.   3. Women's rights—India.   4. Feminism—India.
I. Kumar, Nita, 1951– .   II. Series: Feminist issues
(Charlottesville, Va.)
HQ1742.W653   1994
305.42'0954—dc20   93–44077
                                                CIP

Printed in the United States of America

To Irfana and Nandini
for the good times together,
and more to come

Acknowledgements

This book has been made possible by funding from the Ford Foundation in 1988, a travel grant from Brown University in the same year, a fellowship from the American Institute of Indian Studies in 1989-90, and conference funds from the Wenner-Gren Foundation in 1990. In addition, during 1990-91, the Centre for Studies in Social Sciences, Calcutta, has let me use their facilities.

My contributors deserve thanks not only for giving this book its substance, but also for their patience, their cooperation and congeniality, and for the inspiration that I derive from their work. I am very grateful for the comments on my Introduction and on the book in general from Sunil Kumar, McKim Marriott, Som Mazumdar, Gail Minault, William Sax, Lawrie Sears and Mandira Sen. As it happens, I was able to incorporate only some of their comments, but whether directly used or not, all of them gave me ideas to reflect on.

Finally, it is true that at a personal level, my interest in feminism has been further fuelled by the active lives and concerns of our two daughters, Irfana and Saraswati Nandini, and this book is dedicated to them.

South Point Vidyashram   NITA KUMAR
Banaras   1994

Contents

Introduction

NITA KUMAR

I

THE IDEA FOR this volume originated from my past work on Banaras artisans,from the writings of other South Asianists studying North India whose work somewhere resonated with mine, and from my growing familiarity with feminist theory. In my book on popular culture (Kumar 1988) I described the self-perceived world of these artisans. Although the processes of colonial-elite domination and hegemonic construction were addressed in my book, it focused rather on the struggle of subordinate groups towards the construction of identity in radical, little recognized ways.If that was an insightful approach for its time, foreshadowing the more recent literature on protest and resistance, my second achievement was a negative one. I simply left out a vital dimension of reality because it did not stare me in the face, and because I could not interpret much of the evidence offered by my informants. The artisans of Banaras are all typically male, which became my justification for excluding women from my study, even while speaking of the 'people of Banaras', 'Banarsis', and so on. Yet women are vital to the production processes and to the creation of the work and leisure worlds that I had described, in various hidden but fundamental capacities. My informants excluded them in their representations and I did not notice the significance of their exclusion. Later, on taking up a study of education in Banaras, although women once again seemed to deserve little attention, I was wiser and could investigate gaps and silences.

The irony of this neglect of women lies in its conceptual nature. I have been interested in artisans particularly because they are an unrepresented, unknown category who exemplify in their practices most of those things currently being looked for under 'protest': assertion of autonomy through unconventional (non-modern, non-progressive, 'backward') lifestyles, the expression of freedom through distinct work and leisure habits, and so on. These were not recognized as subversion, challenge, or protest because they are simply not the kind of subversion, challenge or protest we are accustomed to. The irony is that the same, now well-known, argument applies to women. Within any community, say, the weavers, the women are a dominated stratum and assert their autonomy, subjecthood and freedom exactly as male weavers do in the larger society, that is, through distinct work and leisure routines, speech and dress codes, cultural practices and lifestyle. These practices of the women are not recognized by the men as constituting protest, and are either denounced as vulgar, lower, 'theirs', or else are silently marginalized, just as is done to artisan culture by dominant classes.

This blindness is not to be found only in my own work. In most studies that focus on the identities of dominated groups there is a failure to theorize sufficiently from the empirical data recovered. These data are rich in their revelation of subcultures and popular cultures, rituals and ceremonies, everyday life and habits that carve out and maintain spaces within which these dominated groups can assert themselves with limited freedom and dignity. These are not practices and activities that originate simply as responses to control by more powerful classes. Nor are they expressions of 'primordial', 'traditional' preferences and affiliations. The data show clearly that these 'subaltern' practices as well as the normative discourses that condemn them as peripheral, backward and other negative attributes are both discourses that develop in tandem, each speaking to the other continuously even if clashing volubly only seldom. Neither is primary; both are constitutive as well as reactive. We may agree that these subversive discourses are being discovered in many different sites in South Asia, but we may question whether they have been theorized sufficiently into a statement of subversion and subjecthood that could also include women. The irony is that we in the South Asian social sciences are particularly well placed to develop such a praxis of the subject, given the parallel situations of a colonized subject, a peasant or a worker in an incompletely formed class society, an untouchable in a caste structure, and a woman in a patriarchy; each at the bottom of his or her own hierarchy. This is also true given our long history of interest in these various processes of domination.

I found that some of my close colleagues were working on similar tasks, even as we engaged with different problems. Raheja, Gold and I, for instance, returned from our second rounds of field work within a couple of years of each other, having each continued to work on old locations (Saharanpur, Rajasthan and Banaras, respectively) with new foci. At the broadest level, our latest concerns included unveiling the covered, listening to the muted, looking for hidden meanings—all discovering a separate, parallel discourse for women within the larger context of a normative, more familiar male-centred discourse. It was this convergence of interests that led me to organize the first panel at the New England AAS meetings at Washington, D. C., in 1989. The goal at this point was to move forward from the previous discussion of women as 'paradox'—the benevolent-malevolent model—to see latent models in the parallel, subversive use of symbols by actors in hidden ways; indeed, to see actors where none had been acknowledged as existing.

An accepted view by now is that protest does not have to take only well-recognized forms but that it can appear in various other permutations of daily life: evasive tactics, counter-cultures of language, genres of song and dance, myths full of double entendres, private correspondence and diary writing, and many pressure tactics of both the Scott model (James Scott 1988) and others. These discoveries were important but did not seem to be going anywhere theoretically. The application of these more general interests to the case of South Asian women particularly has been limited. For me the applicability became evident when stimulated by recent feminist writings. Most of the ones I found useful have nothing to do with South Asia; indeed they are squarely located in the Western problematic (for instance, Campbell 1992; Flax 1990; Gergen 1988; Hawkesworth 1989; McNay 1992; Nicholson 1990; O'Brien 1981; Sanday 1988; Scott 1988; Tong 1989; Walby 1990). Yet they are far from irrelevant: given the central issues in women's studies, they raise questions that can be applied and adapted.

This book will appeal of course to those who concur with my approach to the study of South Asian women, but it is aimed particularly at (*i*) those who work on South Asia but have taken no interest in women as yet, or equally, in women as historical beings (rather than in women as signs), with the conviction that South Asian studies cannot proceed without taking cognisance of the subjectivity of women. And (*ii*) those who are interested in feminist scholarship but not particularly in South Asia may find that the case of South Asian women illustrates the overall problem of women's subjectivity extraordinarily well. The papers are based on empirical research that give rich and up-to-date evidence on the specificities of South Asian culture(s) and power(s). My Introduction, on the other hand, while also discussing these essays, is grounded in the problematizations of a Western-based feminist theory, and a Eurocentric postmodernism. This is not because I tend to be unreflexively derivative but because I think this is the direction that South Asian women's studies should take: not to reject feminist and critical theory in the fear that they threaten to model our data in their own images, but to question, modify and adapt the theory to make sense of specific South Asian discourses. As I see it, this would serve the purpose of more incisive analysis as well as of building a bridge to both non-South Asian feminist work and non-feminist South Asian work.

The problem addressed is a larger one familiar to history and anthropology: How do we conceptualize women (or any subject) and write about them? If I may sum up, there are a few given ways to proceed. One way is to make women further the object of our gaze, by enlarging the scope of each particular discipline and including them in topics, further objectifying them (Krishnamurti 1989). Another is to see them as actors and subjects, with the will, rationality and meaning to re-make the world, in short, to give them the prerogative of males (Forbes 1988). A third is to focus on the structures within which they exist and which seemingly control them without a chance for them to exercise agency, especially patriarchal, ideological, discursive structures (Chatterjee 1989). Yet a fourth is to look at the hidden, subversive ways in which women exercise their agency even while outwardly part of a repressive normative order (Oldenburg 1991).

As the very hierarchization suggests, my preferred postition is the last, and while I separate the third and fourth approaches because scholarship tends to do so, I regard them as inseparable for any but heuristic purposes such as the present discussion. For scholars there has been a clear weighting of the opposite ends of the scale: normative discourse and control on the one; subversive discourse and resisting spaces on the other. One may suggest that scholars do not talk of what they have not weighted because they have not investigated it. But of course it is not *possible* to investigate it if the prior theorization does not exist, apart from the methodologies being understood as at variance. Even within a village, given a similar length of time and the identical approach of participant-observation, data on female health or life expectancy are collected through one set of questions, that on ritual songs or proverbs through another procedure. This may seem incontrovertible and relatively harmless, but the wider conclusions generated, in so far as they proceed to theorize without explicit acknowledgement of the prior choices made can have deleterious effects. The discussion of colonial discourse and of nationalist discourse, for instance—just as of patriarchal discourse—is invaluable, but cannot be valorized into the 'history of women'. The circumscribed perspective on women represented by such discussion reflects the control exercised on women by the discourse itself, and presents, particularly for serious but unprepared students, an unfortunate limitation of agenda.

In the second part of the Introduction I search for the subject through a series of three questions; in the third I review the seven essays in this collection to juxtapose their contributions against each other and make what may be seen to be a sharper analysis for the purposes of this book.

II

The title *Women as Subject* raises the first and obvious question of whether it is desirable to *have* women as subject. Is it desirable to replace the masculine, rational, free subject (as the subject exists today) with a feminine one? I posit the question in this way largely to pull the rug from under the feet of my potential critics who, quite familiar with the Foucauldian and postmodernist critique of the subject as a Western Enlightenment-bred, rational, free, masculine agent who comprehends all in his gaze, would challenge the very title itself. I stand by the title because it gives rise to a very valuable discussion which lies at the heart of the matter, and because it constitutes a problematic issue that will not go away simply by being ignored.

This issue is no less than the status of protest, resistance and autonomy, as expressed through consciousness, experience and agency, therefore, of the nature of power itself. Perhaps all scholars directly interested in subordinate groups, including women, are now wiser in realizing that simply an enthusiasm for reconstructing the history of these neglected constituencies is not of much value. The effort is in fact riddled with dangers on all sides. If the scholar escapes collusion with colonialism and European historicizing epistemology, there is 'the classic figure of Western humanism . . . readmitted through the back door' (O'Hanlon 1988: 191). If she scrupulously attends to the subordinates' expressions of identity through their lived-in practices, she is in danger of falling into 'an essentialism arising from the assertion of an irreducibility and autonomy of experience, and a simple-minded voluntarism deriving from the insistence upon a capacity for self-determination' (ibid.: 198). It is clear that for any scholarship that strives to go beyond the positivist, orientalist, nationalist and other passé and objectifying categorizations, there must be a discussion of the subject.

In addition, there is, as always, a particular problem for women's studies. For studies of South Asian societies, it is Orientalism and Western ethnocentrism that must be recognized. For studies of subaltern groups, it is the colonialist, the nationalist, the marxist-determinist, and the Western humanist model that must be avoided. For studies of women in South Asia, it is all this that must be recognized and avoided plus the phallocentrism

of all dualisms that constitute Western (and Western-derived 'indigenous')
thought.

> This is the risk. The effect of the Law is to build the structure
> of the subject, and as soon as you say, 'well, the woman is
> a subject and the subject deserves equal rights', and so
> on—then you are caught in the logic of phallogocentrism
> and you have rebuilt the empire of the Law. So it seems that
> women's studies can't go very far if it does not deconstruct
> the philosophical framework of this situation, starting with
> the notion of subject, ego, of consciousness, soul and body,
> and so on (Derrida 1987: 193, quoted in Hekman 1990: 68).

The problem of the nature of subjectivity to be ascribed to women is a
difficult one, just as it is—even more so—for those interested in the history
of the objectified in general. To resurrect the Cartesian subject in another
form is to engage in a perpetuation of 'the oppressive effects of an
epistemology based on the principle of a clear and unambiguous distinc-
tion of subject and object in knowledge' (Gallop 1985: 15-16). It is not
only that the subject/object dualism relegates women to an inferior position, it is that all dichotomies are hierarchical, and should be replaced by
knowledge that is pluralistic. In such a vision the subject remains, because
as long as we acknowledge the existence of consciousness and of language
itself, we have to retain the notion of a subject. But this subject is a radical
departure from the Cartesian subject-knower and actor, not merely a
reconceptualization of it. As Kristeva puts it: 'We are no doubt permanent
subjects of a language that holds us in its power. But we are subjects *in
process*, ceaselessly losing our identity, destabilized by fluctuations in our
relations with the other, to whom we nevertheless remain bound in a kind
of homeostatis' (Kristeva 1987: 9).

The very dichotomy between subject and object that may be described
as Cartesian and characteristic of the Enlightenment is a departure perhaps
from an older concept of the subject that characterized ancient and medieval thought (Ong 1967: 225-26). The dichotomy is challenged by the now
familiar postmodernist argument that we should not imagine knowledge
to be some abstraction that is created from the process of an autonomous
subject working on a separate object, but, rather, that knowledge, along
with subjects and objects, is constituted collectively through forms and
discourse. The dichotomy is also challenged (or challengable) through a
tenet quite central to many strands of South Asian thought: knowlege is in

no case unitary and acquirable through one correct method; rather it is plural and heterogeneous, with 'truths' being the norm, not Truth.

Recognition of this leads us to a situation where we cannot replace men's truth with women's truth, men's voice by women's, or subject as presently constituted by a new subject differently constituted. Constituting women as subject entails making them a part of a system that gives power to men and accepting a philosophical system where men are central. Such a system may not be characteristic of the South Asian reality at all, and to accept it is to play a losing game on two fronts: in failing to empower women by bestowing on them a self-defeating subjecthood; and in failing to recognize the subject spaces that do exist for women within South Asian discourse. In the first instance, the dualism may be resisted by paying attention to a philosopher like Foucault who has rejected the 'philosophy of the subject', not so much as by simply ignoring subjects as by re-evaluating subjectivity. Foucault does not overtly discuss femininity in his writings, but his practice is usefully illustrated in, for example, his discussions of sexuality. The essentialism that characterizes some feminist attempts to institute a female subject versus the technique of Foucault is described by Hekman as follows:

> His perspective has been useful to feminists who have sought to define precisely how feminine sexuality has been constituted in our society. But to move from an objection to the patriarchal domination of definitions of feminine sexuality to the attempt to define essential feminine sexuality is self-defeating . . . Feminists can and should oppose the discourse on sexuality that characterizes the modern episteme because it is a discourse that defines women as passive objects. It does not follow from this, however,that we must presuppose an essential feminine sexualtity. To do so is to remain trapped in the Enlightenment epistemology that is defined in terms of essences and absolutes (Hekman 1990: 72).

The same danger of remaining trapped in Enlightenment epistemology and essentialism is what the Subaltern Studies project has also displayed, and being an innovative and daring project, it is naturally expected to teach other similar ventures how to avoid its mistakes. Peasants, labourers and tribals have all been made to display, in the effort to raise them to the status of subjects, questionable essential qualities that characterize them beyond conflict and history. This leaves the project short of its goals because the

determinism of economistic and materialistic readings of action is simply
replaced by an ahistorical idealism (O'Hanlon 1988:212).

A tentative answer to my question, Should we simply posit a feminine
subject to replace the masculine one? then, would be no because:

(*i*) Doing so would not remove the essential dualism that
       characterizes modern, Eurocentric knowledge; what is
       needed is to conceptualize the category 'subject' itself differently.
(*ii*) to continue with the dualism even while instituting a female subject
       that refuses domination by a male subject will not fulfil the
       feminist agenda of rescuing women from an underprivileged po-
       sition in both knowledge and society.
(*iii*) Other efforts to perform a similar operation for other groups, say,
       by the subalternists, have demonstrated the failure inherent in such
       an effort.

So if the subject is not free, autonomous, rational, identifiable and
predictable like modern Western man, the question that arises is: How do
we fashion an appropriate subject?

The first way to do so is to adopt a modified postmodernist, particularly
Foucauldian approach. Foucault's approach consists of dispensing with
the subject in favour of geneology, 'a form of history that can account for
the constitution of knowledges, discourses, domains of objects, etc., without having to make reference to a subject which is neither transcendental
in relation to the field of events or runs in its empty sameness throughout
the course of history' (Foucault 1980: 117). A modified Foucauldian
approach would emphasize that strand in his thought which discusses the
subject as constituted, as formed by discourse, but also the subject that
resists, that can inevitably fashion other discourses (although none would
equal Truth). In other words, since history consists of practices that fuse
knowledge and power, individuals and groups can comprehend their
'subjection' to be at the hands of not an absolute, but one of a plurality of
discourses, one that is deploying—typically in the case of women—one
of several knowledges to define status.

A modified Foucauldian approach would also retain the subject for, let
us say, political reasons, being unable to live up to the epistemological task
of giving up subjectivity on having been denied it for so long and just
discovering it. For the relatively new approach of a feminist social science
(and for the relatively new politics of feminism) the postmodernist questioning of subjecthood is a luxury, it seems at times, that we cannot afford;
or as Braidotti (1987:80) puts it , 'in order to announce the death of the

subject one must first have gained the right to speak as one'. This philosophical inability in the face of political need is of course an ongoing tension for feminist writing (see Stephens 1989; Tharu 1989) and indeed for writing about other underprivileged groups as well. O'Hanlon's comments on the political use of a subaltern identity bears such a close resemblance to the point I am making of the political use of a feminine identity that I quote them in full:

> We must also bear in mind the siren attractions of the idea of the self-constituting human subject, in a political culture in which the free and autonomous individual represents the highest value.To lay claim to this highest value for our subaltern peoples represents an overwhelmingly attractive and apparently effective move, creating possibilities for retributive polemic along the lines of primordial being and distinctive identity, which far outstrips any to be had in a nuanced focus upon practice alone. We can be sure, moreover, that none of the genres of dominant historiography, with their own much more towering subject-agents are about to perform any act of deconstruction upon themselves, thus giving us very little incentive at all to refrain from taking up the same metaphysical weapons in our own cause (O'Hanlon 1988: 197).

Our adoption of a Foucauldian approach would be modified first, then, by our feminist interests, which in turn have to acknowledge their politics. Feminist scholarship is necessarily political in its implications, but it cannot be so at the expense of the necessary qualifications that underlie theorization because that would be to defeat the very purpose of the politics. Even while we want to act for the liberation of women, we must acknowledge that women, as such, have neither been liberated nor repressed. Rather there has been a succession of discourses about femininity, about purity, virtue, honour and womanhood that have displayed knowledge and power differently at different periods. The pattern of these discourses have been androcentric and patriarchal: man as the subject, the rational knower. The constitution of man as subject as been a power ploy. So must the constitution of woman as subject be seen to be.

I have no philosophical or epistemological argument to make regarding my installation of women as subject. I do not maintain that there are any subjects or objects *per se*. There are only people creating and becoming part of historically constituted relationships of power and knowledge. Women are historical beings first and 'women' second. However, in *particular* historical and social contexts women are incontrovertibly part of a system where they are inheritors of certain roles, caught up in a web of symbols that define their being. They perceive the system in certain ways, accept it or challenge it and realign the symbols for themselves. These discoveries are yet very new in the social sciences and partly for that reason give rise to extremist claims. But of course the Truth of women is not superior or morally more valid than that of men. There is no Truth of 'women'.

In other related contexts, our approach would be anti-colonial, subalternist, and South Asian with aims that go beyond the Foucauldian agenda, but are not contradicted by it.Let us examine some of these concerns a little further. A carefully constructed anti-colonialism can deal with the problem of binary opposites set up by the more doubtful term 'postcolonialism' (McClintock 1992; Shohat 1992). Both Foucault and postcolonialism seem to posit systems where the inequality of relations (legitimated by the state and by colonialism, respectively) creates a world in which 'things move, rather than people, a world in which subjects become obliterated, or, rather, recreated as passive objects, a world in which passivity or refusal represent the only possible choices' (Harstock 1990: 166-67). Here I find that a feminist modification of postmodernism is exactly what anti-colonial historical studies do, or should do: 'to develop an account of the world which treats our perspectives not as subjugated or disruptive knowledges, but as primarily and constitutive of a different world' (ibid. : 171).

A subalternist reading that seeks to reinstate people without apparent power into strategists within history, which is how I read women as being, must likewise locate new idioms for alterity (Suleri 1992: 1-15). It is not just that the structure of power is apprehended only by returning the dominated subject to the stage and locating power in the confrontation between domination and subordination. It is that the very paradigm of margin against centre is unhelpful, hierarchizing, as it does, experience. 'Alteritism represents the detail of cultural facticity by citing otherness as a universal trope, thereby suggesting that the discursive site of alterity is nothing other than the familiar and unresolved confrontation between the historical and the allegorical' (ibid. : 13).

Finally, we come to the troublesome question of what a South Asian approach to the subject would look like. We in South Asia or who write about South Asia with empathy do not have our own discourse in any case, feminist or otherwise. We use the Western discourse, the colonial discourse, the Enlightenment modernist discourse, or, at best, the postmodernist discourse. Not only are we as feminists in danger of objectifying the 'non-Western' woman as the Other, we are not rendering her sufficiently complex by thus categorizing her in implicitly negative terms. More important, in our attempts to escape instituting the masculine subjectivity of the rational Enlightenment and to overthrow the dichotomies that we recognize to be hierarchical, we are not asking the prior questions about South Asian reality. Has there been a modernism in South Asia comparable to the European one? Has it, or another process, resulted in similar monolithically constructed dichotomies as in the West that are similarly injurious to women? Is the normative subject of South Asian history as clearly masculine? Does masculinity itself bear the same characteristic marks of rationality, independence, freedom and action that it does in the West?

Precise or tangential answers to these questions have been given only by those whose subject matter has been myths (O'Flaherty, Gold), folktales (Sax, Wadley), literature (Nandy), psychoanalytical data from patients (Kakar, Roy), and the rare, rich ethnographic data from a village. The overall thrust of suggestions on this score is that dichotomies such as body/spirit, mind/matter, inside/outside, and so on, including those of male/female are less rigorously constructed in India than in the West. That there is neither such a clearly delineated normative male subject nor does the expectation arise that everything that does not display the Western man's rational, unitary qualities is necessarily inferior, strange and other. That neither masculinity nor femininity necessarily bear the same characteristics as they do in the West, nor do they have the same relationship to each other.

Having said that, we realize that all this is less helpful than it could have been, since a sociology of South Asian women—or of South Asian men for that matter—has still to be accepted, even where it has been proposed in a limited way (see Marriott 1990, 1991, 1992a, 1992b). The nature of South Asian history has been such that a search for the indigenous degenerates into a quest for the authentic, which has almost certainly never existed anywhere, but in eighteenth- and nineteenth-century India became particularly obfuscated under colonial impact. Precisely those features that we find captured and labelled 'South Asian' turn out, when scrutinized with sufficient historical acumen, to be colonial constructions, or responses to them, or developed through their influence. Or, given the weight of historical research in this direction, we suspect that the 'indigenous' is of dubious innocence even where it has not been demonstrated as so being.

That would of course still leave it as South Asian if only we could abandon the search for authenticity. Apart from historical discontinuity, there is the fabled regional variation, and the less recognized class antagonism (Kumar 1992) that puts a spoke in a South Asian project's wheel. What makes for an authentic identity for one South Asian is nonexistent for another, and often *consciously* so, with a deliberate effort at marginalization.

Two points of recognition to be re-stressed here are that there is no 'South Asian' outside history; and that South Asian reality means socio-economic processes as well, which may or may not be described together with cultural constructions.Thus as Patricia Jeffery and Roger Jeffery maintain in an earlier study, a young woman's position is weak partly because of a cultural South Asian distaste of physiological processes and partly because of the demands of a labour-intensive economy (1989: 150-52). Or as Mies has argued, women's position has worsened, de-mographically and economically, with the very development of capitalism (1988: 29).It is economic processes, again, which largely produce the ideological paradox of nationalism minus bourgeois humanism, and pro-duced the reform movements that used woman as symbol to ease the process of national liberation and modernization (see Mani 1989; Chak-ravarty 1989; and Chatterjee 1989, among others).

I am more sympathetic than most historians to the anthropological project of modelling the many variations of South Asian discourses, and of how they combine, relate, collide and conflict. I am also aware, together with some anthropologists, of the theoretical need to take a position regarding the 'specific historio-discursive determinations' of culture (Ivy 1993: 245-47). Should I say, then, that as we cannot discover or retrieve properly wherein lies South Asian characterization of the subject, the object, the male and the female, let us continue to work with Western concepts as do the rest of the social sciences, and steer clear, at least, of the dangers of essentialism, ahistoricism and Orientalism? To the extent that I espouse application of a modified postmodernism, yes. I do not maintain that postmodernism signals the end of theory or goes beyond the historical constitution of theoretical paradigms. I also think that there can be no escape from challenging Western-based theories, whether colonial or post-, continuously, and looking at the actual South Asian data to interpret what these are saying, as all the essays in this volume do. South Asia has its own discourses of gender and power (the particular configu-rations of which have been always historically constructed, in the last two centuries partly by colonialism), and it is the complex notion of *discourse* with its attendant connotations that we apply, not any *particular* conclusions regarding modernity. Such analysis must necessarily be done in numerous different ways, undoubtedly discipline-based. The appropriate subject for feminist studies in South Asia has to be at least South Asian, although we may be far from sure of what this entails, and although we take the aid of postmodernist theory to ask the first questions.

III

At the simplest level, these essays can be divided by basically two approaches, the anthropological, and the historical. Both these, however, as well as the sociological essay by Jeffery and Jeffery, are characterized by a straining at disciplinary boundaries, which is crucial in the constitution of a female subject. They all, for instance, take seriously the use of language as a means for retrieving feminine subjectivity. In the South Asian case this is usually done in a sociologically oriented way: by assessing the contexts, referential meanings, and often hidden implications of a particular usage by women that differs radically from the usage by men. Although woman in this case is a subject who has made her own selections in language use and is manipulating them purposefully, it can be asserted that she is neither free, nor autonomous, nor necessarily an agent with the power to act. Her language signals her consciousness, her will, and most likely her protest, but the larger implications of this for normative discourse do not add up to revolt and the overthrowing of authority.

This approach is an expansion of the use of linguistic methods in the style of an earlier ethnosociology. To remember an old and pioneering work, David Schneider's *American Kinship* (1968), relied extensively on linguistic analysis (that he sought to establish an autonomous space for culture which I do not support is another matter). Much Chicago-based anthropology took clues from his work and bore results in stimulating and radical interpretation of South Asian social life: radical in the sense of challenging normative Eurocentric rationalist discourse. Again, it is the method, not particular conclusions, that I am discussing here. All the best in the work that followed in later years, concentrated, as far as I am aware, on men, or on the male-centred order. Progressively some scholars trained in Chicago, or Chicago-style anthropology, do apply these ideas to their studies of women. I suggest simply that the intensive, very serious atttention paid to linguistic categories and usage by this approach could be fruitfully extended to the world of women—without the single-mindedness of insisting on a separation of culture from politics and history.

Another approach in our essays is that of a discursive textual analysis, where the very existence of a text is evidence of the consciousness being looked for. As in the case of language, there need be no evidence of 'action', thought/writing is action. Women's writings, as has been demonstrated again and again, express what they nowhere else manage to articulate or, yet more difficult, act upon. A diary, correspondence, autobiography, or perhaps published piece, as well as myth or tale, displays to us evidence of that submerged but struggling notion of a subject-identity that is otherwise displayed by radical action. These texts, even when revelatory of no very radical messages, can be read for the doubts, confusions and aspirations that characterize the fashioning of a non-normative discourse.

A second discipline-based approach that seeks to construct an appropriate subject is the historiographical one. I have already offered theoretical comparisons with the subalternist effort, and in methodology a direct parallel exists. For both women's history and the history of peasants, tribals and labourers, men or women, the academic effort is one of progressive sophistication in expanding the sources of historical data, analysing these data in ways to make them reveal more, weighing and adjudicating the biases of the data and establishing that there could have been people in the past who if not actors and agents *could* have been actors and agents. That they did not lack consciousness or will; that they had parallel discourses; that these discourses had varying relationships with dominant ones, sometimes loyalist, sometimes subversive, sometimes scornful and silent, at other times directly challenging. The historiographical effort needs not only this breakthrough in using new data but a further theoretical widening of agenda because it is after all only when history is recognized to be also about certain routines and patterns that do not conventionally constitute 'events' that the history of the majority of the people in the world will get written at all.

This collection is rich in ethnographical and historical detail. I have tried scrupulously to discuss and indeed include approaches that are theoretized or may be theoretized on the basis of empirical data, and not merely critical and meta efforts, to borrow a phrase from Jonathan Spencer (1989). The deconstruction of controlling discourses, colonial, nationalist, modernist and gendered, whether undertaken within the postcolonial, postmodernist, poststructuralist or 'post-foundationalist' rubrics is enlightening, even exciting in its analytical brilliance. It has come to seem repetitive to me, however; unilateral in its perception of agency; elitist in its choice of sources and interpretive strategies; and hopelessly dualistic in its indifference to the many alternative discourses that dominate experience.It also has connotations of negativity: it has become all too easy to discuss at length what an appropriate subject for feminist studies—and for historical and anthropological studies in general—should *not* be, and indeed what we are *not* to constitute ourselves to be. We know we are not orientalist, nationalist, marxist-determinist, functionalist, culturalist or postmodernist theorists. The more difficult question is, What are we? To be aware of the pitfalls of defining an 'is-ness' is not to reject the possibilities of women's history. My interest in the question of how we fashion an appropriate subject and the preceding discussion of possible approaches as Foucauldian, historiographical, linguistic, and ethnographical are all based squarely on an understanding of actual work that has been and is being done, and is represented here.

I would like to summarize the kind of feminine subject we are talking about in the light of these essays. Firstly, the subject must be South Asian,which is suggested without being complacent about what it implies. Ann Gold and William Sax are the only ones who state head-on that they are working with different epistemologies. Gold actually sums up what she considers to be characteristics of gender identities in South Asia, of which one important point is the lack of a sharp differentiation between male and female roles. Sax likewise speaks of the 'radically un-Cartesian assumption that governs much of Indian thought—that the world is fundamentally one'. For both Gold and Sax, these and other such observations are not made in the spirit of finality, either as axioms or conclusions. Rather, they arise from the kind of subject matter both are considering, chiefly, creation myths and folktales, and are used as assumptions which may be borne out by further interpretation. The burden of proof, in other words, is fully assumed by them. Gold freely admits to a situation of male biological, political and economic dominance. That is, of the various constitutive elements in South Asian history, some may bear resemblance to the Western patriarchal order with its dualistic ideology, while others may contrast sharply in their fluidity of identity characterizations.

Patricia Jeffery and Roger Jeffery's essay throws further light on this issue by displaying clearly that the demographic and development literature,within which they started off investigating the issue of women's autonomy, with its Western points of origin, does violence to the complexity both of the social structure and of the individual's will to act. This literature,concentrating on pre-chosen variables, as it does, underestimates the impact of the social constraints and the subjugating discourses within which women operate. Through an excessively narrow definition of autonomy, it also misunderstands what women assess in their best interests as possible and desirable to do. The course to adopt is clearly to modify, if not revolutionize, many of the assumptions within the demographic literature regarding universalist definitions of 'autonomy', 'control', 'progress' and even 'education'.

Gail Minault and Gloria Raheja have chosen to write on purdah and kinship, respectively, which must necessarily be understood in South Asian terms; but the matter does not end there. Even a South Asian perspective such as was recovered by cultural-symbolic anthropologists may have a male and a female version. As the myths collected by Sax and Gold reveal about procreation and violence, Raheja and Minault's examination of purdah and kinship demonstrate both to be aspects of the social world about which information has hitherto been available chiefly from the exigesis of male informants. The absence of female constructions, as Raheja and Minault show us, is not because they do not exist but because they were not theorized as existing, not searched for, and not analysed. In other words, there may be a first need to evoke a South Asian epistemology, or to discuss South Asian representations, but that can hardly give us a respite from tasks at hand. A further differentiation may need to be made, not only between a Judaeo-Christian and a Hindu/Muslim model (to adapt Gold's terms), but within the South Asian model, among discourses of class, power and gender. The 'South Asian' turns out to be a heterogeneous category on many levels.

Of the active educationists discussed in the paper by Kumar, some have been totally silenced in the institutional records, and some have found it necessary to speak in a male patriarchal voice that conforms and elicits support from men for ventures actually oriented to women's progress. These are not notably South Asian processes. There are also women, however, who have seemingly been marginalized as saints and ascetics, who have found that these identitites provide excellent avenues for action. The saint-ascetic discourse is indeed culturally constructed. Moreover, it is only attention to cultural configurations that reveals to us the spaces within these discourses, which enable women to act, and the logic they employ in doing so. Any notion of freedom, autonomy and power that did not rely on the precise meanings of these terms in their cultural contexts would leave us weakened in our retrieval of the subject.

Secondly, these essays have not focused specifically on social structures and hegemonic discourses, which are seen as necessary constitutive elements of the subject. None of the papers in this volume is predominantly about colonialism, even though for the historical essays of Minault, Kumar and Flemming, the colonial situation, together with its nationalist and reformist responses, forms a necessary backdrop. Again, no essay is exclusively about other's constructions of women—partial, distorting, misplaced, injurious—that is, about controls on women ranging from the subtle to the explicit, by implication, about what women were not or what they could not do. But in emphasizing this, I do not mean to suggest that our decision is a retributive one, that is, to offer the exaggeration of women's agency, only to fall into the trap made familiar by nationalist and much subalternist history writing.

Rather, the constructions of an authoritative voice—of male kin, reformers, social leaders, and so on—are seen as crucial to the project, even if they are not the focus. In some cases, as for Minault and Kumar, these authoritarian voices form the very evidence which allows, given its explicit biases and distortions, for an interpretation of the subject. Minault explicates how in the parallel world of the zenana, there is neither an obliviousness to male discourse, nor an indifference to it, nor in any sense subjection to it; but rather a creative—if often frustrated—interplay of silence, collaboration and protest. Kumar's essay highlights that certain gaps and even actual conflicts in historical records become striking when approached with the notion of the 'underside' of history. In other cases, the voices of authority keep our interpretaion in balance. The degree and efficacy of agency can never be measured fully, but may be comprehended realistically only in the context of domination. As Jeffery and Jeffery succinctly put it, it is only in comparison with larger structures that our subjects—and their weapons—come to be defined as weak, which brings us to the realization that weak subjects, weak weapons and weak efforts cannot be expected to bear forth powerful results.

For our contributors, Gold, Raheja and Sax, the focus of analysis is an alternative discourse expressed through song and story.The subject that emerges is one that resists vocally by fashioning her own narratives, but an assessment of the status of these as resistance can be made only with reference to dominant discourses. Only when set against the normative voice is there any meaning to the reversals embodied in the subject's narratives. One may complain that it is not clear how these strategies of resistance operate. The alternative model of the women may look like resistance but in fact it may be totally suppressed and powerless. The social structural constraints on the ability to act may be far greater than a posited compulsion to act as glimpsed through speech. In some cases, it may be pointed out, as in the essay by Sax, there is no evidence of any compulsion to act whatsoever, to protest in any way, rather, evidence of actual victimization, as suicide victims fall at the hegemonic structure's stake year after year.

We have subjects, in short, who act, as action is commonly understood, but it is more likely that we have subjects who at best 'merely' speak. In both cases there is a larger structure that binds them—and is unquestionably dominant, powerful and controlling—so much is implied in the very enquiry about women as subordinate. The jump we have to make is to envision how in both these, and other cases as well, there is an attempt to assert themselves within this structure of power, through the posing of alternative models, sometimes deceptive in their mutedness. But in all cases there is partial alignment with these very dominant structures, so that autonomy is never complete, it is often ambiguous, and is probably not always desired.

Another reason why it is essential to devote attention to larger social and discursive structures, whether we are historians, anthropologists or any other kind of scholars, is that these structures give us clues as to where the fault lines lie in otherwise monolithic constructs, where spaces exist that may be widened and utilized; what the portents of change are. Again, Jeffery and Jeffery state this the most explicitly when they wonder: What will happen when all the girls are educated? When they, as educated mothers-in-law, interact with educated daughters-in-law? When the needs of farming do not necessitate shared hearths? Other essays also demonstrate similar reasoning. Minault shows that it was precisely the Islamic reformist stress on a hypothetical equality before God that could be used by women to push for education. Kumar, likewise, points to all the spaces in normative Hindu discourse for women, even widows, to act within, utilizing them for their own purposes. Flemming describes the situation for three Christian women that definitely applies to many women. They are poised between different social and cultural backgrounds, historical identities and formative influences, each of which could be authoritarian in itself but is also available as a space within which to manoeuvre and develop.

At one level, rituals of rebellion have their own meaning, not only for the dominant ideology but also for the subordinated women. This is brought out clearly for speech genres by Minault when she makes a semi-utilitarian analysis, showing how zenana speech helped to cope with the pressures of everyday life. Raheja argues that there is contestation and negotiation in the very nature of songs and proverbs, and one also derives from her analysis a sense of the everyday 'function' of these parallel articulations of family and kinship roles. It is a misjudgement of the nature of normative discourse to believe that it can so effectively suppress and so completely ignore subordinate discourse that the latter merely reinforces authority. To speak in an alternative voice is already to assert a subjectivity and be active in the creation of one's own world. Women in Rajasthan, Saharanpur or the Garhwal have seemingly gone on singing the same alternative songs generation after generation; and while there is value in these songs as rituals of rebellion, there is surely some negotiation of change in their situation, and history exists for them as well. In order to discover this we must pay careful attention to larger social and discursive structures. Since these tell us of the very spaces within which women act; we have a glimpse of potential and possible enlargements and perhaps transformations of their spaces. A cross-sectional view, such as most of us are typically obliged to adopt, may show us a very powerless subject, but a subject may be powerless only at a given point or in the short run.

Thirdly, there is the vision, developed to different degrees in these essays, of what we may call the discovery of agency. It is linked crucially to the power of normative structures and cannot be separated for any but heuristic purposes. What the subject-agent looks like differs from one case to the other. In some cases, women act but do not speak: the women educationists in Banaras have left no records of their efforts or experiences; such writings as there are in journals and school souvenirs are deliberately impersonal. They echo the male patriarchal voice with such formality that when contrasted with the radicalism of the same women it seems like a conscious muffling of a subjective voice.

The women interviewed by Jeffery and Jeffery, likewise, seem not to have any alternative discourses; regarding the control of economic resources and choices in reproductivity, their opinion seems to coincide exactly with their menfolk's. But one can glimpse the incongruencies. Firstly, we know not to expect an articulated difference on each subject. The village women of Bijnor may seem relatively unadventurous when discussing money matters, but may have turned to spitfires when speaking of their husbands' moral transgressions. Secondly, even on the questioned topics, these women do speak out, even if guardedly, and moreover they act. What is relevant for us is that given what I consider to be a degree of academic rheumatism induced by the formal training into separate disciplines that we experience, each scholar looks beyond the answers that emerge on the surface. A search for agency necessitates this. Jeffery and Jeffery look at local language use when conventional academic terminology shows itself to be inappropriate. Kumar turns to women's oral reports in the absence of any historical evidence of their activity in a certain period.

Whatever their disciplines, all the contributors also use parallel methods from anthropological, historical, linguistic and literary analysis. This irreverence for established disciplinary boundaries could and should go further in the search for a female subject.

Excepting the essays by Jeffery and Jeffery and Kumar, most of the essays are about women who are very vocal, but may not translate their speech into action. Flemming's women use both speech and action as weapons for their purposes, and Gold's extraordinary Shobhag Kanwar is suspected of using both. But the rule is that we must discover voices that range from the mildly defiant to the eloquently challenging, both seemingly silenced or marginalized through the exercise of a more powerful discourse. Our essays make an advance in the older exercise of elaborating on this marginalization and silencing (Chatterjee 1989; Mani 1989; Chakravarti 1989) by describing how subjectivity gets constituted through the articulation of alternative perspectives. The analysis is based on new and persuasive data, linking up the struggles of a fluid, unformed, dominated subjectivity with the discourse of larger hegemonic structures in ways that allow us to glimpse further recourses for speech and action. A discourse, after all, comprises both power and knowledge. Neither is the prerogative of those in control. Women's discourses must be read as their alternative knowledge and also as necessarily exercising power as well, presently or potentially.

Let me summarize with regard to our primary question: What would 'women as subject' look like? Our discontent with the male subject as presently constituted and with the necessity for searching more carefully in the past and for listening more closely to half-silent voices have already told us of some salient characteristics of this subject. 'It' is discontinuous and apparently contradictory, not consistent, unified, or freely choosing but a palimpsest of identities, constituted and reconstituted, constantly in flux (see Pathak and Rajan 1989). There is no 'it' to pin down; the very category of 'woman' is predicated on a society's shifting discourse of sexuality. As in all discourse, this knowledge of sexual difference, of what a woman is, is socially and politically constructed, is present in institutions and structures, as well as in everyday speech. As such, this knowledge constitutes equally men and women, the only difference being that men are politically dominant, and our task is to give weight to women.

As stressed at the beginning, although we continue to speak of a subject, this is not the familiar masculine subject with an operative will. The perspective we can adopt is of alternative discourses, where signs indicating a woman's subjugation exist, are seemingly accepted, passively or actively, but are most often changed. New spaces are constantly created from within which women can speak and create in their own terms their own definitions of autonomy and power. What seems to us to be on the outside, namely, normative hegemonic discourse, is easily available to us and simple to deconstruct. What seems to us to be on the inside, private, hidden and silenced, is mysterious and indistinguishable. Not only can we not interpret it right away, we cannot even locate it easily. It even needs a jump of the imagination, a wielding of methodology that makes us uneasy, being trained in a tradition oriented to other kinds of discoveries. Further, our acceptance of the normative is so mechanical that we seldom question its contradictions or ambiguities. These same paradoxes in non-normative discourse make it problematic for us and confuse us into wondering if it can be taken seriously.

The subject we want is fashioned by discourse, but is not a passive recipient of it, certainly not of its symbols and meanings which typically contain the broadest messages of the discourse. Even when the terms of the discourse seem unchanged, the slight displacement of a symbol from its conventional positioning is enough to codify completely different, opposing meanings for the subject. This could be one expression of her agency, and must be looked for with a sensitivity to the use of symbols. At another extreme there could be action, or invocation to action, that is positively challenging. The whole spectrum of protest, from daily 'private' acts and intentionally ambiguous language to elaborate myths and execution of violent oppositional deeds, should be seen as part of the same structure of power as that which creates the dominant discourse. Because we know that power is not located at any one level but diffused throughout the system, because power is never unilaterally exercised, both parties to its exercise constitute it and respond to it.

Only in these terms can we install a subject that would both have agency and be comprehensible as a collaborator. Let me point to a few important differences with the male subaltern subjects of the Guha volumes. Whereas both the subaltern and feminine subjects display the same complexities: they are simultaneously empowered and powerless, active and passive, constituted and constituting; one difference is that in the women's case, the lack of separation from the 'enemy', the collusion with the enemy and the non-identification of the enemy is even greater (see MacLeod 1992). Women are in many instances indistinguishably part of the normative male discourse, including the construction of it, even as they are utterly absent from it in other instances. A second point of difference is the extreme heterogeneity of the people called 'women'; unified not by class or region,

Nita Kumar

history or culture, only tenuously by biology (see O'Brien 1981), and not at all by age.

Our discussions of what would be our appropriate feminine subject have been, we hope, conducted with care: an agent, yes, but one constantly sought to be objectified by repressive 'malestream' discourse, as well as by economic and political structures in most cases, and in the representations of academics and ideologues. In each particular instance, we constitute her subjectivity by noting what her alternative discourses are saying or suggesting, and why; realizing all the time that there is no larger fixed category of 'woman' who has any essential characteristic whatever; recognizing the tension in this ethically somewhat irresponsible position towards feminism.

References

Braidotti, Rosi. 1987. Envy: Or with your brains and my looks. In Alice Jardine and Paul Smith, eds., *Men in feminism,* pp. 231-41. New York: Methuen.

Campbell, Kate, ed., 1992. *Arguments in the disciplines.* Philadelhia: Open University Press.

Chakravarty, Uma. 1989. Whatever happened to the Vedic *dasi?* In Kumkum Sangari and Sudesh Vaid, eds., *Recasting women: Essays in colonial history.* Delhi: Kali for Women.

Chatterjee, Partha. 1989. The national resolution of the women question. In Kumkum Sangari and Sudesh Vaid, eds., *Recasting women: Essays in colonial history.* Delhi: Kali for Women.

Derrida, Jacques. 1987. *The post card: From Socrates to Freud and beyond.* Chicago: University of Chicago Press.

Flax, Jane. 1990. *Thinking fragments: Psychoanalysis, feminism and postmodernism in the contemporary West.* Berkeley: University of California Press.

Forbes, Geraldine. 1988. The politics of respectability: Indian women and the Indian National Congress. In D. A. Low, ed., *The Indian National Congress.* Delhi: Oxford University Press.

Foucault, Michel. 1980. *Power/Knowledge.* New York: Pantheon.

Gallop, Jane. 1985. *Reading Lacan.* Ithaca: Cornell University Press.

Gergen, Mary M., ed., 1988. *Feminist thought and the structure of knowledge.* New York: New York University Press.

Gold, Ann Grodzins. 1989. Stories of *shakti:* Interpreting female violence in some Rajasthani traditions. Paper presented at the AAS meetings, Washington D.C., March 1989.

Guha, Ranajit., ed., 1982-89. *Subaltern Studies* vols. 1-6. Delhi: Oxford University Press.

Harstock, Nancy. 1990. Foucault on power: A theory for women? In Linda Nicholson, ed., *Feminism/postmodernism.* New York: Routledge.

Hawkesworth, Mary E. 1989. Knowers, knowing, known. Feminist theory and claims of truth. *Signs* 14, 3.

Hekman, Susan J. 1990. *Gender and knowledge: Elements of a postmodern feminism.* Cambridge, UK: Polity Press.

Ivy, Marilyn. 1993. (Ef)facing culture; a reply to Greg Urban. *Public Culture* 245-47.

Jeffery, Patricia M., and Roger Jeffery, and Andrew Lyon. 1989. *Labour pains and labour power.* London: Zed Books.

Kakar, Sudhir. 1978. *The inner world.* Delhi: Oxford University Press.

Krishnamurti, J., ed. 1989. *Women in colonial India: Essays on survival,work and the state.* Delhi: Oxford University Press.

Kristeva, Julia. 1987. *In the beginning was love: Psychoanalysis and faith.* New York: Columbia University Press.

Kumar, Nita. 1988. *The artisans of Banaras: Popular culture and identity, c. 1880-1984.* Princeton: Princeton University Press.

—. 1992. *Friends, brothers, and informants.* Berkeley: University of California Press.

MacLeod, Arlene Elowe. 1992. Hegemonic relations and gender resistance: The new veiling as accommodating protest in Cairo. *Signs* 17, 3 (Spring).

Mani, Lata. 1989. Contentious traditions. In Kumkum Sangari and Sudesh Vaid, eds., *Recasting women: Essays in colonial history.* Delhi: Kali for Women.

Marriott, McKim, ed. 1990. *India through Hindu categories.* New Delhi: Sage.

—. 1991. On 'constructing an Indian ethnosociology'. *Contributions to Indian Sociology* (n.s.) 2: 295-308.

—. 1992a. Alternative social sciences. In John MacAloon, ed., *General education in the social sciences: Centennial reflections,* pp. 262-78. Chicago: University of Chicago Press.

—.1992b. Personal communication.

McClintock, Anne: 1992. The angel of progress: Pitfalls of the term 'post-coloni-alism'. *Social Text.*

McNay, Lois. 1992. *Foucault and Feminism: Power, gender and the self.* Cambridge, U.K.: Polity Press.

Mies, Maria, Claudia von Werlhof, and Veronika Bennholdt-Thomson. 1988. *Women: The last colony.* London: Zed Books.

Nandy, Ashish. 1980. *At the edge of psychology.* Delhi: Oxford University Press.

Nicholson, Linda J. 1990. *Feminism/Postmodernism.* New York: Routledge.

O'Brien, Mary. 1981. *The politics of reproduction.* London: Routledge and Kegan Paul.

O'Flaherty, Wendy Doniger.1980. *Women, androgynes, and other mythical beasts.* Chicago: University of Chicago Press.

O'Hanlon, Rosalind. 1988. Recovering the subject: *Subaltern Studies* and histories of resistance in colonial South Asia. *Modern Asian Studies* 22, 1: 189-224.

Oldenburg, Veena T. 1991. Lifestyle as resistance: The case of the courtesans of Lucknow. In Douglas Haynes and Gyan Prakash, eds., *Contesting power: Resistance and everyday social relations in South Asia.* Delhi: Oxford University Press.

Ong, Walter. 1967. *The presence of the word.* New Haven: Yale University Press.

Pathak, Zakia, and Rajeswari Sunder Rajan. 1989. Shahbano. *Signs* 14, 31: 558-82.

Raheja, Gloria Goodwin. 1988. *The poison in the gift.* Chicago: University of Chicago Press.

Roy, Manisha. 1975. the concepts of 'feminity' and 'liberation' in the context of changing sex roles: Women in modern India and America. In Dana Raphael, ed., *Being female: Reproduction, power and change.* The Hague: Mouton.

Sanday, Peggy Reeves. 1988. *Female power and male dominance: On the origins of sexual inequality.* Cambridge, U.K.: Cambridge University Press.

Sax, William. 1989. The many forms of Nandadevi. paper presented at the AAS meetings, Washington, D. C., March 1989.

Schneider, David. 1968. *American kinship: A cultural account.* Englewood Cliffs, N.J.: Prentice-Hall.

Scott, James. 1988. *Weapons of the weak: Everyday forms of peasant resistance.* New Delhi: Oxford University Press.

Shohat, Ella. 1992. Notes on the 'post-colonial'. *Social Text.*

Spencer, Jonathan. 1989. Anthropology as a kind of writing. *Modern Asian Studies* (n.s.) 24: 145-64.

Stephens, Julie. 1989. Feminist fictions: A critique of the category 'non-Western woman' on feminist writings on India. In Ranajit Guha, ed., *Subaltern Studies,* 6, pp. 92-125. Delhi: Oxford University Press.

Suleri, Sara. 1992. *The rhetoric of English India.* Chicago: University of Chicago Press.

Tharu, Susie. 1989. Response to Julie Stephens. In Ranajit Guha, ed., *Subaltern Studies,* 6, pp. 126-31. Delhi: Oxford University Press.

Tong, Rosemarie. 1989. *Feminist thought: A comprehensive introduction.* Boulder,Colorado: Westview Press.

Wadley, Susan. 1975. *Shakti:* Power in the conceptual structure of Karimpur religion. Series in Social, Cultural, and Linguistic Anthropology, no. 2, Department of Anthroplogy, University of Chicago.

——. 1977. Women and the Hindu tradition. *Signs* 3, 1.

Walby, Sylvia. 1990. *Theorizing patriarchy.* Oxford: Basil Blackwell.

1

Gender, Violence and Power :
Rajasthani Stories of Shakti

ANN GRODZINS GOLD

Preface

THE ANGRY, weapon-wielding female divinities who people India's rich
mythology present compelling images. Such larger-than-life figures
emerge from and interact with real peoples' minds, hearts and gender
politics; the realities of sword-wielding, skull-garlanded goddesses somehow interpenetrate the realities of their worshippers. Many questions
might then be posed—and many answers proposed—as to the nature of
this interpenetration. There is no lack of scholarly attempts to explain these
figures' existence and meanings, whether in psychoanalytic, religio-his-
torical, or sociological terms. Hindu images of divine female fury may be
viewed as emerging from projected terrors of boys overawed by their
sexually frustrated mothers' all-consuming love; or as manifestations of
destructive and creative harmonies that sustain the universe; or as projec-
tions of a patriarchal kinship system that fears and suppresses female
sexuality while exalting motherhood.[1] In one culturally sensitive explora-
tion of females in the realms of oral traditions, A. K. Ramanujan describes
the way that an ordinary woman literally swells into a goddess in righteous
anger, and suggests that Hindu culture understands all women to have such
capacity (1986).

In this essay I offer no causally oriented formulations explaining how
lives become story or stories enter lives. My limited aim is to point out
some patterns, and highlight what I am convinced are shifting, complex
and analytically elusive relationships.[2] To do so I shall juxtapose expansive
questions about the relationship between culturally transmitted images and
human lives with a compact set of materials—narratives drawn from a
Rajasthani myth, a Rajasthani legend and a tidbit of Rajasthani village
gossip.[3] A single specific image links the three narratives: a female arm
brandishing a weapon. But the severed or threatened necks vary: her sons',
her own, her husband's.

I begin with an elementary, schematized consideration of some prime 'paradigms and paradoxes' of gender identity in Hindu South Asia. There follow three stories of *shakti* encountered in a single village in Rajasthan during fieldwork in 1979-81 and 1987-88. The stories are set, respectively, in mythic time, in history, and in human memory. Each represents a strong female—divine, transfigured, or mortal. Her actions are in each case moulded, with varying results and implications for herself and those around her, by patterns of gender relations given in cosmology and society. In concluding I suggest some ways the stories of female fury comment on broader cultural configurations.

One paradox I will not consider—although it no doubt lies at the root of this essay's existence—is the fascination India's violent goddesses exercise on Western minds. Judaeo-Christians have no comparable figures in their mythologies—no such divinely capable and sexually aggressive creatrices, no such gruesomely determined saviouresses, no one much indeed between Joan of Arc who was burnt as a witch (see Elshtain 1987) and the ever popular Halloween-style spooky witches consistently portrayed in today's children's literature as friendly, misunderstood and harmless. It is not surprising that goddesses with bloody tongues, weapons in their multiple arms, garlanded with their victims' skulls, have figured largely in constructions of an exotic Asia, along with the neatly complementary stereotype of perfectly passive, submissive wives. Although such cross-cultural fascinations are passed over here, I shall in the end briefly touch on another perhaps related but more immediate inter-cultural encounter: that between Western female fieldworkers and the strong, self-possessed Indian women who have been our teachers. In truth, however, that too is another long story.

Cosmology, Gender and Power: South Asian Configurations

When social scientists attempt to generalize about gender differences and the position of women in India—particularly in contrast to the West—they often highlight certain evidently paradoxical aspects of the Indian case. Susan Wadley's classic essay on 'Women in the Hindu Tradition' states:

> Clearly Indian women present a paradoxical situation for the interpreter of South Asian society. The view of the Hindu woman as downtrodden represents one behavioral reality; her participation in the highest political and social arenas is another undeniable reality (1977:113).

Ashis Nandy speaks of the same paradox in his essay 'Woman versus Womanliness in India': 'Why do some women in India reach the pinnacles of public power and recognition while women in general have kept out of large areas of public life?' (1980:42).

Coming from different disciplines and experiences, Wadley, a female American cultural anthropologist, and Nandy, a male Indian social psychologist, both locate sources for the configurations they note in the same characteristics of Indian culture and cosmology. All animating power is female in Hindu cosmology. The word for power is *shakti* and it can be used to refer to energy or strength. It is also a name of the goddess.[4] 'Womanliness', to use Nandy's term, is associated with energy, animation, and creative artistry—not weakness. As Nandy puts it, 'the ultimate authority in the Indian mind has always been feminine', while the Indian male, according to Nandy, identifies with 'what he sees as the passive, weak, and masculine principle in the cosmos' (1980:36).

It is therefore in South Asia 'natural' or cosmologically appropriate for women to attain and exercise supreme power. A woman prime minister is no surprise; no one worries that she might not be up to the task. In 1979-80 I often heard people in Rajasthan casually refer to Indira Gandhi as *shakti* and explicitly identify the male assistants serving her interests with the lesser male deities who accompany and serve the goddess.

But what evidence is there for identity or continuity between mortal women who are not prime ministers and manifestations of an all-pervasive female power? Both psychological studies and studies of spirit possession in South Asia reveal links between female lives and mythic images. Based on his work with upper class Western educated Hindus who have sought psychotherapy, Alan Roland has observed that 'integral to the socially contextual ego-ideal for Hindu Indians is a strong mythic orientation' (1988:253). He finds that 'women especially, traditionally experience everyday relationships within the framework of myths' (1988:297). Roland argues that myth is not used symbolically by his patients but metonymically—that it is continuous with everyday reality rather than a representation of it. Roland gives the example of a patient who narrates an experience where she ministers to a sick sister, and saves her life, by becoming the mythic heroine, Savitri, who outsmarted Death himself.

A number of studies of spirit possession and healing point to real women's vivid identification with goddesses. This identification is not always with life-giving female myth models (as with Roland's patient), and often expresses both sexuality and rage. Gananath Obeyesekere reports: 'Many Sinhala women who come to be exorcised suffer from severe repressions of both sex and aggression. In rituals there is a myth model that helps to express this problem' (1981:102). In an earlier case study he describes a woman who, when possessed, threatens to assault people and eat them up (1977:249). Sudhir Kakar writes of a possession case observed in Rajasthan that 'Urmilla's expression of rage against her husband and his family is also a rage against her feelings of powerlessness. . . . her identifications are with the powerful figures of the father, the mother-in-law and the Mother Goddess' (1982:79).

While such evidence draws largely on cases that could be viewed as deviant, slighter but pervasive continuities between women and goddesses are traceable in everyday life. Women's devotional songs typically describe female divinities who like the same things they do (such as jewellery, clothes, fine food, and kind attention from loved ones), and who experience the same emotions. Many Hindu women have the names of goddesses (as men do of gods); those who do not, in Rajasthan, commonly have 'Devi', meaning 'goddess' as a middle name. Ethnography suggests that such naming is more than empty custom. Describing a family scene among urban Punjabis in Delhi, Veena Das writes:

> One day Lakshmi, a baby three months of age, was wailing loudly. Her grandfather carried her around in his arms, swinging her and making all kinds of baby sounds. The baby seemed inconsolable. At one stage he said, 'Oh, baby, you are Lakshmi. You are the Goddess. They why do you cry?' As it happened, the baby stopped crying, at which the grandfather turned to me and said, 'See, she needed to be reminded who she was.'

Das argues that this episode, although treated in a 'lighthearted way', actually 'resonates with ideas that are well formed at the level of myths' (Das 1989:268).[5] In the village of Ghatiyali, Rajasthan, where I lived, I was often told that babies of both sexes were like deities to their parents. In Ghatiyali, the way people talked of goddesses seemed to me to mix familiarity and intimacy with respect for their potency and violent capacity—a capacity not necessarily embodied in weapons. When, on one of my early walks through the village, I met a woman accompanied by a child with a deformed leg, she pointed to it and said to me, shaking her head, '*Mataji Mataji*'. Naive as I was—and coming from America where issues of child abuse were just beginning to surface—I thought this woman was telling me that the child's mother had crippled her. As some awkward dialogue soon revealed, she was herself the mother, and she was telling

me with a mixture of resignation, respect and resentment that this affliction
was the work of the goddess.

Elsewhere, in the context of describing shrine cures, I tell of a patient
who attributes his son's paralysis to what he called the 'quarrel' and the
'arrow' of an offended goddess. First the goddess had healed the youth;
then she had reafflicted him. The father speaks of the goddess with mingled
anger, bafflement, and adoration, 'like a thwarted but still fervent lover',
I wrote (Gold 1988:171).

I had a three-year-old friend named Kusum during my 1979-81 residence (a leggy schoolgirl in 1988, a new bride in 1991). Kusum used to
like to come to my room and look at American magazines; whenever she
saw something unfamiliar, amorphous, colourful, and weird—like a Pi-
casso sculpture or a woman with hairdo, make-up and clothing in the latest
Parisian fashion—she would tap it with one finger repeating '*Mataji*
Mataji'.

Mataji is a respectful term for mother but is used to refer to the goddess
in all her forms and names.[6] In most rural Rajasthani shrines, *Mataji* is a
stone often smeared with red paste and draped in gaudy cloth, her only
anthropomorphic feature a pair of striking eyes. Kusum clearly saw the
goddess as something strange and gaudy—sharply unfamiliar but by that
very token recognizable; she did not fear, but liked to name her. Whether
as chaotic form and colour, as the source of an innocent child's affliction,
or as a potential benefactress requiring attentive coaxing; the goddess
appears at once to be unfathomable yet intimately known.

If we acknowledge existing links and identifications among goddesses,
women, and *shakti* as power, the paradox pointed to by Wadley and Nandy
still remains at least partially unexplained. Why are women subordinated
in household hierarchies, kept in seclusion, subjected to discrimination on
the job market? Why are sons preferred to daughters, and the health of
male children of greater concern than that of females? Why, since the
introduction of amniocentesis, has the problem of aborting female babies
become a major ethical issue? The speculations that follow are intended
only to suggest patterns, not to propose answers or solutions.[7]

Part of the explanation evidently lies on the 'other side of the coin' from
everything already mentioned. If women have an excess of power, a
corresponding excess of sexuality, and the potential to swell into angry
goddesses, men have a strong interest in restraining them.[8] Hence the
infamous advice from the classical Hindu book of moral law, the *Laws of
Manu*, that a woman must be subjected to lifelong control by male kin.
Hence the urgency to marry daughters before they attain puberty, the

inauspiciousness of widows, the pervasive male fear of women drainin their vital fluids and life force.[9]

But fear of women as agents or possessors of *shakti* does not account for other factors in the complex of Indian women's apparent subordination. For example, there are socially and religiously salient reasons for the strong preference for sons that have to do with the nature of patrilineal descent and inheritance, patrilocal marriage and ancestor worship; with village exogamy and dowry; with women being considered unfit to study Sanskrit or offer sacrifices—to name just a few elements.[10] None of these seem based on an understanding of power as female, and uncontrolled female power as dangerous; rather a scenario of male biological, political and economic dominance emerges—one much closer to the patriarchal orientations of the Western world.

However male dominance in Hindu South Asia does not imply sharply differentiated male and female gender identities. This is really Nandy's chief point about 'woman versus womanliness': men may be motivated to cultivate womanly traits for positive reasons.[11] Moreover, sources of female power are sometimes located in just that self-restraint and suffering imposed on women by their subordinate roles, but analogous to the self-restraint and suffering embraced by male ascetics to increase spiritual power.[12]

Let me sum up. In South Asia

(i) Power is cosmologically associated with female gender.

(ii) Goddesses are female powers both alien and intimate, not separate and unreachable from the human world, and sometimes incorporated into mortal female identities.

(iii) Women are socially, politically, economically, and ritually disadvantaged.

(iv) Suffering is understood to be a source of power, and women are better at it than men.

(v) Gender identities are relatively fluid.

I have attempted here to approximate some of the striking strands composing Hindu views of gender in an account that is neither exhaustive nor definitive. I do not imagine these views to cohere as a monolithic construct shared by all Hindus. They might rather be understood as culturally available and selectively engaged. The stories of *shakti* that follow are expressions that respond to, interpret, manipulate and substantiate these and other strands too subtle or pliable to be easily enumerated.

Three Narratives of Sword-Wielding Females

THE CREATRIX BEHEADS HER SONS

I recorded this creation myth in January 1988 in the course of a rambling, tape-recorded interview with Madhu Natisar Nath, an old man in his seventies belonging to a caste of yogi-magician-farmers (Naths) with whom I have worked extensively (Gold 1992). Although Madhu Nath is at times a professional performer of tales, he told me this myth conversationally. It was our discussion of his yogic earrings that evoked the creation myth. Rajasthani Naths are Shaivites, and Madhu said that the thick crystal rings in his slit ears were a form of the divine couple, Shiva and Shakti, who are often worshipped as stylized genitals: 'The ear is the *yoni* (vagina) and the earring is the *lingam* (phallus), so it is a form (*rup*) of Shiva-Shakti'. He continued:

> So was the creation of the earth. On the earth were seven oceans. Of its own accord in the water a flame stood up and in it was Niranjan Nirakar [Spotless Shapeless] and a girl, Shakti. And he said to Shakti: 'Let's go create the earth'. He took the form of a tortoise and got some mud and made the nine continents with it. Then he said, 'Shakti, I've made the earth, now you make life.'
> She said, 'I have no mate. How can I do it alone?'
> He said, 'Do it the best you can because I don't have a body. Do it according to your desire.'
> Then Shakti was wandering alone, there were no birds and animals, she was all alone. She said, 'My left hand is female and my right is a man,' so she slapped the right on the left and got three blisters: Brahma, Vishnu, and Shiva emerged from the blisters.
> She said to Vishnu: 'Be a ruler,' and to Brahma, 'You study.' And Shiva had set up his yogi's campfire [that is, he had begun to practice ascetic meditation] and she thought, 'I've had three boys. There is still no one to be my mate. They are my sons. They are my own sons, but I will accept them as my husbands.'

She went to Brahma with her hands joined and said,
   'Marry me.'
'Mother, you are my mother, how can I marry you?'
She said, 'You fucker!' And she cut off his head with her
   disc and burnt him up.
She went to Vishnu and the same thing happened.
She went to Shankar who thought, 'She has killed my two
   brothers. If I refuse she'll kill me too. She's my mother.
   I'll agree to anything and stay alive.'
'Sure, I'll marry you but first calm down. I'll marry you but
   first give me a promise.'
She had three eyes. 'Give me the middle one.'
So she gave it to Shankar. 'Now, let's get married.'
'First bring my brothers back to life and the thirty-three
   million goddesses and gods and fifty-two Bhairujis so that
   they can enjoy the wedding.'
So she clapped again and brought Brahma and Vishnu back
   to life and created the goddesses and gods and
   Bhairujis . . .

[Note that the narrator who has called the goddess Shakti up until now,
refers to her after her wedding as Parvati, the name of Shiva's consort.]

Parvati had no vagina so Shankar scratched her with his nail
and made her a vagina and they collected the blood in a pot
and dyed some cloth and Shankar accepted it as ochre
[*bhagava* because it came from Parvati's *bhag*] and from
this time the Nath yogis wear this colour of cloth.[13]
Parvati kept asking Shiva to make love to her.
Growing annoyed by her demands, he cut off his penis and
threw it up in the air.
Then she spread out her vagina [*bhag*] and sat on the ground
and when Shiva's penis fell back down it stuck there and
from that time it was worshipped in that way.
So Lord Shiva's *lingam* was staked in this *yoni*.
None of the couples were having children.
So Shiva and Shakti called them all and said worship this
lingam and *yoni* and pour water over it and drink it. Then
they had children.

Much could be said about this myth.[14] Here I shall ask only how it might help us think about gender relations in cosmology and in society, and about gendered modes of violence. A mother is sexually aggressive towards her sons.[15] Thwarted, her sexuality becomes dramatically and effectively murderous, but the resulting deaths are only temporary.[16] Shakti's violence to Brahma and Vishnu persuades Shiva to try bargaining instead of refusal, and Shakti is quite willing to bargain. The assaulting, decapitating goddess quite readily relinquishes some power (her masculine power, her third eye) in order to achieve her goal of creation. Cooperation, not murder, is the way to get things done, but it is negotiated only after a violent display.[17]

The erotic mother then becomes transformed into an equally lusty wife. In this myth erotic-violent and non-erotic-procreative females are not two different beings.[18] This Shakti is a mother, the mother of everything; she is also a sexually eager wife and her serial sexual aggressions—first as mother and then as wife—are the means of creating and perpetuating life. They have no permanent negative or frightening consequences. Shiva's self-castration in the second half of the myth seems to balance his brothers' beheadings in the first. Both result from Shakti's sexual aggression, but both are ultimately beneficial.

The myth gives an origin story for two things important to the caste of the teller: the red-orange cloth they wear and the worship of *lingam* and *yoni* (neither of course unique to Naths). Renouncers' robes are a highly valued symbol of detachment from the world, and from women; here they are dyed in vaginal blood—perhaps the blood of Parvati's defloration. In ordinary life this blood is very polluting and dangerous stuff.[19] This could well be viewed as a clear case of male appropriation of female generative power.[20] But alternatively it might express male and female complementarity. Throughout this story the need for mutuality, for pairing—as expressed in the beginning—rather than for domination of one sex by the other, seems to resonate. In accepting the colour emblematic of their identity as dyed in vaginal blood, yogis thus acknowledge an intimacy with female body substance even as they outwardly reject contact with women.

This myth from a regional oral tradition shows us female violence as readily reversible and having positive results, while female sexuality is fully creative. Although Shakti's excessive sexuality, both as mother and wife charters both decapitation and castration, the outcome is gender mutuality on several conceptual planes: it takes a pair to accomplish cosmic world-creation; coupled mortals must worship the pair Shiva-Shakti in order to get children; divine creative coupling is modelled by the teller's earrings; emblems of his yogic identity and microcosms of a paired universe.

HADI RANI BEHEADS HERSELF

In the story of Hadi Rani we encounter a very different configuration of female power and human violence. Sexual exuberance is not merely muted, but annihilated. Here the female-wielded weapon is turned on the female self, even as it punishes, defeats and emasculates the male. The emasculation here leads not to union and fecundity but to separation, although in that separation is victory. Born into a domestic setting, female power is curtailed from the beginning. Unlike Shakti, Hadi Rani has a mother and a father, a caste and a lineage. Yet transfigured as Shakti, she becomes in the end a singular being.

In the tale of Hadi Rani, a popular Rajasthani folk heroine is located in an unrestful era of Rajasthani history, during the Mughul emperor Aurangzeb's reign (1658-1707) when Rajput princes were resisting or capitulating to Delhi's casteless rulers. One powerful symbolic medium for either mode of interaction was women—that is, to give a bride or not to the Muslim royalty. During my stay in Rajasthan in 1979-80 I heard Hadi's story from members of both sexes. It was usually told to back up an argument about the ways women surpassed men, or else to demonstrate the awesome and peculiar valour of Rajput women (women of the 'warrior' caste). I never recorded these tales, so my quotable sources for what follows are a printed version of Hadi Rani's story in English from a cheap compendium of 'true romances' about Indian women and a Rajasthani book that summarizes Hadi's story as preface to a set of verses in her praise.[21]

Hadi's birth and childhood closely follow a pattern common for women warriors in India.[22] Her father wanted a son but a daughter was born (his only progeny). He never treats her like a girl, but gives her instruction in sports and martial skills, calling her 'my eldest son'. Her father is reluctant to get her married, for to do so he must admit she is a daughter. But, she makes her own choice, begging her father to accept the offer of a military chief in the service of the ruler of Udaipur. He is much older than she, but she admires his military prowess and valour.

After her wedding ceremony, Hadi goes to her husband's house for the consummation of her marriage, as is still the custom. Simultaneously a neighbouring princess asks for help from the kingdom of Udaipur to keep the Mughul emperor from taking her, by force, as a wife.

The messenger bearing this news and requesting Hadi's new husband to come at once with his troops arrives at the door of the new couple's bridal chamber. Her brideroom, whom she married for his valour, attempts to defer until morning his departure for war. Hadi is enraged: 'Wear my bangles, and give me your sword and sit secure in the circle of these four walls; and don't ever call yourself a Rajput,' she cries, shaming him into going (Shamsuddin 1977:23-24).

But her husband hesitates a second time at the city gates, sending a messenger to ask Hadi for a remembrance to assure him of her *satitva*—her truthfulness or fidelity. By implication, it would also be a pledge for her to become a sati should he die in battle.

Hadi is enflamed by this double insult: that her husband should question her honour and also reveal a further lack of eagerness for war. She seizes a sword from the wall and—admonishing the messenger to deliver her last remembrance—beheads herself in a single stroke, with the words 'Victory to the Goddess!' on her lips.

A weeping soldier carries the platter to her husband. Her husband ties the head around his neck (or in other accounts to his saddle), as he might have tied the kind of token he expected, a handkerchief or a ring. Stunning the enemy with this gruesome sight, he fights valiantly to a Rajput victory and his own death, while Aurangzeb is 'forced to return to Delhi, empty-handed' (Mahiyariya 1978:3).

Nathu Singh Mahiyariya, a male poet of the early twentieth century, honours Hadi's divine triumph with one hundred and thirty-one four-line Rajasthani verses in rhyme. Mahiyariya's poetry plays with heavily gendered images, not just switching their implications (as the simple 'wear my bangles and give me your sword') but adding and subtracting qualities from them so that the female becomes 'ferocious' without losing her feminine modesty and the male becomes ashamed, like a woman, even in his public deeds of battle. A few vivid examples follow:

Hadi is anchored to modesty	*Hadi langar laj ro*
Her neck sliced, she still keeps the rules	*kat hi nibhayo nem*
Her face-veil is sticky with blood	*ghunghat ragtan bhinjiyo*
So the wind cannot blow it away.	*pavan udave kem* [14]
[From heaven Hadi speaks]	
Now that you've opened the enemies' throats	*piu ariyan ghar kholiya*

O Husband, come open for me	*ab to kholo ay*
Hadi's wedding wristbands;	*hadi bandhiye dorare*
I sit and wait in heaven.	*baithi surpur many* [19]

When her mother heard the news about	*hadi hathan sir diyo*
Hadi giving her head	*suni badhai may*
She cried to her husband, Hada,	*kahiyo hada piv nun*
'How joyful a daughter's birth!'	*hansti hansti jay* [41]

When Hadi's head reached her husband	*sis pugayo piu kane*
The blood-soaked earth turned mud	*thayo ragtan kic*
But Hadi's eyes stayed dry	*rahiyo pan bahiyo nahin*
So her eye make-up didn't smudge.	*kajal nainan bic* [56]

Cowardly men lowered their heads	*nica sir kayar naran*
Their shame spread throughout the world.	*thaya jagat vikhiyat*
Hadi having given her head	*hadi sir detan huvo*
Women raised up theirs.	*sar unco triy jat* [68]

She kept up India's moral courage	*dharam rakhyo hindhavan ro*
She kept her honour before the world,	*jas rakhyau sansar*
Hadi did not keep her head, but	*hadi sir rakhyao nahin*
She kept her lineage great.	*kul rakhyau balihar* [130][23]

Let me point out a few of the more obvious changes rung on gender stereotypes in these verses:

Rajput women should stay inside (keep purdah) and if they must go into public they should cover their faces and lower their heads. But Hadi emerges from purdah as a bodiless, bloody, but with a still demurely covered head. This is surely an ironic comment on female coyness as a pose, as a masking of superior power. Moreover, Hadi's valour of which the emblem is her head on the field of battle inspires all men to take up a pose of shame and gives all women the right to be bold.

Female adornment is an explicitly acknowledged form of restriction, signifying women's submission to men (although women also celebrate their beauty as a form of power). But here the eye make-up with which Hadi was adorned for her wedding night becomes a symbol of her absolute courage, contrasting with male weakness. The male messenger weeps;

Hadi's husband's feet are stuck in bloodied mud, but Hadi's eyes are tearless, her beauty intact but totally inaccessible. Further, Hadi only conditionally grants her husband the right to open her wedding wristbands as a prelude to their marital union—after he has opened the enemies necks.

Sons are wanted to carry on a lineage; the birth of a daughter is not joyful (because a daughter does nothing for her family but cost them in dowry). But Hadi the only daughter has saved the reputation not just of her husband's house, but of her parents'. She is known, significantly enough, by her father's name. Her mother is vindicated for giving birth to a daughter, and she wants her husband to know it.

Women are caught up in concerns of home and family, while men are capable of selfless acts of valour. Yet Hadi's husband cannot give up his attachment, Hadi can. It was, moreover, his questioning of her capacity for becoming a sati that propelled Hadi to her moral height.[24] Many of Mahiyariya's verses contrast Hadi's single act of purely selfless valour with her husbands battlefield exploits which are described as 'giving-and-taking'. This phrase evokes a concept of war as a kind of commerce, a morally debased activity against which Hadi's pure giving stands out as peerless giving without taking. It would seem that by cutting off her own head Hadi has thoroughly emasculated her husband, denying him his sexual rights as well as his martial glory. Nothing he does on the field of battle can compare with her single act, and the poet tells us this again and again, seeing it moreover as a triumph for the whole race (*jati*) of women. Even as she empowers him to defeat the Muslims, she defeats him with her moral superiority.

Despite all of these subversive themes, it is nonetheless clear that Hadi Rani died to perpetuate a system in which male warfare was the supreme value. Her female energy was ultimately set in the service of male politics. But only by ignoring the subtleties of Hadi's tale, and the poetics of her praise, might we conclude that there is nothing more to be learnt from her violent death.

SHOBHAG KANVAR THREATENS HER HUSBAND

When I first knew Shobhag Kanvar she was a married woman about 55 years old with two grown sons and two married daughters.[25] Her life-course has been much like that of thousands of high-caste women in rural India, patterned by her kinship identities as a daughter, wife and mother, mother-in-law and grandmother, and lived in terms of those relationships.

There are, however, ways in which Shobhag Kanvar is not ordinary. Although totally illiterate, she possesses more knowledge about rituals and knows more worshipful stories and songs than most women in her large, multicaste village, giving her a certain status there as a religious expert. As a devotee of the Rajasthani hero-god Dev Narayan—considered to be an incarnation of Vishnu—Shobhag Kanvar was deeply involved in his worship at a shrine just outside her village, and equally involved with a mixed-caste group of that deity's devotees. The central figure among this group was the shrine's charismatic priest—a man of about Shobhag Kanvar's age, and of a different, lower caste. Although the terms of their relationship were never fully clear to me, part of it was certainly economic; Shobhag Kanvar assisted women pilgrims at the shrine, and in return the priest gave her a substantial share of the offerings made there.

In 1979-81 when I first knew them, this priest and several of his male followers came to Shobhag Kanvar's courtyard every day for tea and sat often for more than an hour, talking freely with her. During festivals, Shobhag Kanvar with many other pilgrims would spend the night at Dev Narayan's shrine, singing songs in his praise. Shobhag Kanvar did not define herself as a rebel, but as a devotee, and her bearing implied an impeccable propriety. But her behaviour was by ordinary standards not appropriate for a woman of her caste.

Village gossips told a story about Shobhag Kanvar set years earlier that explained to them how she attained her freedoms—a story notably different from the ones she herself narrated (Gold 1994a). One day, they said, Shobhag Kanvar's husband had had enough. He forbade her to continue her participation in the group of Dev Narayan's devotees. They had strong words and she appeared to accept his authority. However, that night after he was asleep in his bed, Shobhag Kanvar took down the family sword from its place on the wall, climbed astride her husband's chest, and poised the weapon over his neck.[26] 'Let me continue to worship Dev Narayan as I have been,' she demanded. He complied. The image, of Shobhag Kanvar holding the sword over her husband's neck, is both climax and punch line of the tale.

It always made me uncomfortable to hear this gossip about a woman I knew well who, moreover, considerably intimidated me with her mixture of honeyed charm, deep knowledge, and occasionally manipulative behaviour. One main strategy in Shobhag Kanvar's complex life was to claim that she never infringed the rules of propriety. The only way to get along with her was to agree that this was so, despite all evidence to the contrary. Her husband, as the gossips constructed their encounter, violated her self-image by accusing her of misconduct and thus aroused her rage.

The image of a wife astride her husband's chest resonates in village folklore with a bawdy insult song (*gali*). Here are a few lines:

That lewd hussy X's wife lifted a load, yes!
She climbed on his chest and pissed on his mustache,
Yes-oh-yes!
She climbed on his chest and pissed on his mustache,
Yes-oh-yes!
Get away wanton woman, what have you done?
Yes-oh-yes!

dari ra dari ra X-bali syun lunchi bhio unchi han!
charh chhati munchya par muntyo,
han ka han ra!
charh chhati munchya par muntyo,
han ka han ra!
dhur malan jadi yo kidho kai?
han ka han ra!

This outrageous and semi-nonsensical ditty, like most of its genre—is sung by women about one another—substituting different husbands' names. Women seem to be gleefully celebrating here a self-image quite different from that of reticent, dutiful wives. Was this song in the mind of the scandalmongers who envisaged Shobhag Kanvar's threatening her husband? It might well have been. But the image of a sword-wielding, emasculating female also echoes the creatrix myth, and even the story of Hadi Rani, who by doing it to herself really does it to her husband—simultaneously robbing him of his honour and his wedding night pleasures as she saves him from his own weakness. In Shobhag Kanvar's life story resistance both to confinement and to devaluation have been perpetual strategies which may be why village gossips sat her in that mythic pose.

Like Shakti the creatrix and Hadi the queen, Shobhag Kanvar was acting for religiously appropriate ends. She was merely insisting that her husband allow her to continue her devotional activities. The very activities to which her husband objected netted her considerable earnings which she poured into home-improvements, enhancing the value of male-owned property to be sure, but equally making her own life far more comfortable. Certainly the economic independence Shobhag Kanvar reaped from her work at the shrine added weight and edge to the sword that village tongues liked to imagine her wielding.

Concluding Thoughts on Women, Goddesses and Violence

In *Notes on Love in a Tamil Family*, Margaret Trawick reveals an intricate tapestry of subtle interpersonal relationships, observing there that 'the battle between the male and the female modes of existence was not waged exclusively on a mythological level' (1990a:70). She narrates this brief episode concerning herself and Padmini, one of the main female characters in her family, a woman she describes much later in the book as 'having burned herself out in anger' (194): 'Once, when we were picking vegetables in the garden, I came upon a praying mantis. I commented that among these bugs, the wife devours the husband.

'"That's just the way it should be," said Padmini, unsmiling' (1990a:71). Many anthropologists who work closely with Indian women have received similar messages.

In the presence of Shobhag Kanvar I always felt myself both favoured and manipulated, generously educated and not so subtly mocked. No male in her household held any similar sway over me. Yet in the presence of these men—her husband, her husband's elder brother, and other male in-laws—she would veil her face and murmur her words. She described this behaviour as her 'Rajput *dharma*' and no doubt it was so for her. But to a foreign observer her purdah gestures seemed a self-conscious pose, sometimes humorous and sometimes bitter, but never impinging on her sense of self-worth.

Despite all the verbal and physical deference that South Asian women accord to the husband-god and the ideology of female subordination, they also retain and communicate a sense of gender virtue and virtuosity that can manifest as both moral and physical, or both. And these women effectively transmit their convictions of self-worth to the foreigners in their midst (Gold 1988, 1994b; Harlan 1992; Raheja and Gold 1994; Trawick 1980, 1990a). In concluding I want to suggest that the female capacity for violence evident in the three narratives considered here is linked to women's positive self-evaluations as well as to the evident ideological and material disadvantages that women suffer in their daily lives.

In the myth of a creatrix beheading her sons, female desire becomes murderous, but procreative necessity and vitality reverses any deathly implications. Power subsumes violence; violence is only a strategy of power; the creatrix kills, negotiates, and restores.[27]

In the legend of Hadi Rani beheading herself, a bride sacrifices her own gratifications to channel her energy as power to support male valour, but demonstrates as she does so a moral superiority that makes her not only better at suffering but better at war. Rather than terror of uncontrolled female violence, Hadi's legend reflects a subtler, more insidious fear of women's superior self-control. Hadi Rani overcomes her sexuality, and is able to put her public moral conscience above her private desires, when her husband fails to do so. Another strong theme in her legend—used both by female oral narrators and the male poet—is the assertion of female worth: a daughter's birth is joyful.[28] This claim counters the devastating devaluation of women being expressed in the preference for sons.

The story about Shobhag Kanvar threatening to behead her husband engages a bawdy image of acknowledged wanton anti-modesty. But because Shobhag Kanvar's violence was at once in the interests of religious commitment (*dharma*) and profit (*artha*), it is also acknowledged to have positive results. Both shrine and household were prospering at the time that gossip was going around, and certainly some jealousy as well as grudging awe were at work in spinning the tale.

All three images of female violence both embody and confound the paradoxes we began with. They unite positive and negative evaluations of female power as creative and destructive. Particularly vivid is the way each story differently confounds prescriptions for female modesty, confinement, and deference according to which most rural North Indian women live their lives. Social codes dictate that women, as wives, stay inside, keep themselves covered, and do not address husbands directly. But these narratives as manifestations of *shakti* all subvert or deny such conventions of restraint. The creatrix does not act shy before her intended husbands; later in the myth she spreads her legs wide to catch Shiva's penis after he has thrown it up in the sky. Hadi Rani's veiled head rides ironically in the public domain of battle. Shobhag Kanvar, envisioned in gossip, straddles her husband's chest.[29]

This tour through myth, legend, and village hearsay, then, leaves mixed impressions. These are impressions not only of male terror at decapitating, castrating women but of male acknowledgement of a cosmic gender parity and of female creative energy; not only of male exploitation of women's self-sacrifice, but of an ironic resistance to the terms of male superiority articulated by males as well as females; not only of wives perfectly controlled by their husbands lest they destroy family honour, but of wives overriding just such restraints for the good of their families. Gender relations in South Asia as elsewhere, in stories and in social life, are perpetually configured, transacted, reconfigured and may never be comprehended from a single perspective. By presenting three Hindu images of female fury I have offered but fragments of that complex and fluctuating world. I hope I have arranged those fragments to reveal something about the ways that narrative realities sometimes converge to the advantage of a disadvantaged sex.

Notes

This essay has shifted shapes many times, reflecting its elusive subject matter. Throughout these metamorphoses, I have received valuable comments, critiques, and suggestions in more places and from more persons than I shall be able to remember. I must, however, particularly thank Wendy Doniger O'Flaherty, Nita Kumar, Michael Lambek, Barbara Metcalf, and Margaret Trawick for comments delivered in formal and informal contexts. Milton Singer's invitation to participate in a workshop on 'Gender, Reason, and Nuclear Policy' at the University of Chicago in winter 1989 was the initial impetus for contemplating these images. From participants in the Chicago workshop and from members of the University of Rochester Department of Anthropology where I offered a considerably different version in fall of 1990, I received provocative and thoughtful responses. I am solely responsible for the essay's present form. A shortened and simplified version appears as 'Power as violence: Hindu images of female fury', in *The other fifty percent: Multicultural perspectives on gender relations*, edited by Mari Womack and Judith Marti (Prospect Heights, Illinois: Waveland Press, 1993).

1. For some articulations of these diverse approaches see, for example, Bennett 1983; Kakar 1978, 1989; Kinsley 1987; Kondos 1986; Shulman 1986.
2. In a compelling set of essays circling around several tellings of a South Indian myth of 'rape and revenge', Margaret Trawick (1990b, 1991a, 1991b) takes us a long way towards understanding these complexities.
3. In previous work I have looked specifically at women's traditions to explore female self-images, although arguing that these were readily accessible to and sometimes evoked by men (Gold 1994b). Here, by contrast, the voices that produced the stories under consideration are predominantly but not exclusively male.
4. Animate, diversified nature, *prakriti*, is also female: and as *prakriti* is opposed to an originally inanimate, undifferentiated substance or selfness or man: *purusha*. Illusion, *maya*, the power that spins the universe along in delight and ignorance, is female. *Maya*, like *shakti* is a name of the goddess. In its positive aspect it is entrancing art; negatively it is a deathly snare; see Gold 1991; O'Flaherty 1984; Siegel 1991.
5. See also Trawick 1990a for meaningful appreciation of names in a Tamil family.

6. I never heard anyone call or refer to their genealogical mother as *Mataji;* often affectionate circumlocutions like 'Big Sister' were used.

7. Let me stress the partial nature of my discussion here—intended as a background to the narratives that are my focus. There is a vast literature on women's status in South Asia well beyond my scope to summarize or even cite here. Volumes I have found useful and illuminating include Desai and Krishnaraj 1987; Kishvar and Vanita, eds. 1984; Papanek and Minault, eds. 1982.

8. The literature on female crime in India, including homicide, is scant but sometimes revealing. Some studies suggest dispositions to violence located in women's passions and characters, while others stress tensions leading to violence in familial situations. See, for example, Rathi 1989; Shukla and Saxena 1987; Sohani 1989.

9. See Carstairs 1975 for classic ethnographic testimony to such fears; elsewhere I show that female sexuality is very differently construed in women's songs (Gold 1993b).

10. But see Valeri 1990 on power and gender in Java where he complexly argues that women are superior to men in terms of destructive power and therefore inferior in terms of positive value.

11. Elsewhere Nandy argues brilliantly that the British made Indians feel self-depreciating about their feminine side, until Gandhi was able to turn the tables by stressing positive aspects of womanliness not only in Indian culture but also in Western Judaeo-Christian traditions (1983).

12. For some extensive explorations of this theme see Wadley, ed. 1980. Gandhi asserted more than once that women were better at self-suffering—his ethical version of effective asceticism—and better too at non-violence (*ahimsa*) than men: 'Has she not greater intuition, is she not more self-sacrificing, has she not greater powers of endurance, has she not greater courage?' (cited in Rudolph and Rudolph 1983:38) and again 'Woman is the incarnation of *ahimsa. Ahimsa* means infinite love, which again means infinite capacity for suffering' (cited in Rudolph and Rudolph 1983:61). Gandhi's role in politicizing Indian women is generally acnowledged.

13. Sanskritist Wendy Doniger O'Flaherty expressed some astonishment at this 'extraordinarily blasphemous' folk etymology equating the Sanskrit root of 'god' (as in *bhagwan* and *bhagava*) with a word for 'cunt' (*bhag*).

14. See Sax 1991 for a beautiful translation and extensive discussion of a related Shaivite creation myth from Garhwal.

15. For sexually aggressive mothers in Indian mythology and psychology see, for example, Kakar 1978; Vatuk and Vatuk 1979.

16. Mythic violence is frequently reversible, like violence in a tragedy where the cast bows after the curtain or violence in an arcade game when another quarter brings the dead to life. This reversibility or cyclicality must be kept in mind

but I do not believe it makes comparisons with other images of violence untenable.

17. See O'Flaherty 1980 for rich, multifaceted analyses of myths about the appropriation of the goddess's third eye. Heroines who must have removed, or spontaneously lose a third breast, or a horn on the forehead, when they meet their fated husband are common in Hindu mythology.

18. See Gold 1993b for female beings as split between sexual and fertile in the scholarship on gender in India, and for an argument that women's oral traditions frequently offer less divided images. Here, however, it is a male bard who fuses the two.

19. In Rajasthan the low-caste drummer's wife spends the night outside the nuptial bedroom and takes away the bloody cloth in the morning. See Raheja 1988:134-37 for more about this inauspicious cloth; see O'Flaherty 1981:270 for its fearsome nature in Vedic times.

20. See, for example, Bloch and Parry, eds. 1982.

21. See also Harlan 1992 for an interpretation of Hadi's legend as told among Udaipur Rajputs.

22. Hansen 1988 discusses and exemplifies this pattern. She argues that female power in the Indian world view can be fully benevolent, showing that India's many 'Joans of Arc' had exemplary careers as masculine daughters and politically engaged wives and widows.

23. Mahiyariya's difficult Rajasthani verses are by good fortune accompanied by explanations in simple Hindi—both of words and of deep meanings—from which my translation has benefitted greatly.

24. Other legendary husbands who test their wives' capacity for sati live to regret it; see the story of Bharthari and Pingala in Gold 1992.

25. See Gold 1993a for more about Shobhag Kanvar.

26. Rajput families keep swords, dating from a more glorious and lamented past when Rajput men fought heroically in the service of local overlords. The weapon is emblematic of an era when male power among Rajputs had deeper foundations than it does today.

27. For explorations of violence in symbolic and social perspectives see Das and Nandy 1986; Girard 1977; Riches 1986.

28. The hagiography of another Rajasthani heroine, Karni Ma, begins with the baby incarnate-goddess quickly punishing a family member who laments the birth of a girl (Ujwal n.d.).

29. Modern Indian fiction by women portrays similar conjunctions of shocking immodesty and sometimes violent power; see, for example, Mahasveta Devi 1987; Mukherjee 1989. See also many eloquent personal narratives in Tharu and Lalita, eds. 1991 in which women writers describe their own inner conflicts and small and large triumphs over restrictions imposed by gender.

References

Bennett, Lynn. 1983. *Dangerous wives and sacred sisters: Social and symbolic roles of high-caste women in Nepal.* New York: Columbia University Press.

Bloch, Maurice, and Jonathan Parry, eds. 1982. *Death and the regeneration of life.* Cambridge: Cambridge University Press.

Carstairs, G. Morris. 1975. *The Twice-born: A study of a community of high-caste Hindus.* Bloomington: Indiana University Press.

Das, Veena. 1989. Voices of children. *Daedalus* Fall: 263-294.

Das, Veena, and Ashis Nandy. 1986. *Violence, victimhood, and the language of silence.* In Veena Das, ed., *The word and the world.* New Delhi: Sage.

Desai, Neera, and Maithreyi Krishnaraj. 1987. *Women and society in India.* Delhi: Ajanta.

Elshtain, Jean B. 1987. *Women and war.* New York: Basic Books.

Girard, Rene. 1977. *Violence and the sacred.* Baltimore: Johns Hopkins University Press.

Gold, Ann Grodzins. 1988. *Fruitful journeys: The ways of Rajasthani pilgrims.* Berkeley: University of California Press.

———. 1991. Gender and illusion in a Rajasthani yogic tradition. In A. Appadurai, F. Korom, and Margaret Mills, eds., *Gender, genre, and power in South Asian expressive traditions.* 102-135. Philadelphia: University of Pennsylvania Press.

———. 1992. *A carnival of parting.* Berkeley: University of California Press.

———. 1994a. Purdah is as purdah's kept: A storyteller's story. In Gloria Goodwin Raheja and Ann Grodzins Gold. In *Listen to the heron's words: Reimagining gender and kinship in North India.* Berkeley: University of California Press.

———. 1994b. Sexuality, fertility and erotic imagination in Rajasthani women's songs. In Gloria Goodwin Raheja and Ann Grodzins Gold. In *Listen to the heron's words: Reimagining gender and kinship in North India.* Berkeley: University of California Press.

Hansen, Kathryn. 1988. The virangana in North Indian history, myth, and popular culture. *Economic and Political Weekly* 23 (April 30): 25-33.

Harlan, Lindsey. 1992. *Religion and Rajput women: The ethic of protection in contemporary narratives.* Berkley: University of California Press.

Kakar, Sudhir. 1978. *The inner world.* Delhi: Oxford University Press.

———. 1982. *Shamans, mystics and doctors.* New York: Alfred A. Knopf.

———. 1989. *Intimate relations.* Chicago: University of Chicago Press, Delhi: Oxford University Press.

Kinsley, David. 1987. *Hindu goddesses: Visions of the divine feminine in the Hindu religious tradition.* Delhi: Motilal Banarsidass.

Kishvar, Madhu and Ruth Vanita, eds. 1984. *In search of answers: Indian women's voices from Manushi.* London: Zed Books.

Kondos, V. 1986. Images of the fierce goddess and portrayals of Hindu women. *Contributions to Indian Sociology* 20(2): 173-197.

Mahasweta Devi. 1987. Draupadi. Translated in *In other worlds: Essays in cultural politics* by Gayatri Chakravorty Spivak, 179-196. New York: Routledge.

Mahiyariya, Nathu Singh. 1978. *Hadi Satak*. Jaipur: Sohanlal Jain, Jaipur Printers.

Mukherjee, Bharati. 1989. *Jasmine*. New York: Grove Weidenfeld.

Nandy, Ashis. 1980. *At the edge of psychology: Essays in politics and culture.* Delhi: Oxford University Press.

———. 1983. *The intimate enemy*. Delhi: Oxford University Press.

O'Flaherty, Wendy Doniger. 1980. *Women, androgynes, and other mythical beasts*. Chicago: University of Chicago Press.

———. 1981. *The Rigveda: An anthology*. Harmondsworth: Penguin.

———. 1984. *Dreams, illusion and other realities*. Chicago: University of Chicago Press.

Obeyesekere, Gananath. 1977. Psychocultural exegesis of a case of spirit possession in Sri Lanka. In Vincent Crapanzano and Vivian Garrison, eds., *Case studies in spirit possession*. 235-294. New York: Wiley.

———. 1981. *Medusa's hair: An essay on personal symbols and religious experience*. Chicago: University of Chicago Press.

Papanek, H. and G. Minault, eds. 1982. *Separate worlds: Studies of purdah in South Asia*. Columbia, Mo.: South Asia Books.

Raheja, Gloria Goodwin. 1988. *The poison in the gift*. Chicago: University of Chicago Press.

——— and Ann Grodzins Gold. 1994. Introduction: Listening to Women. In *Listen to the heron's words: Reimagining gender and kinship in North India.* Berkeley: University of California Press.

Ramanujan, A.K. 1986. Two realms of Kannada folklore. In Stuart Blackburn and A.K. Ramanujan, eds., *Another harmony*, 41-75. Berkeley: University of California Press.

Rathi, Sushila. 1989. Psycho-social factors in female homicide. In Leelamma Devasia and V.V. Devasia. *Female criminals and female victims: An Indian perspective*, 113-24. Nagpur: Dattsons Publishers.

Riches, David. 1986. The phenomenon of violence. In David Riches, ed., *The anthropology of violence*, 1-27. Oxford: Basil Blackwell.

Roland, Alan. 1988. *In search of self in India and Japan*. Princeton: Princeton University Press.

Rudolph, Susanne H., and Lloyd I. Rudolph. 1983. *Gandhi: The traditional roots of charisma*. Chicago: University of Chicago Press.

Sax, William. 1991. *Mountain goddess: Gender and politics in a Himalayan pilgrimage*. New York: Oxford University Press.

Shamsuddin. 1967. *The loves of Begum Sumroo and other true romances*. Delhi: Orient Paperbacks.

Shukla, K.S., and Rekha Saxena. 1987. Women and crime—A perspective. In K.S. Shukla, ed., *The other side of development: Social-psychological implications.* 115-33. New Delhi: Sage.

Shulman, David D. 1986. Battle as metaphor in Tamil folk and classical traditions. In Stuart Blackburn and A.K. Ramanujan, eds., *Another harmony: New essays in the folklore of India,* 105-30. Berkeley: University of California Press.

Siegel, Lee. 1991. *Net of magic: Wonders and deceptions in India.* Chicago: University of Chicago Press.

Sohoni, Neera K. 1989. *Women behind bars.* New Delhi: Vikas.

Tharu, Susie and K. Lalita, eds. 1991. *Women writing in India*: 600 B.C. to the Present. vol. 1. New York: The Feminist Press.

Trawick, Margaret. 1980. On the meaning of *shakti* to women in Tamil Nadu. In Susan S. Wadley, ed., *The powers of Tamil women,* 1-34. Syracuse: Maxwell School of Citizenship and Public Affairs.

———. 1990a. *Notes on love in a Tamil family.* Berkeley: University of California Press.

———. 1990b. Untouchability and the fear of death. In C. Lutz and L. Abu-Lughod, eds., *Language and the politics of emotion.* 186-206. Cambridge: Cambridge University Press.

———. 1991a. Wandering lost. In A. Appadurai, F. Korom, and Margaret Mills, eds., *Gender, genre, and power in South Asian expressive traditions.* 224-26. Philadelphia: University of Pennsylvania Press.

———. 1991b. Rape and revenge. Unpublished paper presented at the 20th Annual Conference on South Asia, Madison, Wisconsin.

Ujwal, Kailash Dan. n.d. *Bhagwati Shri Karniji Maharaj.* Jodhpur: Jodhpur University Press.

Valeri, Valerio. 1990. Both nature and culture: Reflections on menstrual and parturitional taboos in Huaulu (Seram). In Jane M. Atkinson and Shelly Errington, eds., *Power and difference: Gender in island Southeast Asia,* 235-72. Stanford: Stanford University Press.

Vatuk, Ved P., and Sylvia Vatuk. 1979. The lustful stepmother in the folklore of Northwestern India. In Ved P. Vatuk, eds., *Studies in Indian folk traditions.* 190-221. New Delhi: Manohar.

Wadley, Susan S. 1977. Women and the Hindu tradition. In Doranne Jacobson and Susan S. Wadley, eds., *Women in India: Two perspectives,* 113-39. Columbus, Mo: South Asia Books.

———. 1980. *The powers of Tamil women*: Syracuse: Maxwell School of Citizenship and Public Affairs.

2

Women's Speech Genres, Kinship and Contradiction

GLORIA GOODWIN RAHEJA

> Women's speech practices make visible a crack,
> a fault line in the dominant male discourse of
> gender and power, revealing it to be not monolithic but
> contradictory and thus vulnerable. (Gal 1991: 196)

AS ANTHROPOLOGISTS BEGAN to attend to the contrasting expressive genres in which men and women construct representations of marriage patterns, sexuality, deference behaviour, the 'solidarity' of patrilineal kinship groupings, exchange relationships among kinsmen and so forth, diversity within and among gendered perspectives on such kinship practices became a focus of attention. The heterogeneity of these varying perspectives on kinship, within particular cultures, is no longer open to question. Some of the speech practices in which this heterogeneity is located have been described by Abu-Lughod (1986; 1990), Bloch (1987), Briggs (1989), Das (1988), Grima (1991), Karp (1988), March (1984), Messick (1987), Narayan (1986, 1991), Raheja (1991), Raheja and Gold (1994), Sharma (1980: 20), Trawick (1986; 1991), and others. The critical theoretical issues, however, are not simply the discovery of heterogeneous representations, or the recovery of 'the female voice'; it is rather the tracing of the relationships among these diverse perspectives that constitutes a more difficult interpretive problem.

In this essay, I examine several aspects of the speech practices of rural North Indian women, focusing on two genres of oral expression in which aspects of patrilineal kinship are commented upon, critiqued and resisted.[1] I suggest that women's ritual songs and proverbs make visible the contradictions within dominant North Indian discourses concerning kinship, marriage and gender, and in doing so begin to subvert the authority of those discourses. In pointing out the contradictions within North Indian patrilineal kinship that are reflected upon in women's speech genres, I draw attention also to two interpretive problems embedded in analyses of such perspectival multiplicity. The first of these problems concerns the degree to which the critiques posed in women's verbal practices can be viewed as exemplifying a unitary female voice or a unitary female subjectivity.[2] Gal has taken up this issue in relation to women's use of language, and she has pointed out that the resistance found in women's linguisitic genres is often contradictory and ambiguous; but this heterogeneity within women's speech practices does not prevent them from becoming sites of struggle about kinship, gender definitions, and power (1991: 176-78, 192-93). The proverbs and songs of rural North Indian women that I examine in this essay are multiply voiced. Women speaking as daughters or sisters on the one hand, and wives and daughters-in-law on the other, comment differently on the contradictions within North Indian kinship that frame women's containment within patrilineal definitions. Yet women's speech practices as a whole differ from men's in that even in their heterogeneity, they nonetheless persist in revealing the contradictions (and vulnerability) of the dominant discourse.[3]

The second of these interpretive problems concerns the nature of such struggles, and the question of whether the alternative representations of gender and kinship embedded in these speech practices constitute a potent challenge to the dominant discourse, or whether they should more properly be viewed as 'rituals of rebellion' (Gluckman 1963) that, as Guha puts it, 'reinforce authority by feigning defiance' (1983: 31) in a temporary, contained and innocuous 'reversal' of the otherwise authoritative and unquestioned cultural discourse.[4] Pursuing an argument that resembles Gluckman's on this particular point, Block (1987) summarizes three alternative representations of gender and kinship in a Madagascar society, and argues that the representations that seem to challenge the predominant value placed on descent through males in favour of relationships through women exist only in order to be expelled and then brought under the control of the discourse of patriliny, which is thereby legitimized and rendered persuasive. In an effort to address the same set of issues, Messick (1987) describes a Moroccan women's discourse of gender and kinship embedded in the process of weaving, suggesting that this discourse represents an expressive world that is distinct from the dominant patriarchal ideology. She characterizes this female perspective on kinship as a 'subordinate discourse' rather than an alternative or competing ideology. The latter, she argues, 'would entail an explicit elaboration of an oppositional conceptual order, and might give rise to efforts at suppression by upholders of the dominant ideology'. Women's subordinate discourse, however, 'is not likely even to be noticed, much less elicit active suppression' (1987: 217).

Thus, for both Block and Messick, the alternative moral perspectives encoded in women's speech and ritual pose no potent threat to patrilineal ideology, and effect no transformations in women's everyday lives.

In her review of research on the links between language, gender and power, Gal (1991: 177) suggests that women's speech practices may be seen as resistance to a dominant cultural order (rather than mere 'rituals of rebellion') when they propose alternative models of the social world, and when these strategies of verbal expression are practised and valued despite denigration or attempts to suppress them. The active denigration or suppression of these expressive forms might be viewed, then, as an index of the threat they pose to the dominant representations of kinship and gender. In northern India, attempts to denigrate or suppress women's expressive forms have surfaced in certain specific circumstances. There does, minimally, appear to be an ambivalent attitude towards women's songs. On the one hand, ritual songs are viewed as auspicious and necessary to the performance of many rituals; there is a Hindi proverb that despite its misogyny counts the singing of auspicious songs as one of the good qualities of women: 'Woman, you have four hundred thousand bad attributes, but three good ones: singing auspicious songs, maintaining virtue, and producing sons' (*tirya tujh me tin gun, avagun hai lakh char; mangal gave, sat rache, aur kokhan upje lal*).[5] Yet in many instances, attempts are made to silence women's song. Songs that redefine women's sexuality in positive and celebratory terms rather than as dangerous to males and to male kinship solidarities (Raheja and Gold 1994) may be viewed by men as 'bad songs' (*bura git*) that should no longer be sung by 'our educated girls' (Flueckiger 1991: 92-93). In the early twentieth century, the singing of such songs was viewed as a serious feminine shortcoming, and women's lack of formal education was the imputed source of this moral failing, in women's didactic literature of the time (Kumar 1991: 21). In nineteenth-century Bengal, songs and other forms of women's popular culture were often critical of women's position in Bengali society. 'Often stark and bitter in expressing the plight of women in a male-dominated society, the poems and songs popular among the lower social groups were, at the same time, tough, sensuous or bawdy, in an idiom specific to woman' (Banerjee 1989: 131-32). From the mid-nineteenth century, however, as Banerjee discovered, Bengali men, influenced both by colonial education and by nationalist sentiment, attempted to arouse public opinion against these expressive genres, and there were concerted efforts to denigrate and suppress them as 'corrupting', indecent, and unworthy of proper Hindu women.

Gal recognizes that women's responses to powerlessness may sometimes have the effect only of reproducing the forms of their subordination
(1991: 183), yet she recognizes also the possibility that women's speech
genres do not always simply 'reflect' or reinforce an already constituted
social order; speech genres may function as strategies in ongoing negotiations and contestations in kinship and gender identities.[6] In this essay, I
view rural North Indian women's proverbs and songs as potent forms of
resistance to dominant cultural representations. I do not view them as a
'safety valve' that would effectively limit the possibility of actual resistance. With Scott (1990: 191), I view such discursive forms, and the
alternative normal sensibilities encoded within them, as 'a condition of
practical resistance rather than a substitute for it'. I outline the terms in
which these forms expose and critique the contradictions within North
Indian kinship, and indicate the ways in which they articulate a subversive
moral perspective that is invoked by women as they negotiate their
identities within the constraints set by patrilineal kinship in northern India.

Proverbs, Songs and Women's Use of Language

Veena Das has written that very early in their lives, North Indian women
learn that their use of language must be different from that of men. While
they learn that great circumspection is necessary in using words that reveal
the tensions in their experience of kinship relations, or words that undermine the authority of the official discourses of patriliny, they also learn
that there are ways in which resistance to those discourses may be com-
municated. Das suggests that as a girl reaches sexual maturity, she learns
to communicate through non-verbal gestures, through particular speech
intonations, and through the reading of subtle meta-messages in ordinary
language. Mothers admonish their daughters early on to learn the nuances
of such communicative practices: 'What kind of a daughter are you, if you
cannot read the way the eye of the mother points?' (Das 1988: 198). In
women's songs and proverbs, however, resistance to patrilineal discourse
of kinship and gender is not covert, subtle and silent but overt, explicit and
articulate.

In rural North India, groups of women sing primarily at the births of
sons, at weddings, and at various annual festivals. Songs are sung on two
different kinds of occasions. Women sing as the ritual events of a wedding
unfold, usually in close proximity to the male-dominated formal ceremonies. At these times, women quite literally have to compete to let their
voices be heard. At the *phera*, the central core of the wedding ritual, at
which the bride is formally transferred from her natal kin to her husband's

family amid ritual acts of deference to the groom's side, women of the bride's side just a few feet away in the same courtyard sing *gali*, songs abusing the groom's family, in which obscene joking about the sexual proclivities of the groom's mother is the most common theme. It is not unusual for the men of the groom's family to become angry at this, to call for a halt, only to be rebuffed and assailed by yet more bawdy abuse. When the bride's mother's brothers come to give gifts just before the wedding is to take place, they stand just at the threshold of their sister's husband's house, and behind her the women of the neighbourhood sing 'songs of the mother's brothers' gifts' in which their generosity, and thus their honour (*izzat*) as well is denigrated. Just outside the door, behind the mother's brothers, men of both sides have gathered and there is among them, inevitably, a raucous band, playing loudly and cacophonously as if to drown out the women's song, stopping only when the women's songs are finished.

At the birth of a son, while a son's marriage party is away at the bride's village, and at the festivals of Holi and Tij, singing and dancing sessions called *khoriyas* are held at night in courtyards from which males have been barred. 'Dancing songs' (*nachne ke git*) or 'sitting songs' (*baithne ke git*) are sung on these occasions. Unlike other genres of women's songs, both of these almost always take the form of long verse narratives in which the tragic consequences of a husband's failure to transfer his loyalties from his natal kin to his new wife is the most frequent theme. At the very time that the groom is accepting a bride in *kanya dan* ('the gift of a virgin', the prescribed form of the marriage ritual), according to which ideology the wife should be assimilated to and defer to the kin of her husband, his own mother and aunts and sisters are singing of the morally problematic aspects of such a transformation.

The internal patterning and the formal structure of the songs likewise highlight the competing voices and multiple perspectives. As Gold has pointed out, the verses of many North Indian women's songs are 'chorused conversations' in which conflicts and opposed perspectives are enacted in alternating question and answer conversations among kinsmen (Raheja and Gold 1994). Thus one song may articulate as many as five or six different points of view on a situation or relationship. In the North Indian villages in which I worked, such songs typically depict conversations in which the voices and differing perspectives of husband and wife, the husband's mother, his sister, and the wives of his brothers may all be heard.

Though they are often interpreted as tokens of an abstract and essentialized 'folk mentality', proverbs in northern India, as elsewhere, are strategic speech acts through which speakers comment purposively and strategically on particular social situations (Briggs 1988:101-35; Burke 1973: 291-96; de Certeau 1984: 18-21).

Proverbs are used with great frequency in rural North Indian speech. Most are used by both men and women, but there also exists a large number of proverbs used almost exclusively by women (Christian 1891: xxvii-xxix, Fallon 1886: 299-320). Many, though not all, of these proverbs used by women are commentaries on kinship relations, either overtly and explicitly or metaphorically. Such usages occur in ordinary conversations, most frequently among women, though they may also be used in speaking to or in the hearing of men. Women also used proverbial utterances in conversations with me, to draw my attention to particular conventions concerning kinship relationships and to their own perspectives on them.

Particular proverbs about women and kinship (though not, signifi-cantly, those used primarily by women) were sometimes cited in colonial documents, as evidence of female passivity and submission to the dictates of 'tradition', and of the oppression of women in India. Such citations form part of a larger colonial discourse on women and tradition, a discourse that attempted to provide a moral justification for colonial rule. Colonial reports on the practice of sati, for example, often stress women's submis-sive and unquestioning obedience to the dictates of 'religion', and their identity as passive bearers of a fixed, reified, and univocal 'tradition' (Mani 1984: 1989). Such colonial documents also tend to infantilize women, often speaking of the widow as a 'tender child', even though most satis were women over the age of forty (Mani 1989: 97-98, Yang 1989). As Partha Chatterjee has pointed out, representing Indian women as voiceless and oppressed provided a rationale for British colonial intervention:

> [A] central element in the ideological justification of British colonial rule was the criticism of the 'degenerate and bar-baric' social customs of the Indian people, sanctioned, or so it was believed, by their religious tradition. Alongside the project of instituting orderly, lawful and rational procedures of governance, therefore, colonialism also saw itself as performing a 'civilizing mission'. In identifying this tradi-tion as 'degenerate and barbaric', colonialist critics invari-ably repeated a long list of atrocities perpetrated on Indian women, not so much by men or certain classes of men, but by an entire body of scriptural canons and ritual practices which, they said, by rationalizing such atrocities within a

complete framework of religious doctrine, made them appear to perpetrators and sufferers alike as the necessary
marks of right conduct. By assuming a position of sympathy
with the unfree and oppressed womanhood of India, the
colonial mind was able to transform this figure of the Indian
women into a sign of the inherently oppressive and unfree
nature of the entire cultural tradition of a country. (Chatterjee 1989)

The 'protection' of weak and passive Hindu women became, then, a
strategy of colonial domination, and gender characterizations became
vehicles for moral claims on the part of colonial administrators, missionaries, and so forth (Mani 1989; O'Hanlon 1991).

Though colonial proverb compilations often note when a particular
proverb is used primarily by women, there is no commentary on the
relationship between proverbs about kinship and gender used by men (or
perhaps by both men and women) and those used by women. Features of
women's speech are thus recorded in the colonial archive, but they are
never seen as challenging the supposedly dead weight of the 'tradition'
that oppresses them. Women are thus never represented as reflecting upon
tradition or as giving voice to a distinctive perspective on it.

Like women's songs, however, proverbs used by North Indian women
in ordinary speech frequently interrogate the dominant discourse by exposing the contradictions in its representations of women in patrilineal
kinship. If songs are confined to ritually marked spheres that are somehow
set apart from everyday life, proverbs insert those interrogations into
everyday life and into the conversations and conflicts in which kinship and
gender identities are negotiated and struggled over.

Proverbs and Songs: Exposing Contradictions[7]

The songs and proverbs that I heard in the North Indian villages of Pahansu
and Hathchoya focus attention most frequently and consistently on three
sets of contradictions within North Indian discourses of patriliny: contradictions connected with a woman's shifting ties to natal kin and to conjugal
kin; those connected with the paradoxes of stressing the importance of
marriage for both men and women, while simultaneously devaluing the
conjugal bond in favour of pre-existing relationships (particularly those
among men) in the patrilineal unit; and those surrounding the position of
a norm of silence and submission to one's husband even in the face of
moral transgression on his part.

The first of these contradictions concerns the transfer of a woman from natal home to conjugal home in this patrilineal and virilocal milieu in which village exogamy is practised. In northern India, marriage is spoken of as a *kanya dan* ('gift of a virgin'), the unreciprocated gifting away of a daughter along with lavish gifts for herself and for the people of her *sasural*, her husband's house. She is given away in the course of a complex set of ritual actions designed to effect her transformation from 'one's own' (*apni*) to her natal kin to 'other' (*dusri*) and 'alien' (*parayi*) to them. The woman is often said to undergo a transformation at the wedding, in which she becomes the 'half-body' of her husband, of one substance with him. His kinsmen become her kinsmen, and her ties with her own natal kin are transformed as well; people in Pahansu say that unmarried girls share a 'bodily connection' (*sarir ka sambandh*) with their natal kin, but that after the marriage, there is only a 'relationship' (*rista*).[8] Trautmann has characterized this cultural understanding of marriage and the 'gift of a virgin' as a 'patrilineal idiom of complete dissimilation of the bride from her family of birth and her complete assimilation to that of her husband' (Trautmann 1981: 291).

The present analysis of the commentaries that women compose, in song and proverb, on this patrilineal idiom builds on the observations of Jacobson (1977), Vatuk (1975) and Dube (1988) on this point, and follows their analyses of the limits of 'patriliny' in rural North India. Jacobson argued that structural analyses of the patrilineal and patrilocal aspects of North Indian kinship, and interpretations that stress the completeness of the transfer of a woman from natal to conjugal kin, overlook the complexity of a woman's kinship relations. Though, she argues, much of the ritual and ideology of rural North India does indeed stress patrilineality and the priority of a woman's ties to her husband's kin, many less formalized though no less important ideas and practices, such as extended visiting at the natal village, foreground the permanence of a woman's ties to parents and to brothers. Vatuk's explicit critique of the emphasis on the lineal, corporate nature of North Indian kinship includes the argument that the 'unbreakable bond' between a woman and her natal kin is related to the latter's obligation to supply her with gifts that ensure her security in her husband's home. And Dube, in her discussion of the production of women as gendered subjects in the Indian patrilineal milieu, points out that the particular contradictions within the kinship system produce an ambiguity surrounding women's transferral from natal kin to conjugal kin. While the lifelong tie between brothers and sisters is emphasized in ritual and in everyday talk, young girls are nonetheless prepared for life in the husband's home by being told that a woman should be like water which, having no shape of its own, can take the shape of the vessel into which it is poured, or that she should be like soft and malleable clay that has no form until it is worked into shape by the potter. Thus, on the one hand, ritual perpetuates ties with the natal kin, while on the other, women are in many ways expected, as Dube points out, to discard their loyalties to natal kin, to be formed and shaped anew in the husband's family.[9] The more that women place themselves at a distance from their natal kin, the more vulnerable they may be to harsh treatment in the conjugal village; the natal place continues to be viewed as a place of refuge and of succour throughout a woman's life.

The poignancy of women's separation from natal kin is vividly drama-tized in North India at the moment of *bidai* ('departure'), when a newly married girl first leaves her natal home in the company of her husband and his male kinsmen. Both men and women present at this time are apt to weep at the sight of the heavily-veiled young woman being carried to a waiting automobile or water-buffalo cart, and the women of the bride's natal village sing 'departure songs' (*bidai git*) at the doorway as she leaves. Many of these songs are reflections on the contradictory expectations concerning natal and conjugal relationships.

BIDAI GIT 1

Refrain [Bride's natal kin][10]
Dear girl, today you've left your father's house,
Today you've become 'other' (*parayi*)
The streets in which you spent your childhood
Have today become *parayi*.

[Bride speaking]
My grandfather cries, my grandmother cries,
The whole family cries.
My younger brother cries,
Your sister born from the same mother (*ma jai*)
Has left and gone away.

[Verses in which the bride speaks are repeated, using kin terms for FeB, FeBW, FyBW, and so on]
  The second line of the refrain of this song ends with the words *parayi re.* (*Re* is a vocative particle that commonly appears in these songs.) The second line of the bride's verses ends with the words *ma jai re.* The replication of the same sound pattern, the rhyme, in these two verses

ironically foregrounds the dissimilarity in the meanings of the relationship enunciated by the bride's natal kin and by the bride herself. *Parayi* and *ma jai re* share the same sounds, but this aural similarity serves to heighten the contradiction between the two representations of women in patrilineal kinship relationships. An ironic awareness of this contradiction lies at the heart of this song of departure.

BIDAI GIT 2

Refrain [Bride speaking]
Don't let your mind be filled with sadness.
Mother, I'll meet you again.
I'll call my *dadas* (HFM) *dadi* (FM).
I'll call my *tayas* (HFeBW) *tai* (FeBW).
I won't remember my *dadi*, Mother, I'll meet you again.
I won't remember my *tai*, Mother, I'll meet you again.

[In the following verse of this song, the bride says that she will call her husband's mother 'mother', her husband's sister 'sister', and so on]

This second song of departure expresses an ironic perspective on the same set of contradictions not by juxtaposing two contradictory perspectives, but by making utterances whose actual intended meaning is precisely the opposite of its conventional and literal meaning. The poignant irony of a bride saying, 'I won't remember my *dadi*, I won't remember my *tai*' lies precisely in the fact that all the women singing this song know that she will never forget, and though she may call her husband's father's mother *dadi*, as the ideology of *kanya dan* may enjoin her to do, her experience as she utters that word in her conjugal village is worlds apart from the experience of saying it in her own natal home.

BIDAI GIT 3

Two water pots are on my head.
A beautiful golden pendant is on my forehead.
Call me back quickly, Mother,
Beg with folded hands.
My heart is not here in my husband's mother's house,
My heart is not here with this foreign man.
Call me back quickly, Mother,
Beg with folded hands.

We played with dolls together,
But then I went off to my *sasural.*
Call me back quickly, Mother,
Beg with folded hands.

[First verse is repreated a number of times, changed only by the substitution of the names of other ornaments worn by married woman]

This third song of departure vividly portrays a woman's sense of belonging fully neither to natal home nor conjugal home. The first two lines invoke conventional and often recurring images of desire and fulfillment, and the pleasure of attracting and pleasing one's husband; an image of a woman gracefully drawing water at a village well often, in women's songs, precedes a happy flirtatious encounter, and songs of conjugal happiness frequently include long lists of the ornaments worn by a married woman that mark her body as sexual and pleasureful (Das 1988: 201; Gold 1992). This song of departure begins with these images of conjugal pleasures, but the desires and expectations are evoked but not fulfilled: the husband is a 'foreign man' and the bride cannot bear to stay with him. She has become *parayi* to her own natal kin at the time of marriage, but the man to whose house she has gone is a foreigner to her.

I spoke about these songs in 1988 with Simla, a woman about my own age who had been married into Pahansu about twenty years before, and who had given birth there to four children, one of whom was already married and about to give birth to Simla's first grandchild. We talked about why so many women felt the poignancy of such songs, and she said to me, very slowly and deliberately as she looked around the house in which she had spent more than half her life:'You know, we never call our *sasural* ['house of the mother-in-law'] one's own house. We only call our *pihar* [natal home] one's own house.' Simla's ironic tone speaks here to the fissure she seems to experience between the patrilineal convention that married women become 'one's own' to their husband's family and 'foreign' to their natal kin on the one hand, and women's continual experience of 'foreignness' in their *sasurals* and feelings of longing for the natal kin on the other.

The acknowledgement of this fissure, the awareness of a contradiction within the conventions of patrilineal ideology, is inserted into everyday speech and everyday moral assessments through women's use of proverbs. A very commonly heard proverb used by both men and women asserts the patrilineal idiom of the complete dissimilation of the woman from her natal kin: 'Daughter, daughter's husband, and sister's son; these three are not

one's own' (*dhi jamai banjaye tinon nahin apna*). Yet in speaking of the
emotional and pragmatic difficulties of this dissimilation and the assimilation into the *sasural*, women frequently invoke a countervailing proverbial claim: 'The daughter and the son are one's own, and the
daughter-in-law is "other" ' (*dhi put to apne bahu begani*).

An ironic view of the substitutability of natal kin by the husband's kin
found in the second *bidai git* is echoed in a very commonly heard women's
proverb:

> *sath sas nanad sau hon, ma ki hor na in sun ho.*

> If a woman had sixty mothers-in-law and a hundred
> husband's sisters, none could compare to her own mother.

Three Hindi proverbial couplets also point to women's experience of
this contradiction in the patrilineal description of a woman's easy transferral from natal home to conjugal home.

> *sun sun ke teri bath saheli, soch hua meri man ko,*
> *kar ke byah gharon nahin rakhte babal apni dhi ko.*

> I have heard what you said, friend, and pondered it in my heart,
> That after getting her married, a father doesn't keep his daughter
> in his house.

In feigning surprise at the obvious fact that in North India a married
daughter does not remain in her natal home, this proverb, like the songs of
departure, focuses on women's complex experience of what appears, from
the male perspective, as an unproblematic transferral of women from one
patrilineal kin group to another.

> *ujhar ho ghar sas ka, jo bair kare har bar,*
> *pihar ghar subas base, jab lag hai sansar.*

> May the house of my mother-in-law be ruined,
>   she who always creates enmity.
> May my natal house prosper, as long as the
>   world endures.

Though the patrilineal ideology of *kanya dan* enjoins a woman to
abandon her loyalties to her natal kin and see herself as 'one's own' to her
husband's kin, the second rhymed couplet articulates a critique of that
injunction. As it gives voice to a curse on the *sasural* and a blessing on the
pihar, this proverb, like the preceding one, invokes a sense of the persistent

close ties to a woman's natal kin, and the frequent sense of shattered and incomplete solidarity a woman experiences in her husband's house.[11]

A third proverbial couplet also draws attention to such failures of solidarity in the *sasural*.

jeth jethani devar sab matlab ke mit,
matlab bin to koi bhi rakhe na prit.

The husband's elder brother, elder brother's wife,
  and younger brother are all selfish friends.
No one shows affection without some interested motive.

Although women may use this proverb to comment on indications of self-interest in any human relationships and not just those in the *sasural*, it is nonetheless significant that the proverb cites relationships in the conjugal home as primary examples of selfish and interested relationships in arenas in which solidarity ought to prevail.[12]

A woman in rural North India values natal ties at least partly because they are viewed as sources of support if resistance to the demands of conjugal kin becomes necessary. But this resistance may be curtailed if her husband and his kin can effectively limit her contact with her natal kin (Jeffery, Jeffery and Lyon 1989: 31-36).

A second set of contradictions in North Indian kinship that is addressed in women's speech genres concerns the relative valuation that is to be placed on the conjugal relationship on the one hand, and on a man's ties to his own natal kin and the solidarity of that patrilineal group on the other. Marriage is deemed essential in the social, ritual and emotional lives of both men and women. Many proverbs attest to the commonsensical nature of this view:

tiriya purukh bin hai dukhi jaise ann bin deh;
jale bale hai jivra, jaise khet bin meh.

A wife is sorrowful without her husband,
  as the body without food;
Her heart is burnt and heated as a field without rain.

Tiriya bin to nar har aisa rahbatau hove jaisa.

A man without a wife is as a traveller on the road.

At the same time, however, the discourse of patrilineal kinship enjoins the wife to subordinate her desire for intimacy with the husband to his preexisting bonds of loyalty and affection with his natal kinsmen. Kakar

(1978) suggests that in this regard, the wife represents a pernicious threat to the unity and solidarity of the patrilineal unit, and her intimacy with him must not be allowed to disrupt or weaken his ties to his parents and siblings. Intimacy of all kinds, particularly sexual intimacy, is seen as dangerous to this solidarity; and there may frequently be attempts made to limit sexual intimacy if it does in fact come to threaten a man's preexisting loyalties. The ideal wife, then, accepts without question the patrilineal assumption that her husband's natal ties take precedence over the conjugal relationship, and accepts, in consequence, her subordinate position in her *sasural*.[13]

This dominant perspective concerning the valuation of men's natal ties over ties to the wife are exemplified in a number of proverbs that seem to be used primarily by men. The following is a particularly striking example:

> *mai bap ke laton mare mehri dekh juray,*
> *charon dham jo phir ave, tabhun pap na jay.*

> Whoever kicks [i.e. offends or displeases] his parents to
>   strengthen his relationship with his wife,
> His sin will not go away even if he travels to all
>   the pilgrimage places [where sins are said to be removed]

Women's ritual songs, particularly the long narrative 'dancing songs' offer a set of compelling critiques of this view of the threat women pose to the unity of the patrilineal group, and of the consequent devaluation of conjugality and of the worth of women as wives. A dancing song sung at the festival of Tij is typical of a great many such songs that I recorded.

DANCING SONG 1

[*Bahu* to *Sas*][14]
Sasu, someone has come selling fish.
Sasu, everyone is buying some fish.
Sasu, buy some fish and give some to us too.
You give us halva-puri [sweet pudding and fried breads]
    every day, *Sasu*.[15]

Hearing of the husband's coming, a cup of poison.
She drank the cup of poison, and she felt so very sleepy.

[*Bahu*, who has just drunk the poison, to *Sas*]
Tell me *Sasu*, where should I sleep?

[*Sas* to *Bahu*]
Sleep on the top floor, *Bahu*, in the room with the red door.
Lie down and sleep on your bed, *Bahu*.
Away for twelve years, the beloved husband came home.

[Husband to his mother, the *Sas*]
I see my mother, I see my sisters too.
There's one I don't see, Mother, my wife, the daughter of a
   gentleman.

[*Sas* to her son, the husband]
On the top floor son, in the room with the red door,
She's sleeping there, son, the daughter of a gentleman.

[Husband to the *Sas*]
I called her once, Mother, I called her twice,
But still she didn't speak, Mother, the daughter of a gentleman.

[*Sas* to the husband]
Go into the garden and bring in a branch,
Hit her and wake her up, the daughter of a gentleman.

[Husband to *Sas*]
I hit her once with the branch, Mother, I hit her twice.
But still she didn't speak, Mother, the daughter of a gentleman.
The husband took off her veil, to have a look at her.

[Husband to the *Sas*]
Is she dead or asleep, Mother, the daughter of a gentleman.

[*Sas* to the husband]
Go to the garden, son, and cut some sandalwood.
Burn her body, son, the daughter of a gentleman.
He burnt her body, and he came back to the house.
The husband sat at the threshold, wailing out of grief.

[*Sas* to the husband]
Why are you crying, son, wailing so loudly?
I can have my son married four times.
Two fair brides, two dark ones,
I can have my son married four times.

[Husband to the *Sas*]
You can throw all four down a well, Mother.
I don't have that one, the daughter of a gentleman.
The husband spread out his scarf, and lay down to sleep.

[Husband, addressing his dead wife]
Come in a dream, fair one, and tell me all that happened.

[Bahu speaking in the dream]
Husband, every day she gave bread and pudding.
She heard that you were coming, and she gave a cup of poison.
I drank the poison, and I felt very sleepy.
Where should I sleep, *Sasu*, tell me the place.
On the top floor, husband, in the room with the red door.
Go up to the roof, my husband-lord, and shout out to everyone.

[Husband]
Don't listen, men, to your mothers and your sisters.
My mother and my sisters have laid waste to my home.

In this powerful song, we twice hear the voice of the husband resisting the assumption that a particular woman as wife is replaceable and indeed dispensable. When the mother suggests that her son can easily marry four more times if he wishes, the husband rejects this portrayal of the wife as an anonymous cipher, as either irreducibly 'other' to her conjugal kin or as so assimilated to them that her own particular identity is dissolved. And finally, at the end of this Tij song, as he climbs to the roof and proclaims that a man's loyalty to his natal kin must often be subordinated to his loyalty to his wife, he subverts a fundamental tenet of North Indian kinship. In many women's songs, men are represented as feigning adherence to norms concerning the priority to be placed on patrilineal solidarities, while privately valuing solidarity with the wife. In the following dancing song, as in several others that I recorded, public conformity to the requirements of these solidarities is at odds with a man's private subversion of them.[16]

DANCING SONG 2

My mother-in-law is very cunning.
I am my husband's beloved.
I sat at the grinding stone, I ground the grain coarsely.
She rubbed the flour between her fingers, to see how
    coarse it was.
I am my husband's beloved.

When she rubbed her fingers together, she told her son about it.
I am my husband's beloved.
When she told her son about it, he brought a stick with knobs,
    and he beat me gently gently (*dhire dhire*).
When he beat me gently gently, I went into our bedroom.
I am my husband's beloved.

When I was sleeping in the room, he brought a *ser* of *laddus*.[17]
I am my husband's beloved.
When he brought a *ser* of *laddus*, I threw them back to him.
I am my husband's beloved.
When I threw the *laddus* back, he hand-fed them to me
    and I ate one or two.
I am my husband's beloved.

When I ate one or two, I became very thirsty.
I am my husband's beloved.
When I became very thirsty, he brought some water to me.
I am my husband's beloved.
When he brought the water to me, I drank a drop or two.
I am my husband's beloved.

When I drank a drop or two, I became very cold.
I am my husband's beloved.
When I became very cold, he brought a red quilt to me,
I am my husband's beloved.
When he brought a red quilt to me, I became very warm.
I am my husband's beloved.
When I became very warm, he brought a red fan to me.
I am my husband's beloved.
When he brought a red fan to me,
I waved it gently gently (*dhire dhire*).
I am my husband's beloved.

In this song, the husband makes a show of beating his wife to present a public image of acceding to his mother's claims on his loyalty, but he beats her 'gently gently' and then in their own room, away from the gaze of his mother, he brings her food and drink and engages in sexual intimacy, as the last lines of the song strongly suggest. I have elsewhere suggested that embroidered fans (*bijna*) appear, for a number of reasons, in women's songs and in North Indian folk art as signs of sexual intimacy (Raheja, in press). The private sexual intimacy is read by the wife as a negation of the significance of the public beating, since the beating was a sham one staged for the benefit of the husband's mother. In this song, both the beating and the figurative sexual intercourse are done 'gently gently' (*dhire dhire*). This rather prominent linguistic equation in the song might be read as an ironic commentary on another kind of equation that is often made in Hindi between beatings and sexual intercourse. A contemptuous way of describing intercourse in Hindi is *chut marna*, literally 'beating the vagina'. *Marna* is the usual word for 'beating', the one that is used in the song. But the equivalence between beating and sexual intimacy (both are done 'gently gently') that is drawn in the song underlines the fact that a man's adherence to a public and 'normative' devaluation of sexuality and of women as wives may be only a cover behind which other perspectives are given moral credence, overtly by women, though perhaps covertly and furtively by men.[18]

There are a number of proverbs used by women that echo the perspective voiced in these songs, proverbs that enunciate negative moral assessments concerning the patrilineal norms involving the devaluation of conjugality, and the 'replaceability' of wives.

> *mard ka kya hai? ek juti pahni, ek juti utari.*

> What is it to a man? He puts on a new shoe
> and takes off the old.

This particular properb is sometimes heard in conversations in which women criticize a man who exhibits an attitude of disdain for his wife, or undervalues her in relation to his male kinsmen; he regards her as replaceable as a worn-out shoe.

> *chot lagi pahar ki aur toren ghar ka sil.*

> He is hurt by the mountain and breaks up the grindstone.

Women sometimes use this second proverb as a commentary on men's tendency to unjustly place the blame for discord within the patrilineal group upon their wives, a tendency that places priority on the relationships among men while viewing the women as dangerous threats to male solidarity. Although the proverb can be invoked in a variety of situations of misplaced blame, its use by women in contexts in which kinship loyalties are at stake may represent a strategy of resistance to patrilineal values.

The third set of contradictions to which women's songs and proverbs address themselves is connected with the tension women seem to perceive between positing the kinship group as a solidarity unit on the one hand, and defining wives as both the upholders of the honour of that group and as its most subordinate members on the other. Women are expected to be devoted to their husbands even in the face of serious moral transgressions, and wives are enjoined to emulate the figure of Sita, the wife of Rama in the *Ramayana*, who remains steadfast in wifely devotion even as Rama unjustly banishes her from his kingdom.[19] Kakar (1978:66) speaks of a 'formidable consensus' in India concerning the image of Sita as the 'ideal woman'. And the phrase 'she is a second Sita' is, in northern India, a universally recognized appreciative acknowledgement of feminine virtue. Yet women's songs and proverbs from North India appear to challenge the values of unquestioned submission and self-sacrifice that Sita represents.

An extremely common theme in a wide variety of North Indian textual and oral traditions involves the banishment or scorn of barren women, of women whose husbands decide for one reason or another to take a second wife, and of women unjustly accused of engaging in sexual relations outside of marriage. Representations of women's responses to such treatment, and the moral valuations of these responses, differ dramatically in the epic traditions, in popular North Indian folk dramas (*svang*) performed by and largely for males, and in women's narrative dancing songs from Pahansu and Hathchoya. I have elsewhere (Raheja 1991) described the way in which the epic texts and the folk dramas portray the 'ideal wife' as one who unquestioningly submits to such unjust banishment or scorn, and whose response is simply to wait for other male kinsmen, son or brother or father, to rescue her from her adversity and restore her to her husband.

Despite the authoritative nature of these powerful images in North India, the narratives recounted in women's dancing songs set forth a strikingly different perspective on gender, agency and dependency in kinship relations.

DANCING SONG 3 (For the Festival of Tij)

From which direction did the rains come,
In which direction will it rain now?
Indar Raja comes down in the garden
The rains have come from the east,
And it's about to rain in the west.
Indar Raja comes down in the garden.[20]

[*Bahu* speaking]
Mother-in-law, I heard a surprising thing,
That your son will marry again.
Indar Raja came down in the garden.
Mother-in-law, have I come from a bad family,
Or did I bring a small dowry?
Indar Raja came down in the garden.

[Mother-in-law]
No, Bahu, you aren't from a bad family.
And you didn't bring a small dowry.
Indar Raja came down in the garden.
Your colour is a little dark, Bahu.
And my son wants a fair wife.
Indar Raja came down in the garden.

[Bahu]
Sisters, I went to ask my father-in-law,
Is your son to marry again?
Indar Raja came down in the garden.
Father-in-law, have I come from a bad family,
Or did I bring a small dowry?
Indar Raja came down in the garden.

[Father-in-law]
No, Bahu, you aren't from a bad family,
And you didn't bring a small dowry.
Indar Raja came down in the garden.
You are a little dark, my Bahu,
And my son wants a fair wife.
Indar Raja came down in the garden.

[Bahu]
Sisters, I went to ask my husband's sister,
Is your brother to marry again?
Indar Raja came down in the garden.
Husband's sister, have I come from a bad family,
Or did I bring a small dowry?
Indar Raja came down in the garden.

[Husband's sister]
No, brother's wife, you aren't from a bad family,
And you didn't bring a small dowry.
Indar Raja came down in the garden.
Your colour is a little dark, brother's wife,
And my brother wants a fair wife.

[Bahu]
Sisters, I went to ask my raja [husband, lit. 'king']
Tell me, are you to marry again?
Indar Raja came down in the garden.
Raja, am I from a bad family,
Or did I bring a small dowry?
Indar Raja came down in the garden.

[Husband]
No, you aren't from a bad family,
And you didn't bring a small dowry.
Indar Raja came down in the garden.
Your colour is a little dark.
And I want a fair wife.
Indar Raja came down in the garden.

[Bahu]
Raja, who will do the women's rites [*tehale*] at your marriage,
And who will sing the auspicious songs?
Indar Raja came down in the garden.

[Husband]
Wife, my mother will do the women's rites,
And my sister will sing auspicious songs.
Indar Raja came down in the garden.

[Bahu]
Raja, who will send the marriage party,
And who will bear the expense?
Indar Raja came down in the garden.

[Husband]
Wife, my brother will send off the marriage party,
And my father will bear the expense.
Indar Raja came down in the garden.

[Bahu]

Sisters, I went to the roof [to see the marriage party
    return, after the husband has married again]
And how many came in the marriage party?
Indar Raja came down in the garden.
Sisters, there were one hundred and fifty of them,
    without feet and hands,
And I couldn't count all the bald ones. [The wife is here
    reviling the men of the marriage party.]

Sisters, when I heard that the co-wife had come,
I got a fever right away.
Indar Raja came down in the garden.
Sisters, I went to see the co-wife,
A bent and worthless coin in my hand.
[to give the ritual gift to the new bride]

Indar Raja came down in the garden.
I went to the ritual feast for the new wife,
Sisters, I made a rice pudding filled with poison.

Indar Raja came down in the garden.
Sisters, I heard that the co-wife died,
My fever went down right away.

Indar Raja came down in the garden.
Sisters, I went to the lament for the co-wife,
I veiled myself heavily [women generally veil
    while doing this ritual lament].

Indar Raja came down in the garden.
Sisters, outside I was lamenting, but in my heart I was laughing.
And my heart was joyful.

In this song, the wife is placed in a situation not unlike that of the wives
who appear in the epics and *svang* dramas. Yet in contrast to the submissive
posture assumed by the wives in the male-authored folklore genres, the
heroine of this dancing song takes immediate and decisive action in the
face of the threat to her position in her husband's house. The appeal made
by the wife to 'sisters', the women listeners who hear her tale, make it
evident that the wife's actions are indeed valourized. It is not necessarily
the violence, the poisoning of the co-wife, that is being extolled, but the
ability to act decisively when one is treated unjustly. There is no talk of

'fate' here, or of ineradicable ill-fortune, as is found in the *svang* dramas. There is rather, in this dancing song, a definitive moral judgement, and an immediate and potent response to the injustice. And, as in many other women's songs, a woman is represented as having to struggle against the wishes and interest of her husband's natal kin in her efforts to establish and maintain intimacy with her husband and a non-subordinate position in his home.[21] And finally, the heroine of this song does not wait for a son or a brother or a father to save her from her predicament; there are no such male rescuers in this text or in any of the songs I recorded in Pahansu or Hathchoya.

The critique of the patrilineal norm espousing unquestioned wifely submission evidenced in this narrative is not limited to the relatively narrow confines of ritual song. In this case too, both the patrilineal norms and resistance to aspects of the dominant discourse are lodged in proverbs used in everyday speech situations as well.

> *nar sulakkhni kutumb chhakave,*
> *ao tale ke khurchan khave.*

> A proper wife feeds the household first,
> and saves only the leavings for herself.

This proverb plays upon several conceptions of familial well-being and familial hierarchy to reinforce the subordinate position of women within the kinship group. *Sulakkhni* is an adjective that means literally 'having propitious signs' or 'auspicious'. The auspicious wife, one who brings well-being to her husband's line (*kutumb*), is one who eats only the food leftover after the men have eaten; this is a very common expectation for proper feminine behaviour in North India. Precedence in eating is a potent marker of hierarchy in other arenas as well, and the eating of leftovers is a sign of very low status. The woman who accepts her subordinate position, in matters of food and otherwise, and is ready to sacrifice her own well-being for that of others, causes her husband's family to prosper.

While rural women do not totally repudiate this ideal of self-sacrifice and subordination, they do interrogate the discourse that proposes it as an unchallengeable and inflexible injunction. One women's proverb in particular appears as a direct response to the preceding proverb.

> *sharam ki bahu nit bhukhi mare.*

> A wife who is modest and shy always goes hungry.

In the dominant discourse of North Indian kinship, the possession of *sharam* (reticence, modesty, deference, 'shame') is perhaps the most important feminine attribute; one of the most potent criticisms of a woman is that she is *besharam*, without *sharam*. And yet, when they use this proverb, women cast a skeptical eye on this most Sita-like of qualities, and focus only on the deprivation that is often a consequence of the cultivation of *sharam*.

Narrative Potency[22] *and the Strategic Use of Speech*

The songs and proverbs considered in this essay make visible the contradictions within a male-dominated discourse, and thereby envision that discourse as grounded not in a 'natural' and unchangeable moral order, but in a vulnerable and perhaps transformable set of social conventions. The narrative potency of the stories told in women's songs is evident in that the resistance to patrilineal ideology, the alternative perspectives on North Indian kinship found therein, are not confined to intermittent ritual punctuations of social life, but are found in proverbial speech as well, a speech genre which is used in northern India as a potent form of moral commentary. And beyond song and proverb, women may speak in ways that indicate the pervasiveness of these perspectives in more prosaic conversation as well. When in 1990 I naively asked several groups of rural women from the dominant landholding Gujar caste whether they aspired to be like Sita, the paragon of wifely virtue and self-sacrifice, my question was greeted with gales of laughter, and a plethora of anecdotes about outwitted husbands and independent strong-willed wives. No one is like Sita nowadays, they said, and they assured me further that no one has any desired to be a 'second Sita'.

And yet one must take into account the situations in which such utterances are made. When I posed the same questions to other women in the presence of their daughters-in-law, the responses tended to be evasive, or they were cast fairly unambiguously within the terms of the dominant discourse of subordination and dependency; a reply to the effect that women need not emulate the wifely virtues of Sita would perhaps, in those circumstances, diminish a mother-in-law's authority over her daughter-in-law, and women were obviously aware of this as they spoke.

A conversation I had with a Gujar woman and a woman of the untouchable sweeper caste illustrates this sort of strategic self-presentation in a more complex fashion. This conversation took place in the company of an educated Gujar man, himself an anthropologist. I again asked about the desirability of emulating Sita, about deferring to one's husband, and about the importance of women's role in maintaining the honour (*izzat*) of their husbands and brothers by cultivating the quality of *sharam*. This time my question elicited no laughter or mirthful repudiation of Sita, or subtle evasion of the question. Kalaso, the sweeper woman, was extremely circumspect in answering my questions, insisting throughout the very long tape-recorded interview that women of her family and caste did indeed strive to model their behaviour according to the image of Sita; the *izzat* of one's husband and brothers was at stake, she maintained. She made these assertions vociferously and at times almost angrily, as if the very question was a threat to her own honour and that of her family and caste.

Should we read the transcript of this interview as a token of Kalaso's unambiguous internalization of the image of Sita as the ideal woman, an unambiguous internalization of the dominant patrilineal perspective on kinship, gender, and agency and of the terms of her own subordination? Or should we remember that one of our interlocutors was a man of the dominant landholding caste, and that high caste men, in the past and perhaps in the present as well, have often expected to find low caste women who could be persuaded to disregard the value of sexual continence that Sita embodies, and that Kalaso may have had this set of facts in mind as she angrily asserted her own adherence to the ideals represented by the heroine of the *Ramayana?* Was she perhaps not asserting her subservience so much as her defiance of a perceived expectation that she might possibly be viewed as subject to sexual coercion by a powerful male? And should we then regard Kalaso's words not simply as evidence of the penetration of female subjectivity by the terms of the male discourse on patriliny, but as a strategic presentation of self in a specific social arena? And should we regard many of the words of our interlocuters not as fixed and reified and essentialized mirrors of consciousness, but as shifting and purposeful negotiations of identity and relationship?

In this paper, a focus on the way in which proverbs insert the critical perspectives on patriliny found in women's songs into wider areas of social life permits us to regard aspects of women's speech practices in terms of such negotiations. In *The Practice of Everyday Life*, de Certeau reminds us that proverbs, like all discourses, are not inert objects whose meaning can be dissociated from the situations in which speakers enunciate them. They appear in speech as tools purposefully manipulated by their users (1984:19-21), who may at times play intentionally on the ambiguities of their speech to deflect the power of a dominant social order (1984:xiii). Kenneth Burke has also pointed to the strategic nature of proverbs in social life:

74 Gloria Goodwin Raheja

Proverbs are strategies for dealing with situations. In so far
as situations are typical and recurrent in a given social
structure, people develop names for them and strategies for
handling them. Another name for strategies might be attitudes . . . The apparent contradictions [among proverbs]
depend upon differences in attitude, involving correspond-
ingly different choice of strategy (1973: 296-97).

Thus, proverbs and the diverse perspectives on kinship relationships
embedded in them represent resources that speakers draw upon in framing
their own social worlds. While North Indian women may at times speak
in the terms set by the dominant discourse, they also undermine, to some
extent, the script of patriliny as their speech practices sketch a plural rather
than monolithic moral discourse.

Notes

1. Research upon which this essay is based was carried out in two villages of
    western Uttar Pradesh, North India, from 1977-79, and in 1988 and 1990. The
    fieldwork was supported by grants from the Social Science Research Council,
    the American Institute of Indian Studies, the Wenner-Gren Foundation for
    Anthropological Research, and a McKnight-Land Grant Professorship from
    the University of Minnesota.
2. I have elsewhere (Raheja 1991) discussed this issue in relation to interpretive
    practices employed by the Subaltern Studies historians, particularly by Ranajit
    Guha in his essay 'Chandra's Death' (Guha 1987). On the general problem of
    the heterogeneity of subaltern subjectivity, see Das (1989), O'Hanlon (1988),
    and Spivak (1985).
3. In another paper, I described some of the ways in which women's genres of
    oral traditions differ significantly from men's traditions in their representations
    of kinship, gender and agency (Raheja 1991).
4. For a more detailed discussion of the implications of Gluckman and Guha's
    perspectives on this issue, see the Introduction to Raheja and Gold (1994).
    Listen to the heron's words: *Reimagining gender and kinship in North India*.
    (Berkeley: University of California Press).
5. On the positive valuation and auspicious nature of women's ritual song in
    North India, see Henry 1988, 108-11.
6. On the theoretical issue of the constitutive aspects of speech in social life, see
    Sherzer's (1987) elegant explication of a discourse-centred approach to lan-
    guage and culture.

7. All of the songs translated for this paper were recorded in either Pahansu or Hathchoya (western Uttar Pradesh) in 1988 and 1990. I heard many of the proverbs in these villages, some in other places in northern India, and some are taken from two nineteenth-century compendia of proverbs (Christian 1891 and Fallon 1886), and from William Crooke's *A rural and agricultural glossary for the N.W. Provinces and Oudh* (1888). I found these three sources, especially Fallon, to be extremly useful. Fallon contains nearly all of the Hindi proverbs, on any topic, that I have ever come upon. (Fallon's text has been translated into Hindi and edited by Krishnanand Gupta, and published by the National Book Trust of India in 1968). Though I found translations and indications of usage contexts in these compilations to be sometimes misleading, Hindi texts for all the proverbs are provided in each case; when I have drawn on these works, I have therefore amended translations when necessary.

8. The term *rista*, 'relationship' is never used in connection with relationships within a 'lineage' (*kunba*); it is only normally used to characterize relationships through marriage. Thus, a woman's relationship with her own natal kin is characterized, from this perspective, in the same way as a relationship through marriage, because she has been assimilated to the affinal kin of her natal family.

9. For discussions of the ritual ties between women and their natal kin, and the enduring gift-giving responsibilities entailed by them, see Raheja 1988, 93-202 and in press, and Raheja and Gold (1994).

10. All of the songs that I translate here are sung by groups of women without distinguishing, in the performance, the presumed 'speakers' in the conversation that are represented. I note in these translations the speakers that the women identified for me as I worked on the translations with them.

11. There is also a male perspective on women's ties to natal kin, one that appears to respond to the critiques women pose in song and proverb. In the folk dramas performed in the *nautanki* popular theatre of northern India, a frequent theme is a husband's hostility to the wife's brother, and a fear and suspicion that the wife harbours powerful loyalties to her natal kin that could jeopardize his own position. But if a husband cannot fully trust his wife in these plays, brothers also frequently distrust their sisters because they have married into other families and have allegiances there (Hansen 1992:184-88). Two proverbs used, I believe, almost exclusively by men attest to the suspicions harboured by husbands concerning their wives' brothers: *divar khai alon ne, ghar khaya salon ne.* ('As niches weaken walls, so wives' brothers weaken the house'); and *bahu ka bhaiyya puri khaye, bhaiyya ka bhaiyya matar chabaye.* ('The wife's brother eats special fried breads, while a brother's brother has only peas to eat', i.e., a wife will favour her own brother over husband's kin).

12. For further discussion of women's perspectives on the 'solidarity' of patrilineal relationships through men, see Raheja 1991.

13. The power of this particular perspective is illustrated in *Shashthi*, 'The Punishment', a short story by the Bengali writer Rabindranath Tagore, in which a husband unthinkingly utters the conventional sentiment 'One can always replace a wife, but one can never replace a brother' with tragic consequences.

14. *Bahu* is a kinship term meaning 'wife'. *Sas* (or *Sasu*) is 'mother-in-law.'

15. These first lines of the song are not entirely clear to me. It seems apparent though that the mother-in-law is angered by the bahu's suggestion. The following line indicates that upon hearing that her son would soon return after a long absence, the sas poisons the bahu.

16. My reading of this song owed much to Das' analysis (1976) of similar ambiguities in Punjabi kinship.

17. A *ser* is a unit of weight, about two pounds. *Laddus* are sweetmeats made from chickpea flour and sugar, often distributed in North Indian villages at weddings and other festive occasions.

18. One tragic index of the limits to women's resistance is the fact that the heroine of this song must undergo a public beating, however 'gently' it is administered, before she is able to speak up privately to her husband.

19. On the figure of Sita as an exemplary model for Hindu women, see Das 1982; Dube 1988; Kakar 1978, 1989; Mitter 1991; and Roy 1992.

20. The festival of Tij is celebrated in the rainy month of Savan, hence the lines about the rains and Indar Raja (the god Indra) who presides over the monsoon rains. In North Indian oral traditions and pictorial art, the rainy season is represented as a time of erotic encounters and the reunion of lovers. (See for e.g., Wadley 1983) The repeated references to the rains in this song thus function in the same ironic mode as the references to the water pots in the third song of departure translated earlier; they create an expectation here of conjugal intimacy that is thwarted by the wife's realization of her husband's plan to marry again.

21. A second set of significant limitations on women's resistance to the discourse of patriliny are evident in this song and in many of the others we have considered. In these songs, and frequently in everyday life as well, women's struggles are often directed against other women—co-wives, mothers-in-law, husband's sisters—and not against the men who perpetuate this discourse.

22. I have borrowed this phrase from Ann Grodzins Gold (Raheja and Gold, in press), who uses it to describe the way in which the stories women tell in ritual contexts, in Rajasthan, enter into and transform their everyday lives.

References

Abu-Lughod, Lila. 1986. *Veiled sentiments: Honor and poetry in Bedouin society.* Berkeley: University of California Press.

——. 1990. The romance of resistance: Tracing transformations of power through Bedouin women. *American Ethnologist* 17: 41: 55.

Banerjee, Sumanta. 1989. Marginalization of women's popular culture in nineteenth-century Bengal. In Kumkum Sangari and Sudesh Vaid,eds., *Recasting women: Essays in colonial history*, 127-79. New Delhi: Kali for Women

Bloch, Maurice. 1987. Descent and sources of contradiction in representation of women and kinship. In Jane Fishburne Collier and Sylvia Junko Yanagisako, eds., *Gender and kinship: Essays towards a unified analysis*, 324-37. Stanford: Stanford University Press.

Briggs, Charles. 1988. *Competence in performance: The creativity of tradition in Mexican verbal art.* Philadelphia: University of Philadelphia Press.

——.1992. Since I am a woman I will chastize my relatives: Gender, reported speech and the reproduction of social relations in Warao ritual wailing. *American Ethnologist* 19 (2): 337-61.

Burke, Kenneth. 1973. *The philosophy of literary form.* Berkeley, University of California Press.

Chatterjee, Partha. 1989. Colonialism, nationalism and the colonized woman: The contest in India. *American Ethnologist* 16: 622-33.

Christian, John. 1891. *Behar proverbs.* London: Kegan Paul, Trench, Trubner and Co.

Crooke, William. 1888. *A rural and agricultural glossary for the N W Provinces and Oudh.* Calcutta: Superintendent of Government Printing, India.

Das, Veena. 1976. Masks and faces: An essay on Punjabi kinship. *Contributions to Indian Sociology* n.s. 10: 1-30.

——. 1982. Kama in the scheme of the Purusarthas: The story of Rama. In T. N. Madan, ed., *Way of life: King, householder, renouncer*, 183-203. Delhi: Vikas.

——. 1988. Femininity and the orientation to the body. In K. Chanana, ed., *Women: Explorations in gender identity*, 193-207. New Delhi: Orient Longman.

——. 1989. Subaltern as perspective. In Ranajit Guha, ed., *Subaltern Studies*, 310-24. Delhi: Oxford University Press.

de Certeau, Michel. 1984. *The practice of everyday life.* Berkeley: University of California Press.

Dube, Leela. 1988. On the construction of gender: Hindu girls in patrilineal India. *Economic and Political Weekly* 30 April: 11-19.

Fallon, S. W. 1886. *A dictionary of Hindustani proverbs.* Banaras: Medical Hall Press.

Flueckiger, Joyce Burkhalter. 1991. Genre and community in the folklore system of Chhatisgarh. In Arjun Appadurai, Frank J. Korom and Margaret Mills, eds., *Gender, genre and power in South Asian expressive traditions*, 181-200. Philadelphia: University of Pennsylvania Press.

Gal, Susan. 1991. Between speech and silence: The problematics of research on language and gender. In Micaela di Leonardo, ed., *Gender at the crossroads of knowledge: Feminist anthropology in the postmodern era*, 175-203. Berkeley: University of California Press.

Gluckman, Max. 1963. Rituals of rebellion in South East Africa. In *Order and rebellion in tribal Africa*. New York: Free Press.

Gold, Ann Grodzins. 1992. *A carnival of parting*. Berkeley: University of California Press.

Grima, Benedicte. 1991. The role of suffering in women's performance of *Paxto*. In Arjun Appadurai, Frank. J. Korom and Margaret Mills, eds., *Gender, genre and power in South Asian expressive traditions*, 91-101. Philadelphia: University of Pennsylvania Press.

Guha, Ranajit. 1983. *Elementary aspects of peasant insurgency in colonial India*. Delhi: Oxford University Press.

—. 1987. Chandra's death. In Ranajit Guha, ed., *Subaltern Studies* 5, 135-65. Delhi: Oxford University Press.

Gupta, Krishnanand. 1968. *Hindustani kahavat kosh* (a Hindi translation of Fallon 1886). New Delhi: National Book Trust.

Hansen, Kathryn. 1992. *Grounds for play: The nautanki theater of North India*. Berkeley: University of California Press.

Henry, Edward O. 1988. *Chant the names of God: Music and culture in Bhojpuri-speaking India*. San Diego: San Diego State University Press.

Jacobson, Doranne. 1977. Flexibility in North Indian kinship and residence. In Kenneth David, ed., *Changing identities in South Asia*, 263-83. The Hague: Mouton.

Jeffery, Patricia, Roger Jeffery, and Andrew Lyon. 1989. *Labour pains and labour power: Women and childbearing in India*. London: Zed Books.

Kakar, Sudhir. 1978. *The inner world*. Delhi: Oxford University Press.

—. 1989. *Intimate relations*. Chicago: University of Chicago Press.

Karp, Ivan. 1988. Laughter at marriage: Subversion in performance. *Journal of Folklore Research* 25 (1-2): 35-52.

Kumar, Nita. 1991. Widows, education and social change in twentieth-century Banaras. *Economic and Political Weekly* April 27: 19-25.

Mani, Lata. 1984. The production of an official discourse on *sati* early nineteenth-century Bengal. In Francis Barker, ed., *Europe and its others*, 89-127. Colchester: University of Essex.

—. 1989. Contentious traditions: The debate on *sati* in colonial India. In Kumkum Sangari and Sudesh Vaid eds., *Recasting women: Essays in colonial history*, 88-126. New Delhi: Kali for Women.

March, Kathryn. 1984. Weaving, writing and gender. *Man* n.s. 18 (4): 729-44.

Messick, Brinkley. 1987. Subordinate discourse: Women, weaving, and gender relations in North Africa. *American Ethnologist* 14 (2): 210-25.

Mitter, Sara. 1991. *Dharma's daughters: Contemporary Indian women and Hindu culture*. New Brunswick: Rutgers University Press.

Narayan, Kirin. 1986. Birds on a branch: Girlfriends and wedding songs in Kangra. *Ethos* 14 (1): 47-75.

——.1991. husbands as foreigners: Women's songs and subjectivities in Kangra. Paper presented at the conference 'Language, gender, and the subaltern voice: Framing identities in South Asia'. University of Minnesota, April 1991.

O'Hanlon, Rosalind. 1988. Recovering the subject: Subaltern studies and histories of resistance in colonial South Asia. *Modern Asian Studies 22 (1): 189-224.*

——. 1991. Issues of widowhood: Gender and resistance in colonial western India. In Douglas Haynes and Gyan Prakash, eds., *Contesting power: Resistance and everyday social relations in South Asia*. Berkeley : University of California Press.

Raheja, Gloria Goodwin. 1988. *The poison in the gift: Ritual, prestation and the dominant caste in a North Indian village*. Chicago: University of Chicago Press.

——. 1991. Negotiated solidarities. Paper presented at the 20th annual conference on South Asia. University of Wisconsin, November 1991.

——. In press. Crying when she's born,and crying when she goes away: Marriage and the idiom of gift in Pahansu song performance.In Paul Courtwright and Lindsey Harlan, eds., *From the margins of Hindu marriage: New essays on gender, culture and religion*. Oxford: Oxford University Press.

——, and Ann Grodzins Gold. 1994. *Listen to the heron's words: Reimagining gender and kinship in North India*. Berkeley: University of California Press.

Roy, Manisha. 1992. *Bengali women*. Chicago: University of Chicago Press.

Scott, James C. 1990. *Domination and the arts of resistance: Hidden transcripts*. New Haven: Yale University Press.

Sharma, Ursula. 1980. *Women, work and property in North-West India*. London: Tavistock.

Sherzer, Joel. 1987. A discourse-centered approach to culture. *American Anthropologist* 89 (2):295-309.

Spivak, Gayatri Chakravorty. 1985. Subaltern studies: Deconstructing historiography. In Ranajit Guha ed., *Subaltern Studies* 4, 330-63. Delhi: Oxford University Press.

Tagore, Rabindranath. 1990. *Shasthi* ('The punishment').In Kalpana Bardhan, ed., and trans., *Of Women, outcastes, peasants and rebels: Selection of Bengali short stories*. Berkeley: University of California Press.

Trautmann, Thomas. 1981. *Dravidian kinship*. Berkeley: University of California Press.

Trawick, Margaret (Egnor). 1986. Internal iconicity in Paraiyar crying songs. In Stuart Blackburn and A. K. Ramanujan, eds., *Another harmony: New essays on the folklore of India*. Berkeley: University of California Press.

——. 1991. Wandering lost: A landless laborer's sense of place and self. In Arjun Appadurai, Frank J. Korom, and Margaret Mills eds., *Gender, genre and power in South Asian expressive traditions.* Philadelhia: University of Pennsylvania Press.

Vatuk, Sylvia. 1975. Gifts and affines. *Contributions to Indian Sociology* n. s. 5: 155-96.

Wadley, Susan S. 1983. The rains of estrangement: Understanding the Hindu yearly cycle. *Contributions to Indian Sociology* n.s. 17 (1): 51-85.

Yang, Anand. 1989. Whose sati? Widow burning in early nineteenth-century India. *Journal of Women's History* 1 (2): 8-33.

3

Between Two Worlds:
Self-Construction and Self-Identity in the
Writings of Three Nineteenth-Century
Indian Christian Women

LESLIE A. FLEMMING

CORNELIA SORABJI OPENS the introduction to her autobiography, *India Calling*, published in London in 1934, by telling her readers,

> At one of the many delightful visits which I paid in my youth to the Grant Duffs at York House, Twickenham—Sir Mountstuart said of me, making a necessary introduction, 'A Friend who has warmed her hands at two fires, without being scorched.' . . . Yes—it is true that I have been privileged to know two hearthstones, to be homed in two countries, England and India. But though it is difficult to say which 'home' I love best, there has never, at any time, been the remotest doubt as to which called to me with most insistence. . . . Always, early or late, throughout the years, it has been 'India Calling'.[1]

Although scarcely remembered today, Cornelia Sorabji was only one of many prominent elite women born during the latter part of the nineteenth century who moved freely in both Indian and Western settings and who gained public visibility through autobiographical writings in English.[2] Often Brahmins or members of princely families, these articulate, educated women, in their published diaries, letters and autobiographies, not only gave narrative shape to their own life stories, but also forcefully argued the case for changes in the lives of Indian women more generally.

Not surprisingly, a significant number of these women were Indian Christians. Members of a marginal religious community dominated by Europeans, and thus more likely to be educated and literate in English than their non-Christian sisters, these Christian women felt particularly acutely the dual loyalties alluded to by Cornelia Sorabji. At the same time, those dual loyalties gave them uniquely complex angles of vision

from which to assess their own and other women's lives. Of these Indian
Christian women, three have left behind particularly rich autobiographical texts: Krupabai Satthianadhan (1862-1894), the first wife of the
prominent South Indian church leader Samuel Satthianadhan, Cornelia
Sorabji (1860?-1936?), the daughter of Parsi converts to Christianity,
and Pandita Ramabai Saraswati (1858-1922), a Chitpavan Brahmin convert to Christianity, who founded an internationally known Christian
community near Pune.

These women's autobiographical writings, while products of particular
temporal and socio-cultural milieux, are not uniquely Indian. Examples of
women's autobiographical writings abound in Europe, many dating from
as early as the twelfth century.[3] Of the theoretical perspectives current
scholars have developed to study women's autobiographies as social and
cultural phenomena, two are particularly useful for understanding the
writings of these Indian Christians. Mary Mason (1988) provides the first
in her article in the collection *Life/Lines*.[4] Analysing the writings of four
women whose autobiographies reflect what she calls self-identity through
alterity, Mason argues that these women's explorations of their connections with the other significant people in their lives is what allows them to
achieve a coherent sense of themselves. Mason's delineation of the ways
in which the self-construction of American Puritan poet Anne Bradstreet
(1612?-1670) is noted in identification with a religious community is
particularly helpful. The work of Sidonie Smith (1987), is also useful here.[5]
In the third chapter of her book Smith emphasizes the interplay of paternal
and maternal texts in women's self-expression, suggesting that standing
at the intersection of these texts is what allows women to control the written
discourse sufficiently to construct coherent representations of themselves.

In approaching the writings of these Indian Christians, I want to extend
both Mason and Smith's arguments. Firstly, with Mason, I suggest that
unlike most of their contemporaries these women found their primary
identities through membership in communities transcending families or
jatis (hereditary occupation-based kinship groups), and that Krupabai
Satthianadhan and Ramabai, in particular, found their primary identities
in religious communities. Secondly, I suggest that all three of these women
articulated a sense of standing at the intersection of more than one
community. By this I mean that despite their identification with a particular
community, despite their internalization of its values, their adherence to
its norms, and their use of its symbol set in their writings, they all also
identified with competing communities whose values, norms, and symbols
also inform their texts. Building on Smith's analysis, I suggest that gender

issues at least partially informed their understandings of the differences between these communities. More important, I argue that these women were able to construct written selves precisely because they were not rooted in any one community, and that the act of written self-construction reflected a partial attempt to deal with the tensions they experienced in standing at communal intersections.

Illuminating these issues requires asking a series of questions of these women's writings. Firstly, with which community did these women primarily identify? Secondly, at the intersections of which communities did these women see themselves as standing? On what issues did these communities fundamentally differ for them, and where did gender issues, especially, fit in their sense of these differences? To what extent, did these women articulate a conscious choice of the various elements of their communal identities? What sense of tension do these women articulate, and what sense of their self seems to emerge from this tension and from their writings? And, finally, do these writers provide an alternative paradigm of women's roles, in the process of constructing their lives and dealing with tensions within them? As the analysis that follows will show, each of these women provides very different answers to these questions.

Krupabai Satthianadhan

Krupabai Satthianadhan constructed her life and articulated her sense of multiple identities in an autobiographical novel entitled *Saguna*, written in English with the encouragement of a British friend and published in 1892 when Satthianadhan was about thirty (edition referred here is 1895).[6] In a second novel, *Kamala: A Story of Hindu Life* (1894), written just before her death,[7] she provides a significantly contrasting construction of the early life of a young Hindu woman.

Krupabai Satthianadhan was born on 14 February 1862, the thirteenth child of early Brahmin converts to Christianity in the Bombay Presidency. As she tells us in *Saguna*, her father's decision to convert to Christianity, in which he persuaded his young wife to follow him with some difficulty, alienated the couple from both their families, forcing them to seek their primary attachments with other Christians. Krupabai was an exceptionally intelligent and curious child, and after her father's death, she was given an eclectic education, first by her mother and elder brother, then by a pair of eccentric Englishwomen. She completed her secondary education in an Anglican mission high school in Madras, where she was strongly encouraged by an American medical missionary to begin medical training. She was admitted to Christian Medical College in Madras, but dropped out for

health reasons after only one year. Soon thereafter, she married Samuel
Satthianadhan, a member of a prominent South Indian Christian family,
with whose parents she had boarded during her year in medical school.
Active with her husband in his ministry following their marriage, she died
in 1894 at the age of thirty-two.

The product of an unorthodox family, whose parents had already
dissolved the bonds of *jati* and religion, Satthianadhan further attenuated
her ties to traditional culture by arranging her own marriage, against the
then common practice of arranged marriages, with a man outside her own
linguistic and geographic region. Following her parents' example, she does
not locate her primary identity in either her own or her husband's families,
nor does she, in her autobiographical novel, construct her life around the
roles valued for women by Hindu tradition of dutiful daughter, daughter-
in-law and wife. Rather, like Anne Bradstreet, she identifies primarily with
the Indian Christian community, and her relations with that community
provide the primary structure for her life story. At the same time, however,
Satthianadhan acknowledges the validity of some of the values and norms
of the South Indian Brahmin community around her, and both *Saguna* and
Kamala suggest that she considered certain elements of the culture of that
community worthy of emulation.

Satthianadhan does not base her self-construction as an Indian Christian
in *Saguna* on intellectual assent to particular doctrines or on adherence to
certain liturgical or devotional practices. Rather, she depicts the significant
Christians in her life, almost all of whom were males, who contributed to
her religious development. Foremost among these was her father, whose
conversion experience she delineates in some detail. Well aware of the
personal sacrifices for him and the difficult dilemma for her mother that
this move entailed, Satthianadhan nonetheless expresses approval of both
her father's choice and her mother's commitment to fostering a Christian
identity for her family after his death. Also influential was her older sister,
who began her Christian education by telling her Bible stories and tales of
Christian heroes. Most influential of her family members was her older
brother Bhasker, who having supervised her early education, both secular
and religious, extracted from her what she characterized as a promise
governing her life. Articulating two potentially competing roles, Bhasker
asks her 'to speak boldly to your countrywomen, and yet remain as your
sister was, modest, gentle and kind, a real woman' (1895:12). More
important, Bhasker is the mediator of her own internal assent to her
Christian identity. Feeling ostracized by the other girls at the mission high
school, and longing for love from 'Bhasker's God and mine', she experi-

ences a sense of deep bond with Jesus. As she falls at Jesus' feet, she sees Bhasker's face and years him saying,

> 'You have found it. That is right; keep close to Jesus, and
> all will be right.'
> 'Will it last, Bhasker?'
> 'Yes, for ever.' (1895: 186).

Krupabai's identity with the Christian community was cemented through her marriage into the Satthianadhan family. From her year as a boarder prior to her marriage, she developed a strong bond with W. Satthianadhan, Samuel's father, whose conversion experience she also relates, and whom she regards as a second father. During that year, as well as after her marriage, she also felt strong affective ties to Samuel's mother, Anna, whose family had been Christians for four generations, and who initially encouraged Krupabai to begin writing. Although disappointed in her inability to continue studying medicine, Krupabai sees her marriage to Samuel as exemplifying an ideal egalitarian Christian marriage, and she values her involvement with his work as a pastor.

Reflecting the firm ties to the Christian community that govern the narrative in *Saguna*, Satthianadhan openly criticizes much in Hinduism in her depiction of a Brahmin woman's life in *Kamala*. Throughout, the third-person narrator openly deplores Kamala's attribution of all her misfortunes to fate, often refers to the barbarity and inefficacy of Hindu rituals, and applauds Kamala's defiance of traditional norms in maintaining an affectionate relationship with a low-caste family. On the other hand, some elements of the novel suggest that she also partially identified with Hindu values. Paralleling her portrayals in *Saguna* of her close relationships with both her father and father-in-law, the novel *Kamala* provides extremely sympathetic portraits of learned Hindu men, and especially of Kamala's father. The novel also approvingly suggests that traditional Hindu learning enables women to endure their hard lot in life. Detailing Kamala's relationships with her in-laws, the narrator of the novel tells us that all her Hindu learning

> had taught her one lesson, the great lesson of humanity, love
> for others and the need of doing one's duty at any cost.
> However crude the stories and legends were, they all shewed
> how good deeds were rewarded and bad deeds punished
> even in the next life, how humility had its reward, and love,

chastity, honour, and respect for elders were looked upon as
the distinguishing virtues of noble life (1894: 57).

In contrasting the two communities in the two novels, the access of
women to education and their roles within marriage are what most differ-
entiate the Christian and Hindu communities for Satthianadhan. She
especially forcefully criticizes Hindus in *Saguna* for denying education to
women and forcing them to lead intellectually shallow lives. After describing a religious ceremony involving pre-adolescent girls, she challenges the
hypocrisy of educated Hindu men by suggesting that women's lack of
intellectual development is barbaric and uncivilized:

> Poor girls! What can we expect from such impoverished,
> stunted minds? Their mothers are no better, and their fathers
> have very little to do with them. Their starved minds have
> nothing to feed on except such vain, silly thoughts . . .
> No wonder then that they grow vain, flippant, inordinately
> fond of money or stupidly proud of their hoarded gold and
> jewels . . . The refined, civilized mind shudders or looks
> down with pity on the exhibition as a relic of savagery; and
> yet these are the daughters of India whose lot is considered
> as not needing any improvement by many of my country-
> men who are highly cultured and who are supposed to have
> benefitted by western civilization (1895: 30).

In contrast, she knows that her own access to education is liberating.
Not only does she understand the importance of the education given her
in the mission high school, but she sees her study of medicine as necessary
to her attempt to break free of debilitating stereotypes. As she contemplates
beginning her studies, she again alludes to the intellectual shallowness and
narrow world-view of most women:

> What a world of untried possibilities seemed to open out for
> me. I would now throw aside the fetters that bound me and
> be independent. I had chafed under the restraints and the ties
> which formed the common lot of women, and I longed for
> an opportunity to show that a woman is in no way inferior
> to a man. How hard it seemed to my mind that marriage
> should be the goal of a woman's ambition, and that she
> should spend her days in the light trifles of a home life, live
> to dress, to look pretty, and never know the joy of inde-
> pendence and intellectual work (1895:178).

Satthianadhan is equally critical of the dynamics of high-caste Hindu marriage. Depicting such a marriage in *Kamala* in extremely unflattering terms, she portrays the mother-in-law as cruel and oppressive, the young husband as indifferent and unfaithful, and the husband's entire extended family as co-conspirators in Kamala's eventual death. Although in *Saguna* she uses some of the traditional rhetoric of self-sacrifice in assuaging her disappointment in giving up her medical studies and in justifying her decision to marry, she strongly suggests that her marriage is based on a mutually respectful and loving relationship between husband and wife, both of whom are centred in Christ. In such a marriage, in contrast to the Hindu marriage that stifles and eventually murders her heroine in Kamala, she feels able to continue growing intellectually and spiritually. Significantly, she depicts her mother-in-law, Anna Satthianadhan, who was probably less tied to traditional women's roles than her own mother, as extremely supportive of her intellectual development, and of her writing in particular.

In addition to her Christian identity, Satthianadhan also alludes to a sense of national identity. However, the contours of that identity are less well-defined than those of her religious identity, and her writings suggest a stronger sense of competing allegiances. On the one hand, she commends the influence of Western women and expresses her identity with them. She holds in particularly high regard the two Englishwomen who directed her early education, the English missionaries at the Anglican secondary school she attended in Madras, and the American woman physician who encouraged her to take medical training. In her dedication to *Saguna* she singles out her British friend, Elizabeth Grigg, expressing her gratitude for encouraging her to write the work and her 'appreciation of her active sympathy with everything connected with the welfare of India's women'. Clearly, these women modelled for her the freer, better educated, more socially aware women that she wanted Indian women to be. More generally, Satthianadhan's command of written English discourse and her knowledge of English literary texts, on which she occasionally draws for illustrative examples, also suggest her dependence on and approval of Western culture.

Despite acknowledging the beneficial influence and role modelling provided by these Western women, Satthianadhan also alludes to ties with India, and with a variety of Indians, groping towards a sense of identity that transcends *jati* and religion and encompasses all Indians. To begin with, although perhaps partially reflecting Victorian literary conventions, many passages in both *Saguna* and *Kamala* depict the loveliness of the

Indian countryside. *Kamala*, for example, opens with the observation that, 'India may not be a perfect paradise, yet there are in it spots of surpassing beauty and grandeur' (p 1). The text then goes on to describe a twilight setting in the Nasik district (near her original family home). Throughout *Saguna* Satthianadhan expresses a strong sense of identity with Indian Christians of all classes, although she also criticizes overly westernized Indian Christians who refuse to associate with low-caste converts. Equally critical in *Kamala* of the barriers between castes, she approvingly depicts Kamala's relationship with a low-caste family. Most tellingly, in contrast to Cornelia Sorabji, who begins her autobiography with an expression of her sense of dual loyalties, Satthianadhan opens *Saguna* by identifying herself as an Indian. Alluding to her sense of the changes taking place in India, she nevertheless disarmingly assures her readers that,

> In the following pages I shall in my own way try to present
> a faithful picture of the experiences and thoughts of a simple
> Indian girl, whose life has been highly influenced by a new
> order of things—an order of things which at the present time
> is spreading its influence to a greater or less extent over the
> whole of her native land (p 1).

While looking forward to the coming changes in the women's roles brought about by Western influence, of the three women whose writings are under consideration here, Satthianadhan is, in many respects, the most comfortable with her choice of communities, and she presents in her work the strongest sense of the three of a cohesive identity based on acceptance of the norms and values of a minority religious community. Taking Indian Christians, especially her father, brother, husband, and mother-in-law, as models of personal, spiritual, and intellectual development, she articulates a deep sense of Christian identity and a strong sense of the differences between herself and Hindu women. In particular, although she accepted a relatively traditional role as the wife of a church leader, she consciously constructs her marriage as an egalitarian partnership. In contrast she depicts the then prevailing Hindu values for women as stultifying, particularly focusing on the denial of education to women and their subordination in marriage. To a lesser extent, Satthianadhan also includes selected elements of what she sees as Western and Indian cultures in her self-construction. Appreciative of Western culture because of her relationships with some influential British and American women, she accepts the potentially beneficial changes encouraged by Western influence, at the same time that she also maintains a sense of herself as an Indian. If she presents an alternative paradigm, it is one that allows for the fusion of some traditional Indian values, including respect for and intellectual identity with significant male family members, positive valuing of marriage, and sense of identity with a particular religious community, with Western values for women, especially emphasizing education, egalitarian marriages, and access to a public discourse beyond the family.

Cornelia Sorabji

Cornelia Sorabji's construction of her life is contained in her collection of memories, *India Calling* (1934). In contrast to Krupabai Satthianadhan, who concentrated solely on her own experiences in her autobiographical novel, Cornelia Sorabji included in her autobiographical narrative many vignettes of the lives of secluded Indian women. Taken as a whole, her narrative strongly suggests that in addition to structuring her own experiences, she was also attempting to explain, and justify, Indians, especially Indian women, to English readers.

Cornelia Sorabji was the daughter of Parsi converts to Christianity, who, while strongly identifying with English culture, also maintained their ties with the Parsi community. Well educated in English and strongly encouraged by her mother to study law in England, she spend most of her life in India employed by the government as an itinerant legal advocate for princely and high-caste widows and orphans. She never married, and in her later years, she was an articulate spokesperson for women's rights and education for women in both England and India.

As the opening paragraph of her autobiography makes plain, Sorabji clearly saw herself as standing at the intersection of both East and West and as having drawn the best from both. Although she claims that her attachment to India is the stronger, much of the narrative suggests a conscious sense of marginalization within Indian culture and a refusal to accommodate to the usual norms for elite women. Sorabji locates the origin of her sense of differentness from most elite women in her connection with the already marginal Parsi community, which her family retained despite her parents' conversion to Christianity. Alluding to the tradition that the earliest Parsis were allowed to remain in India if they relinquished the Persian language and dress, Sorabji suggests that,

> the interpretation given to the taboo about dress and speech
> has nevertheless helped the 'apartness' as a community,
> which our origin, temperament, and habits of life had made
> inevitable. Our women wear a sari certainly, but it is of silk,

and draped differently from the Hindi sari (over the right
ear, behind the left); while the Guzerathi spoken by the
Parsees is 'Parsee Guzerathi' (pp. 3-4; italics in the
original).

Parsis also differed from Hindus in particular, according to Sorabji, in
that they maintained no parallel to the caste system. Most important, since
Parsi women were never secluded, she had in the women of her community
not only models of public activity and visibility then relatively unavailable
to other Indian women but also a focus for her sense of differentness from
most Indian women.

In addition to identifying with the values that she inherited as a Parsi,
and thereby maintaining a sense of connection with the larger Parsi
community, Sorabji also credits her immediate family with providing her
with a sense of herself as both English and Indian at the same time. 'We
were "brought up English"', Sorabji tells us (p. 7), as she describes the
English furniture and the use of the English language in her home.
However, the gender dynamics in Sorabji's family differed significantly
from those of the families of many other nineteenth-century elite women,
in which the father was often the sole mediator of the new and the Western,
with the mother often clinging to older, indigenous values. Rather, in
explaining the direction that her life took, Sorabji portrays both her parents
as having been equally involved with and appreciative of English culture,
and as having made acquaintance with an English lifestyle an important
part of their children's upbringing. At the same time, however,

> we were taught to call outselves Indians, and to love and be
> proud of the country of our adoption. Thus had our Parents
> conceived, and built upon, a unity which did not at the time
> exist in India . . . (ibid.)

Even so, in strong contrast to Krupabai Satthianadhan, Sorabji suggests that her mother, Francina Sorabji, had a more decisive influence
on her than her father. An early progressive and educator, Francina
Sorabji strongly argued for changes in Indian women's lives and heavily
involved herself in social service work for women. More important,
Francina Sorabji was 'proud of having seven daughters, in a country
where the birth of a daughter was considered a calamity: because "they
were women that India wanted, just then, for her service"' (p. 14).
Equipping her daughters for a life of social service, she encouraged

them to prepare for medical, educational and legal careers. Following a visit by a recently widowed family friend who had been bilked of all her property by an unscrupulous manager, she especially urged Cornelia to study law, in order to be able to press for changes in the legal structures governing Indian women's lives.

In the depiction of her legal career in India, in which she worked primarily as an adviser to the Court of Wards, Sorabji demonstrates that she actualized many of her mother's progressive values. In her work securing the inheritance rights of secluded women, she worked with women who would not otherwise generally have had access to sympathetic or effective legal counsel. In so doing, she followed her mother's example in not challenging traditional structures outright. Instead, she successfully challenged men's abuse of women's rights within those structures, thus achieving incremental change for these women, rather than urging a rending of the entire social fabric.

In portraying her relationships with the women whose legal rights she secured, Sorabji characterizes herself as a conscious agent of change. She suggests that the values of her community and immediate family, coupled with her English legal education, enhanced her strong sense of her difference from most Hindu and Muslim women and encouraged her to want to help them change their lives. Indeed, throughout her autobiography, she emphasizes her differences from the women whom she defended, stressing especially differences in education, religious outlook and degree of identification with older indigenous values. In one of her earlier vignettes, for example, she relates the story of a client who had at first told her an elaborate, made-up tale of her difficulties and then, with questioning, revealed the true circumstances.

> 'Why did you tell me that other tale?'
> Her answer was pathetic. 'We have no one to protect us, we are accursed, everything that happens to us or that we do is cursed. I wanted to tell you something that was not *nagawar* [unlettered].'
>
> 'But the *nagawar* story, the truth, as you told it the second time, is far better for you. Now I can help. There is a way out.'
> I can see her face as I write. She had not lied because she was false, but because she was reaching after—cleverness! She was in revolt against—ignorance! (pp.:77-78)

Seeing herself as modern, rationalist and progressive, in her many vignettes detailing her experiences with secluded elite women, she often speaks for the voice of reason, suggesting that her clients are influenced by blind superstition or uninformed religion. Relating the story of a childless young wife who was about to urge her husband to take another wife, for example, she indicates that through the ministrations of a woman doctor the woman finally became pregnant. However, during her pregnancy she was obliged to follow the traditional custom of not sewing and not covering or shutting anything. After relating the birth of a lovely daughter, Sorabji concludes the vignette with the observation, 'Sons followed, and we could rejoice together that the pessimism of her eighteenth year had been saved from the drastic measures of ignorance' (p.141).

In many of the vignettes, Sorabji also construes her mission as that of working to free Indian women from the constraints imposed on them by indigenous culture. Often she does this, as she relates towards the end of the narrative, by using superstition and custom as the means for bringing about change. After relating, for example, the story of a child whose mother killed him when he had a seizure, for fear that he had a demon that would kill her husband, Sorabji tell us,

> Now when we go into the villages, we can say to the women—'When your child beats his fists and his legs into your face, you think he has a demon. We know that he has not. But this is the way to drive out the demon if you believe he is there.' And we teach the requisite treatment for convulsions.
>
> After years of experience, in untrodden ways, I conclude that the only way to help the illiterate and superstitious is to proceed from the known and accepted to the unknown; to base the enlightenment which you would bring upon the superstition; not to flout the superstition (p.238).

At the same time, however, throughout her autobiography Sorabji also articulates a sense of community with Indian women. Taking real interest in their lives, stories, rituals, problems and needs, through her long association with them, she developed strong affective bonds with women of all religious communities, occasionally even intervening to save their lives or help them escape from destructive family situations. She also articulates a sense of the women's movement in India as an Indian women's movement. Strongly critical of Western women who tried to impose their own perspective on the Indian women's movement, rather than letting Indian women accomplish change at their own rate, she forcefully argued for 'progress in the vernacular, so to speak, not in the language of the Emancipated West' (p.300).

Despite her strong identification with the Indian women's movement, and her desire to work for the welfare of her countrywomen, the issue of national identity was clearly a source of tension for Sorabji. Because of her family's orientation towards English culture, she was decidedly not a nationalist, and she was deeply critical of the leaders of the independence movement as she saw it developing after the turn of the century. Towards the end of the autobiography she particularly criticizes the movement for working against the needs of the poorest Indians, especially in its call for use of the then more expensive handloom cloth. More significantly, because of the aggressive, occasionally even violent, enforcement of the ban on imported cloth by women whom she associated with 'Gandhi's pickets', Sorabji characterizes women's participation in the movement as retarding, even undoing, progress already achieved for women:

> Women picketers did the most harm to the Country, because they set back the clock of progress in the orthodox Hindu and conservative regions where progress was vital, and where the move forward had just begun (p.266).

The tactics of these women were, she suggests,

> against tradition, and exposed the women to implications which were as a rule unjustifiable. 'We had begun to think Education was good,' said orthodox Hindu *Purdahnashins*, 'but if this is what it does to women, ignorance is better' (ibid.).

In addition, she characterized Gandhi as exploited by clever young politicians and as not really giving the untouchables what they want and need most (p.271). Claiming that the 'movement is identifiable with the communism which is sweeping the whole World' (p.275), she concludes this section by proclaiming the civil disobedience movement to have been an utter failure.

Curiously, Sorabji does not mention anywhere in her autobiography tensions over religious identity, either for her parents or herself. In fact, after briefly describing Parsi religious rites and beliefs, Sorabji scarcely mentions religion at all. In contrast to Krupabai Satthianadhan, who depicted the conversions of both her father and her father-in-law, Sorabji provides little detail about her father's conversion or the intellectual or personal struggle that may have accompanied it. Rather, perhaps because her mother was the more influential figure in her life, she simply accepts her father's conversion as a given for her life, without questioning either the reasons for or the consequences of his action. Sorabji does, however, allude to the importance of the Gospel to her mother, suggesting that her mother was motivated by a mixture of religious and social concerns: 'She was never tired of sharing with others the Gospel as she knew it, the Good News—of Christianity, of Health, of Education, of Sanitation' (p.14). Despite her mother's influence on her, Sorabji provides no evidence in the text of any interior spiritual life, of participation in any liturgical community, or even of disagreement with or criticism of the Indian Christian community. In strong contrast to both Krupabai Satthianadhan and Ramabai, Sorabji's self-construction here is practically devoid of any Christian identity, or of any evidence that being a Christian, rather than a Zoroastrian, made any significant difference in her life.

Although lacking a well-defined religious identity, a particular person, with a concrete personality, nevertheless emerges from this self-portrait. To begin with, Sorabji constructs herself as a determined, resourceful person, able to move freely and mediate among secluded women following older, indigenous lifestyles, England-returned, westernized Indians, and the British themselves, both in India and on their home turf. In detailing her many experiences with secluded women involving daring escapades, and in describing, in the latter part of the book, her travels in various parts of India, she portrays herself as intrepid, courageous and adventurous, yet, at the same time, calm and enduring, especially in facing personal danger. Most important, throughout the work, and especially in her descriptions of the lifestyles of the women with whom she works, she constructs herself as modern, sensible, rational, and free—free of the ignorance and superstition that she felt inhibited most Indian women, and able to order her life rationally according to her own dictates.

At the same time, however, Sorabji also seems to have chosen values, norms, and communal identities that make her the most marginalized of the three women dealt with here. As a member of two numerically minuscule communities, she was cut off, by communal ties at least, from the majority of Indians. By remaining single all her life, while liberated from the constraints imposed on married women and therefore able to observe and participate in a much wider cross-section of life than would otherwise be possible, she nevertheless could not share, except vicariously, in the particular problems faced by married women. By constantly moving around the country pursuing a highly visible career, unknown at that time for Western, let alone Indian, women, she had no role models, no colleagues and few peers. Finally, through her strong identification with English culture, she experienced a divided cultural loyalty which, in her opposition to the independence movement in particular, prevented her from sympathizing with many of the concerns of her fellow Indians.

Does Cornelia Sorabji present an alternative paradigm for Indian women? If so, it is one of a woman almost completely detached from the constraints imposed on most elite women of her time, who while sympathizing with the needs of these women was determined to substitute Western values for most of the values emphasized by their cultures. Such thoroughgoing westernization was rarely attainable or even desired by Indian women of Sorabji's generation, and would probably be unusual even today. More important, however, by remaining free of the constraints of marriage, Sorabji models the role of a woman freed from the needs of family and able to dedicate herself solely to the concerns of women more generally. In that aspect of her life, she models a role emulated by many Indian Christian women, and even by some women of other communities, who have similarly remained single in order to focus their lives around social service concerns.

Pandita Ramabai

In contrast to Krupabai Satthianadhan and Cornelia Sorabji, both of whom have left clearly autobiographical texts, Pandita Ramabai's primary self-construction is found in a series of letters written in English to various British friends between 1883 and 1903 (Shah 1977; CLS 1979). Most of these letters are addressed to Sister Geraldine, a member of the Anglo-Catholic women's order, the Community of St. Mary the Virgin (CSMV), whose mother house was at Wantage, England, and whose members ran a large convent and girls' school in Pune.[8] Ramabai's sponsor at baptism, and in some sense her spiritual mother throughout her life, Sr. Geraldine, originally edited a collection of Ramabai's letters in 1917, to which she added letters about Ramabai from some of Ramabai's other correspondents, as well as her own commentary on events and issues referred to by Ramabai in her letters. Finally, the whole collection was re-edited and published in 1977 (Shah 1977).[9]

This collection of Ramabai's letters provides two sources for the details of her life. The first is a short account of her early life that Ramabai wrote at Wantage, at the request of the reverend mother of the CSMV, just before her baptism. This account is reproduced in a letter from the reverend mother to Sr. Geraldine that is included in the collection. In addition, Sr. Geraldine outlines the main events in the remainder of Ramabai's life in the commentary accompanying the letters. Very occasionally, Ramabai alludes to events in her life in her letters.

The daughter of Chitpavan Brahmins, Ramabai was born into a family dominated by a father who believed strongly enough in education for women to willingly risk censure by his community in order to educate his own young wife. Early trained equally to value education for women, Ramabai received from her parents a broad classical education emphasizing grounding in Sanskrit religious and literary texts. Because of the failed marriage of her elder sister, Ramabai's own marriage was not arranged, and she was allowed to remain at home with her parents past the customary marriage age. After the death of her parents and sister when she was about sixteen, she spent the next six years travelling around India with her brother, lecturing on women's rights. Shortly after her brother's death in Dacca in 1880, she married Bipin Behari Das, a Bengali lawyer of a non-Brahmin *jati*, who had been a friend of her brother's. His tragic death from cholera sixteen months later left her with an infant daughter, Manorama. Soon thereafter, she met some of the CSMV sisters in Pune and also came under the influence of Nehemiah Goreh, an influential Brahmin convert to the Anglican church. Encouraged by the CSMV sisters to study medicine, she went to England in 1882, where she took up residence at the CSMV mother house and began her preparations for entrance to medical school. After receiving baptism at Wantage, Ramabai remained in England studying English and teaching Sanskrit at Cheltenham Ladies College until 1886. Abandoning her plan to study medicine because of increasing deafness, she then went to the United States to raise support for a home for Indian child widows, returning to Indian in 1889. After initially establishing her home in Bombay, she soon moved to Pune and then finally to Kedgaon, near Pune, where she gradually built up a complex of widows' shelters, girls' schools, schools for the blind, a home for the aged, and a self-supporting farm serving both Christians and non-Christians. In the latter part of her life, she undertook a translation of the complete Bible into simple Marathi, which she completed shortly before her death in 1922.

Clearly standing at the intersections of several communities, Ramabai was an extremely complex personality, who consciously selected the values and norms of several different and at least partially competing Indian and European communities. Her self-construction in her letters especially reveals three important areas of tension for her: her relationship with the then prevailing culture of her *jati*, her complex religious identity, and her complex relationship with westerners and with Victorian, British culture in particular.

In her account of her early life, as well as in her subsequent letters, Ramabai locates the origin for her selective appropriation of elements of indigenous Chitpavan Brahmin culture in her relationship with significant males in her life, all of whom aided her ability to distance herself from elements of that culture. Her father, risking excommunication from his *jati* in educating his wife and daughters and in refusing to arrange Ramabai's marriage provided her with an early model of stubborn resistance to public opinion: 'He would not heed them and as he was in no way beholden to them, he pursued his own ways' (Shah 1977: 15; Rev. Mother's letter, 11 November 1883). Similarly, her brother accompanied her on her travels around India, sharing in her lectures and critiques of women's roles. Describing those six years and the two thousand miles the two covered, Ramabai notes that, 'Thus we had a good opportunity of seeing the sufferings of Hindu women and were much touched by their sorrows . . . This made us think much of how it was possible to improve the condition of women and raise them out of their degradation' (Shah 1977: 17; Rev. Mother's letter). Her husband was similarly detached from traditional values. Describing their choice of a civil ceremony to solemnize their marriage across traditional caste and regional lines, Ramabai tells us that 'neither my husband nor I believed in the Hindu religion' (Shah 1977: 18; Rev. Mother's letter).

Reflecting her early detachment from the norms of her *jati*, and especially her early formative experiences lecturing in favour of women's rights, Ramabai was strongly critical of most Hindus, and especially of what she considered oppressive Hindu ideology for women. Her critique in *Stree Neeti Dharma*, which she wrote in order to finance her trip to England and the United States, of prevailing indigenous women's roles clearly demonstrates that she was reform-minded even before her conversion to Christianity. In *The High Caste Hindu Woman*, which she wrote in Philadelphia soon after her conversion, she is even more critical of traditional Hindu views of women. Commenting, for example, on the portraits of women in traditional Hindu scriptures, she avers,

> Those who diligently and impartially read Sanskrit literature
> in the original, cannot fail to recognize the law-giver Manu
> as one of those hundreds who have done their best to make
> a woman a hateful being in the world's eye. I can say
> honestly and truthfully, that I have never read any sacred

book in Sanskrit literature without meeting hateful sentiment about women. True, they contain here and there a kind
word about women, but such words seem to me a heartless
mockery after having charged them, as a class, with crime
and evil deeds (CLS 1977: 89).

While the barriers between castes maintained particularly by Brahmins
was a target of her criticism throughout her writings, she was especially
critical of her own caste members for their disregard of education for
women, their prevailing lifestyle that restricted physical freedom for
women, and their treatment of widows. In an early letter from Wantage,
for example, after describing the beauties of nature there, she laments,

but my happiness is not [an] unmixed one. My heart cries
for those poor prisoners in the Zenanas, to whom the com-
forts of Nature, which God in His goodness has bestowed
alike on all creatures, are denied by almost all of my selfish
countrymen. I feel myself unworthy to enjoy this great
comfort and happiness while my dear sisters are almost all
so unhappy and miserable, shut up in the eternal darkness
of ignorance and crushed under domestic 26 slavery (Shah
1977: 81; 12 July 1885).

In a later letter, after detailing the ill treatment of two young women,
she explicity criticizes Hindus for their treatment of widows:

How sad and shameful it is that we should be obliged to see
and hear such things and not be able to protect and help the
poor helpless victims from the heartless cruelty of Hindu
religion and society. We can do nothing but pray for these
poor souls! (Shah 1977: 290; December 1892)

At the same time, Ramabai also remained bonded to some aspects
of her own culture. She expresses respect throughout her life for the
classical Sanskrit literature that had been the foundation of her early
education. Although often criticized by her British friends, she also retained some aspects of Brahmin lifestyle, including abstinence from al-
cohol, vegetarianism, and preference for simple Indian clothing, often
wearing even the traditional white clothing of widows. In her spirited
defence of her retention of these practices, against her friends' accusa-
tion of the sin of pride, she often characterized them as essential to her
personal identity:

> I confess that I am not free from all my caste prejudices, as
> you are pleased to call them. I like to be called a Hindoo, for
> I am one, and also keep all the customs of my forefathers as
> far as I can. How would you, an Englishwoman, like being
> called a proud and prejudiced [sic] if she were to go and live
> among the Hindoos for a time but did not think it necessary
> to alter her customs when they were not hurtful or necessary
> to her neighbours? (Shah 1977: 109; 15 October 1885).

Ramabai's religious identity is even more complex than her relationship
with the culture of her *jati*. Introduced to Christianity in an Anglo-Catholic
context, through the influence of Nehemiah Goreh's writings and, more
important, through her interaction with the CSMV sisters in Pune and
Wantage, she maintained a lifelong relationship with the CSMV sisters
and kept up a warm friendship and continued correspondence with Sr.
Geraldine. Despite these close personal ties, Ramabai steadfastly resisted
much of Anglo-Catholic doctrine and devotional practice. Arguing
strongly and continually for a relatively simple Bible-based Christianity,
she especially rejected the doctrines of the Trinity and the Incarnation,
because she could find no biblical evidence for them. For the same reason,
she also rejected much Anglo-Catholic ceremonialism and private devotional practice. She also resisted the attempts of conservative Anglo-
Catholic male church leaders to convince her of their point of view.
Drawing a conscious parallel with her unwillingness to accept male
domination of Hindu discourse and ceremonial, she argued,

> I am not bound to accept every word that falls down from
> the lips of priests or bishops . . . I have just with great
> efforts freed myself from the yoke of the Indian priestly
> tribe, so I am not at present willing to place myself under
> another similar yoke by accepting everything which comes
> from the priests as authorised command of the Most High
> (Shah 1977: 59;12 May 1885).

Often challenging Anglo-Catholic Christians to relinquish their self-construction as sole possessors of religious truth, she forcefully and repeatedly
stressed the importance of free will, her need to follow her own conscience,
and her sense of dependence directly on God for guidance.

In relying solely on the Bible for her religious authority, Ramabai
implicitly denied the validity of oral and post-Biblical tradition. In doing
so, she was perhaps influenced by the veneration of the written text that

characterized her earliest education. At the same time, she also clearly protested against the ignorance of written texts in which most Indian women were then held, repeatedly asserting that control of the text was central to her religious independence and exercise of free will. In her arguments with conservative Anglicans, she kept for herself the right to impose her own hermeneutic on the text, denying priestly interpretation when it did not match her own ideas:

> I am not bound to believe in comments, I believe in the Word of God only and in the testimony of His Prophets. I am a disciple of Christ, though one of the least, and not of the commentators (Shah 1977: 150; Summer 1885).

At the end of her life, she demonstrated her desire to control the text by also claiming the right to translate the biblical text into a Marathi that, in contrast to the Sanskritized Marathi of previous translations, better suited the needs of the people with whom she worked.

In her interpretation of the biblical text, Ramabai focused primarily on the figure of Jesus. Especially concerned with following Jesus' teachings as the Gospels report them, she declared that the example of Jesus was one of the primary differences for her between Hinduism and Christianity. Tending to downplay the miraculous aspects of the biblical record, however, Ramabai was neither a fundamentalist, nor a believer in the infallible authority of the Bible. Rather, she most clearly venerated the Bible for its record of the life of Jesus.

As her spiritual life matured, Ramabai's relationship with Jesus gradually became more important to her than interpreting the biblical text. While even her early letters allude to her bond with Jesus, and while throughout her life she was clearly an activist rather than a contemplative who spent hours in solitary prayer, nevertheless her later letters provide a strongly articulated sense of a deepening personal relationship with Jesus. Alluding in one letter to troubles at her school, she assures Sr. Geraldine,

> but I am very thankful to the Lord for all these trials and thorns in the flesh, for the more I am beset with trials and difficulties, the closer I learn to draw to and love Him, and experience what a truly blessed life is, 'the life in God with Christ'. This has been my experience for the last four years and it is a great joy to me to find out daily what a truly wonderful Saviour is the Lord Jesus Christ (Shah 1977:322; 9 January 1895).

Perhaps as a way of resolving her dual marginality, as a Brahmin convert to Christianity, and as a Christian who rejected much of the Anglo-Catholic tradition through which she had initially found Christianity, in the end Ramabai arrived at a broad, inclusive Christianity in which sectarian differences were ultimately unimportant to her:

> I believe in the Universal Church of Christ which includes all the members of His body, and am not particular about others being members of different sects . . . I am not prejudiced against any secular belief. I only want to do the right thing and believe the right thing. I am trusting the Lord for everything and He knows how to teach and lead us in the right path (Shah 1977: 25 November 1896, p 335).

Like her relationship with her *jati* and her religious communities, Ramabai's relationship with Western culture and individual westerners was also complex. On the one hand, she had strong bonds with the West. She had converted to a religion brought to India by westerners, she maintained lifelong friendships with westerners, especially the CSMV sisters, she travelled in both the United States and England, and, as a result of her English education, she had complete control of written discourse in English. On the other hand, she was also quite critical of the British, both of individuals and of the government. She was particularly resentful of British women who tried to impose their own lifestyle on her, especially in terms of food or dress, and she frequently criticized them for being unwilling to make similar changes in their own lifestyles. More important, she articulated much of her criticism of the British government in terms of its insensitivity to women's needs. Particularly criticizing the government for its handling of the Rukhmabai affair, a case involving a married Hindu woman, she declares,

> And what a beneficial Government it is that does not care in the least to defend nearly half of the inhabitants of the country from the tyrannical lords whose marital property the women are said to be!

Suggesting that the British government would even have condoned sati, had Ram Mohun Roy, an indigenous reformer, not condemned it, she continues,

It is false to expect any justice for India's daughters from
the English Government, for instead of befriending her the
Government has proved to be a worse tyrant to her than the
native society and religion (Shah 1977: 177; 22 May 1887).

Despite her ties to westerners, and despite her criticisms of both
individual Hindus and Hinduism as a religious community, Ramabai also
still felt close ties to India. These ties are reflected not only in her lifestyle
preferences, but also in her repeated assertion of her strong desire to redress
the wrongs done to Indian women. Ramabai also repeatedly insisted that
her daughter Mano's education be carried out in India. Responding to Sr.
Geraldine's proposal that Mano be educated in England, she expressed her
fear that Mano would lose her Indian identity and declared that, 'I do not
want her to be too proud to acknowledge that she is one of India's
daughters. I do not want her to blush when our name is mentioned, such
being too often the case with those who have made their homes in foreign
lands' (Shah 1977:199; 20 May 1887). Symptomatic, however, of the
complexity of her relationship with Indian culture, although Ramabai
clearly asserted her desire that Mano not become Anglicized, she was
never able to articulate what kind of education she did want for Mano.
After their return to India, Mano was educated at home and in a variety of
English-medium schools in India, never staying in one long enough to
finish the prescribed course. The result was that Mano's education was
eclectic, sporadic, and disjointed.

A very strong sense of the woman comes through in these letters.
Without doubt, Ramabai was extremely independent-minded in thought
and action, and was unwilling to submit to any authority, English or
Indian, male or female. Consequently, Ramabai was a woman simultaneously both empowered by and distanced from several different communities. As a Christian, she was clearly not a contemplative. Indeed,
she disliked protracted religious devotion and preferred energetic action
directed at specific ends. Her identity as a Christian allowed her to
direct, in ways that might not have been possible had she remained a
Hindu, that energy and preference for action into institution building.
Despite her affectionate regard for the Anglo-Catholic sisters who had
introduced her to Christianity, she refused to allow herself to be drawn
into theological debate and sectarian arguments, although she could
clearly hold her own in interpretative arguments and stood firm in her
insistence on interpreting the biblical text for herself.

Clearly she was also both empowered by and detached from Chitpavan Brahmin culture and from India more generally. On the other hand, she consciously chose to retain many important elements of the lifestyle of her *jati*, even as she elected to spend the remainder of her life at Kedgaon after her return from the United States. On the other hand, she rejected the prescribed roles for women of her *jati*, the social and religious barriers between the various *jatis*, and the domination of religious texts and rituals by males. I would argue that her retention of some traditional lifestyle elements and her commitment to Kedgaon increased her credibility with her countrymen and women, enhanced her ability to advocate for changes in the lives of Indian women more generally, and contributed to the support and success of her establishment at Kedgaon.

At the same time, she was also both empowered by and distanced from aspects of Western culture. Respecting the English for their insistence on education for women and their allowance of greater physical freedom for women than most prevailing Hindu norms allowed, participating in their religion and controlling their language, she also strongly asserted her commitment to religious liberty and retained her ability to criticize the British government.

Much more so than Cornelia Sorabji, Pandita Ramabai presents a possible new paradigm for Indian women. Firstly, rejecting the seclusion and concentration on religious devotion traditionally enjoined on widows, she elected and modelled a socially useful role for widows, providing the foundation for that role for child and adult widows at Kedgaon. Secondly, she demonstrated how education and control of the written discourse may empower women. Thirdly, having made a religious commitment early in her life, she took that commitment seriously throughout her life, even while consciously remaining a Hindu and an Indian in some other aspects of her life. While Ramabai's religious choice was not the choice most of her countrywomen would make, Ramabai was nonetheless respected, even by many Hindus, for following through on the consequences of that commitment and remaining devoted to the God whom she had chosen. Thus, detached from and bonded to Indian culture, she was also uniquely able to envision possibilities for change. In working out those possibilities, she did not present a radical challenge to prevailing norms. Rather, like Cornelia Sorabji, and to a lesser extent Krupabai Satthianadhan, she worked for incremental change in Indian culture, pressing for and modelling in her own life significant changes in a few key aspects of women's lives.

Conclusion

Although the three women whose writings have been dealt with here constructed themselves through different media and in different ways, they nevertheless share several significant common elements among them. All three were raised in elite, nonconformist families. At least two of the three were influenced by strong family males, and two of the three spent most of their lives unmarried. All three identified themselves as Christians and saw their Christian identity as a significant area of difference between themselves and Indian women of other communities. Deeply committed to education for women, all three were not only literate in English but also able to find their own voices in that alien language. Addressing an English as well as an educated, although largely male, Indian readership in their writings, they were also able to use the act of constructing texts themselves as a means of enhancing their ability to take charge of their own lives. All three also experienced to a greater or lesser extent the pull of competing religious and national loyalties. While all three were firmly rooted in some part of a larger Indian culture in some way, all three also challenged prevailing paradigms in their respective communities.

Among the common elements these women share, two point to broader issues relating to Indian women's autobiographies. The first of these is the question of the effect of the choice of identity within a particular religious community. As Indian Christians, these women clearly identified with a community that transcended family and embraced a variety of *jatis*. At the same time, each of these women had a different relationship with the Indian Christian community. For Krupabai Satthianadhan, Christian identity was the defining characteristic of her life, and she experienced not only a deep sense of personal relationship with Christ, but also a firm bond with the Indian Christian community that provided real direction to her life. For Cornelia Sorabji, in contrast, Christian religious identity seems to have played a minor role in her life, although it was clearly part of the secular, progressive humanism that seems to have been her real code. For Pandita Ramabai, Christian identity allowed her the freedom to choose among a broad set of norms and values that also included some of those of her natal community. It also helped spur her on to social action on behalf of Indian women and the larger Indian Christian community. More important, for all these women, Christian religious identity, in distancing them from indigenous culture in a significant way, provided the foundation from which to work for both the self-actualization that they articulated in their writings and for changes in Indian women's roles. However, none experienced the kind of radical break with Indian culture that missionary rhetoric suggested should result from Christian identity. Rather, all remained tied in some way to Indian culture, opting instead to work for incremental change in the lives of the women around them.

In addition to the question of the consequences of religious identity, these women's writings also raise the issue of the autobiographer's relationship to her text. Clearly, to some extent, these women pursued different aims in their texts. Krupabai Satthianadhan found in the autobiographical novel a means of solidifying her Christian identity. As the wife of a well-known evangelist, Satthianadhan also used the novel, as well as its companion fictionalized account of a Hindu woman's life, to demonstrate the deleterious effects of indigenous Hindu customs and the benefits conferred on Indians, and particularly on women, by Christianity. Cornelia Sorabji, in contrast, found in her memoirs a means of justifying her unusual life by constructing herself as a change-agent, at the same time that she entertained and enlightened her English readers with vignettes of Indian women's lives. In contrast to both of these, Pandita Ramabai seems to have seen her letters as a way of convincing her English friends, and no doubt herself as well, of the rightness of her particular choices. At the same time, however, as literate women addressing an audience oriented toward colonial culture, all three of these women also articulated a particular view of the other Indian women. In stressing the contrast between educated Christian women like themselves and illiterate, ignorant, physically confined Hindu and Muslim women, these writers not only argued for the need for profound changes in indigenous Indian cultures, but, despite their expressions of divided loyalty, implicity supported and encouraged those elements of the colonial power structure that aided the realization of those changes. In this respect, like the active accomplishments of their lives, their texts become, and were perhaps always intended to be, more than simply expressions of self: they also become, in the hands of reform-minded men and, ultimately, other women, themselves the means to change the worldviews of both women and men. While Krupabai Satthianadhan and Cornelia Sorabji are not widely read today, they had an influential readership earlier in this century. That readership, together with the continued interest, among both Christians and non-Christians, in Pandita Ramabai's life and writings suggests that these texts may indeed have realized their authors' wider goals.

Notes

1. Cornelia Sorabji (1934: ix).
2. In addition to the three Indian Christian women whose autobiographical texts are dealt with here, examples of elite non-Christian women whose autobiographies have been published in English include Sunity Devee, Maharani of Cooch Behar (1864-?).1921. *The autobiography of an Indian princess* (London: John Murray); and Dr. S. Muthulakshmi Reddy (1886-?). 1964. *Autobiography* (Madras: MLJ Press). More recent examples include Vijaya Raje Scindia (b. 1919). 1987. *The last maharani of Gwalior* (Albany, NY: SUNY Press); and Gayatri Devi of Jaipur (and Santha Rama Rau).1984. *A princess remembers: the memoirs of the Maharani of Jaipur* (New Delhi: Vikas, 5th ed.).
3. Julian of Norwich (1342?-1413?), whose revelations of divine love have a strongly autobiographical cast, and Marjorie Kempe (1373-1438), who dictated her spiritual autobiography to her confessor, are only two examples of the many medieval women mystics who have left autobiographical writings.
4. Mary Mason (1988: 19-44).
5. Sidonie Smith (1987: 44-62).
6. Mrs S. (Krupabai) Satthianadhan (1895).
7. Mrs. S. (Krupabai) Satthianadhan (1894).
8. The complex built by the CSMV sisters at Panch Howd in Pune, adjacent to a similar structure for boys built by the Society of St. John the Evangelist, still stands, although the schools are now run entirely by Indians. A few English CSMV sisters are still working in Maharashtra.
9. A.B. Shah, ed. (1977). Quotations from this source will be identified by date. Occasional references will also be made here to a small collection of excerpts from Ramabai's other published writings, Shamsundar Manohar Adhav (1979). Introduction. *Pandita Ramabai* (Madras: The Christian Literature Society). The bibliography of primary and secondary sources on Ramabai is extensive. Hereafter this will be referred to as CLS.

References

Adhav, Shamsunder Manohar. 1979. Introduction. *Pandita Ramabai*. Madras:The Christian Literature Society.

The Christian Literature Society. 1979. *Pandita Ramabai*. Madras.

Mason, Mary. 1988. The other voice: Autobiographies of women writers. In Bella Brodzki and Celeste Schenk, eds. *Life/lines: Theorizing women's autobiography*. Ithaca: Cornell University Press.

Satthianadhan, Mrs. S. [Krupabai].1894. *Kamala: A story of Hindu life*. Madras: Srinivasa, Varadachari and Co.

—-. 1895. *Saguna: A story of a native Christian life*. Madras: Srinivasa, Varadachari and Co.

Shah, A. B., ed. 1977. *The letters and correspondence of Pandita Ramabai*. Compiled by Sister Geraldine. Bombay: Maharashtra State Board for Literature and Culture.

Smith, Sidonie. 1987. Women's story and the engendering of self-representation. In *Women's autobiography: marginality and the fictions of self-representation*, 44-62. Bloomington: Indiana University Press.

Sorabji, Cornelia. 1934. *India calling*. London: Nisbet.

4

Other Voices, Other Rooms:
The View from the Zenana

GAIL MINAULT

T HE PROVERBIAL VIEW of a woman's life in purdah-observing urban society in North India in the nineteenth century was one of hermetically sealed respectability: The woman left her father's house only when carried out in a wedding palanquin, and left her husband's house only when carried out on her bier. In reality, however, zenana life was considerably more sociable. Women in urban areas spent a great deal of time on their rooftops, conversing from one house to another. They visited one another frequently within their neighbourhood or circle of relations, and shared food on festival occasions with a whole network of families, bound together by ties of blood or social and economic obligation. A bride returned to her natal family for several visits during the first year of her marriage, and then for the birth of her first child and possibly for later confinements. Sisters remained in close contact, whatever the vicissitudes of their married lives. Women's networks were largely responsible for arranging marriages, even though the formal negotiation of marriage contracts was the prerogative of men.[1]

How is it possible to get an inside view of zenana life in India in the nineteenth century? The historian is handicapped by the fact that most works from the period, whether literary, historical, or religious, are written by men and represent what might be characterized as the 'hegemonic' or 'patriarchal' view of the zenana.[2] At the very least, such sources represent outsiders' views of the zenana, and thus to rely upon them is problematic. A critical reading of such works, however, permits one to illuminate their ideological stance, while simultaneously reading between the lines for what they reveal of zenana life, even as they criticize or complain about it.[3]

This discussion will draw extensively upon two texts written by Muslim reformers of the late nineteenth century, one from the educated middle class associated with the Aligarh movement, and the other from among the ulama associated with the Deoband school.[4] The first text, *Majalis un-Nissa* by Altaf Husain Hali, first published in 1874, consists of supposed conversations among women in a prosperous, urban Muslim household. The purpose of the work is to dramatize the need for women's education in that social milieu, to condemn superstition and useless custom, and to define the ideal Muslim woman.[5] The second text is *Bihishti Zewar* by Maulana Ashraf Ali Thanawi, published in 1905 or earlier. The reformist ulama of Deoband sought to improve the quality of Islamic education, to increase personal piety, and to spread the observance of Islamic law more widely among Muslims in India. Their advocacy of a reformed Islam led the Deoband ulama to champion women's education in order to suppress many customary practices and to Islamicize women's religious observances. *Bihishti Zewar* was the major vehicle for this reform, a veritable encyclopaedia of religious and family laws, Islamic medicine, and accounts of the lives of pious women. It became a standard guide to religious practice for women in many Muslim homes.[6]

One of the topics that both texts deal with is women's language in Urdu, or *begamati zuban*. They do so in order to indicate that it is incorrect, either uninstructed or un-Islamic. Maulana Thanawi particularly notes that women's language goes against religion:

> She greets the women of the house . . . [M]any do not even take the trouble to speak but simply place their hand to their forehead in greeting. The *hadith* says that this style of greeting is forbidden. Some say . . . simple 'salam'. That too is against the *sunna*. One should say '*As-salamu alaikum*' ['Peace be upon you']. Now just look at the responses:

> 'Keep cool!'
> 'May you live long!'
> 'Remain a beloved wife [*suhagin*]!'
> 'Long life!'
> 'May you bathe in milk and enjoy grandsons!'
> 'May your brother live long!'
> 'May your husband live long!'
> 'May your children live long!'

> It is easy to count off the names of the whole family but difficult to say '*As-salamu alaikum*', which in fact subsumes all the other prayers. Always to oppose the *shariat* is [a] sin.[7]

Hali's critique of women's language is more extensive, and takes the form of a lesson given by a mother to her son, indicating vocabulary that he—as a man —must never use:

> For example: *nauj, dur par, chhain phuin, ab se dur* [all interjections meaning God forbid; heaven forfend], *chal dur* [get out of here; begone], *sidharna* [to go away], *muva* [dead], *picchalpai* [demoness, witch], *bodli* [transvestite, whore], *vari, acchi, bua* [terms of endearment], *bhayya, bhaina* [younger brother, younger sister—also terms of endearment used for other women), *ujra* [ruined, in decline], *marne joga, janihar* [worthy of death, deadly—curses), *pinda* [body], *nikhattu* [worthless, useless], *nagori [unfortunate, without support]*, *bakhtavari* [lucky], *rasna basna* [fortunate, one who stays at home], *jhulsa* [fiery, quarrelsome], *ag lago, bhar men jae* [burn up, go into the fire/stove—curses, the equivalent of 'go to hell'], *dar gor* [into the grave—another curse], and so on. Never use these words in front of anyone! They won't say anything to you, but they will certainly say to themselves that this boy has started talking like a woman from hanging around his mother too long.[8]

What is going on here? And what can we learn from it? Such comments show that there is a whole area of idiomatic usage confined to the segregated world of women from which men are excluded. Their exclusion from this realm may make them feel uncomfortable, but if so, they express their discomfort in disdainful terms. The idioms of *begamati zuban*, as we see from these examples, have to do with the world of the household and with relationships, and are especially rich in interjections, in terms of endearment and abuse, and in forebodings of disaster. Other idioms, discussed later, relate to bodily health and a variety of customs and rituals that reformers also regarded askance. These are the elements of zenana culture that were under the control of women, and they developed their own ways of discussing them. In these matters of the household, women had a special competence, self-sufficiency, and even power.

The language of the zenana, according to these and other lexical and literary sources[9] is earthy, graphic, and colourful. The prevailing linguistic style is straightforward and highly colloquial. Even though there are patterns of deference among women, the flowery and polite phrases of Persianized Urdu do not come into play. The vocabulary from this language lesson, when further analysed, tells a lot about the character of women's lives. An area of rich, varied vocabulary indicates a topic of particular importance—a subject that women feel strongly about, or feel secure and competent to discuss.

To cite a few examples: a woman who did not have to leave her home (*rasna basna*) was deemed very fortunate; but her fortunate state implied family support and domestic responsibilities. A woman without support or companionship was particularly unfortunate (*nagori*). Customs reinforced these ideas. Young girls and women without a full complement of sisters or female relatives would readily 'adopt' female friends as their sisters through customs such as marrying their dolls, exchanging dupattas (*dupatta badalna bahin*), feeding each other cardamoms (*ilaichi bahin*), or breaking a chicken wishbone together (*zinakhi ka rishta*). Such vows of fictive sisterhood also survived their marriages and displacements.[10]

Women's lives were isolated in some respects but not in others. They lived, literally, at the centre of the household, in the courtyard with its manifold activities. Older women managed the household and trained the younger ones in their duties. Women with servants supervised them, checking petty theft and wastage. The amount of domestic work, maintenance, and household production of dishes of food and items of clothing for social occasions was staggering. Their lives may have been claustrophobic, but they were rich in human contact. Comfort was never very far away; on the other hand, neither was condemnation. There were always other women around to talk to, defer to, order around, quarrel with, laugh or cry with, or curse.[11]

The nature of women's verbal exchanges gives a clue to their activities, their beliefs and their values. *Begamati zuban* is sprinkled with terms of endearment and blessing. Women address each other as *bua*, *vari* (my dear/dearest), *bhaina* (younger sister), and *apa* (older sister); but also *bhayya* (brother), *beta* (son), and *sahib* (sir). Using male terms for women indicates particular endearment and also respect. For example, when a daughter has done her lessons particularly well, or produced a fine piece of needlework, her mother might call her *beta* to show special pleasure and admiration. Many blessings take the form not of blessing the woman herself, but of blessing those she holds most dear, such as *kaleja thanda rahe*, or *pet thanda rahe* which mean, literally, 'may your liver/belly keep cool', but figuratively, 'may your children have long lives/be happy/never disappoint you'. Another is *kokh aur mang se thandi rahe*, which means 'may you never become a widow / may your husband live a long time'. Young children may be blessed with *jite raho* or *jam jam jiyo*, 'may you live a long time', but they may also be told *teri ma ka pet thanda rahe,* 'may your mother never lose you/grieve for you'.[12]

Blessing a woman by wishing her husband and children long lives, or honouring a girl or a woman with a male title, are special characteristics of women's discourse. This is not self-deprecation per se, but rather indicates that one's life is important only in relation to others: the males upon whom the woman is dependent, and the children who are dependent upon her. Maulana Thanawi, however, in the passage quoted earlier, condemned such expressions as insufficiently Islamic, because to view women as blessed in terms of their relationships to men and children devalues their relationship to God and goes against the tenet that all believers are equal in His sight. Maulana Thanawi thus emphasizes the egalitarian basis of Islam as opposed to custom, an important element in reformist discourse. Much of the customary usage he so deprecates is a part of patterns of respect and deference, deemed necessary for the maintenance of peaceful relations in large, interdependent families. Thanawi, however, would respond that status and honour derive from God.[13]

The high value placed upon mutual dependence also comes out in anger. Women have no hesitation in telling other women to drop dead, but they hardly ever would wish their husbands or children dead. To do so might call down the wrath of God upon the speaker herself, whereas the following curses are uttered with seeming impunity: *bhar men jae, chulhe men jae* (into the fire/stove— go to hell); *dar gor, gor khaye, duniya se ure* (into the grave/drop dead); *janhar, marne joga* (worthy of death). Imprecations appear in rich variety in *begamati zuban*, indicating that women did a lot of quarrelling. In addition to wishing each other dead, they also accused one another of shamelessness, immodesty and dishonouring the family— just about the worst crimes a woman in purdah could commit. Epithets such as *bodli, randi, kasbi, bazaari, ghungru ki sharik* (transvestite, whore, streetwalker, dancing girl) were usually reserved for the practitioners of the oldest profession; but not necessarily. Similarly, *picchalpai, churel* (demoness, witch), were not always supernatural creatures. Impugning a woman's competence as a housekeeper was a milder form of abuse: *phuar, nikhattu, ate-ki-apa* (incompetent, useless, good-for-nothing, brainless).[14]

Turning to another characteristic of women's language, one finds that coinage tends to be from regional vernaculars such as Khari Boli, Braj Bhasha, Avadhi, and Dakkani rather than Arabic or Persian. Examples of words from Sanskrit-based local languages in *begamati zuban* have already been mentioned: *nagori, phuar, nikhattu*. Others include *surh* (the space of time between children); *sanvarna* (to arrange, prepare, or put right); *bhag* (fate—instead of *qismat*); and *nalijja* (shameless—rather than, or in addition to, *besharm*).[15] The reformers took exception to such expressions, finding *begamati zuban* to be archaic, illiterate, and—what's more—insufficiently Islamic. Hali and Thanawi, among others, were involved in codifying a modern Urdu idiom as well as a reformed Indian Muslim identity. In so doing, they wanted to purge the vernacular expressions that persisted in women's language and replace them with higher status, classical loan words from Persian and Arabic, thereby reinforcing the identity of Urdu as a Muslim language, whether that was their intention or not.

The influence of local languages on women's speech indicates that one can also expect local influences in household customs and rituals, evidence of Hindu borrowings, and a tenuous adherence to the Islamic scriptural tradition. This is most obvious in a large number of customs connected with marriage and childbirth, a rich composite of Hindu and Muslim observances which evolved in the zenana over the centuries. Muslim reformers attacked such customs as being wasteful and un-Islamic, and their advocacy of reform, ironically, provides us with much of our information about these customary observances.[16]

Maulana Thanawi, for example, here describes marriage customs:

> [T]he women of the family gather and confine the girl in a corner . . . Etiquette calls for the girl to be seated on a low platform, for ointment to be placed on her right hand, and for her lap to be filled with rice and *batasha* [a crisp sweet made of sugar syrup]. Rice and sweets are also distributed among those present. From that day on, the women continually rub the girl with ointments. They distribute fried sweet flour balls (*pindiyan*) among the kinfolk. This custom involves much foolishness. The first objection is to the requirement of seating the girl alone. Whether it is hot, whether it is stuffy, whether all the doctors and physicians of the world say she will get sick . . . this obligation must not be missed. This entails the evil of strict adherence to set customs. If there is apprehension about her getting sick, then there is the further sin of causing harm to a Muslim . . .[17]

These are popular customs that partake of Indian traditions rather than Islamic ones, and hence, in his view, to be deplored. The cost of the sweets

and ointments was a minor issue compared to the non-Islamic nature of
the observances. Further:

> The woman of the families gather at the groom's house to
> prepare the *bari* [gifts of clothing and so forth] and at the
> bride's house to prepare the *jahez* [dowry]. In the midst of
> this, any guest who comes from the other family's house,
> whether invited or not, has his or her fare paid. This encour-
> ages the gathering of women and provides another instance
> of unnecessary compulsion. To pay for travel whether one
> wishes it or not . . . is done simply for the sake of osten-
> tation and glory. It is a kind of compulsion forced on those
> who have come to think of it as obligatory. Such ostentation
> and compulsion are obviously against the *shariat*.[18]

The maulana, in his zeal for Islamic correctness, cannot empathize with
women for whom a wedding was one of the few occasions for approved
travel and visiting outside their own four walls.

The composite nature of women's culture also becomes clear from the
complex of activities designed to cope with evil. Women spent a great deal
of time and effort fending off disaster—from the elements, from illness,
from uncooperative relatives and children, and from the general tendency
of things to break down or wear out. This gave rise to a variety of
expressions signifying 'God forbid!' or 'Heaven forfend!': *nauj, dur par,
ab se dur, teri jan se dur,* and so on. In addition, women held a variety of
beliefs which, as Hali commented, 'you won't find in the Quran or *hadith*'.
These beliefs concerned spirits and the evil eye and practices designed to
charm them away, cure illness and generally keep things on an even keel.
To the reformers who enumerated them, these superstitions were anath-
ema. Hali nevertheless provides an account of many beliefs and practices
which he deemed useless:

> If two pieces of metal strike together, it is inauspicious, so
> when cutting with scissors . . . don't strike the two sides
> together. Nor should you rest your hand on the vessel while
> drinking water; that too is unlucky . . . Don't touch a door
> frame while you are standing up, but if by chance you should
> do so, kiss both your hands . . . If you stand a cot up against
> the wall with its legs facing out, it will bring bad luck . . .
> If a broom touches your body, you will become thin as a
> broomstick. If a ladle touches your body, you will become

greedy for food . . . Whenever you give children milk,
curd, or rice [white things] to eat, give them a slight taste of
ashes as well, or else the evil eye will affect them . . . If the
veil of a woman whose child has died touches someone, her
child will become sick, unless she cuts off the corner of the
veil and burns it. If you go to someone's house for a visit,
don't return on the third day. Don't go visiting on Wednes-
day . . . the third, thirteenth, and twenty-third and the
eighth, eighteenth, and twenty-eighth are unlucky, so don't
take up new tasks on those dates . . . And so forth and so
on.[19]

It would be interesting to compare this to a similar list of popular Hindu
beliefs and practices; many of them would doubtless be the same. Reformers were involved in a complex process of cultural critique that, firstly,
judged women's cultural practices as inferior, involving 'superstition' or
'custom' and, secondly, defined what was acceptable in terms of scriptural
tradition. In so doing, they were delimiting the boundaries of acceptable
behaviour on terms of what pious men did, and further defining what is
meant to be either a Hindu or a Muslim.[20]

Many of these superstitions had to do with subjects central to women's
lives: housework, food preparation and eating, marriages, children, visits,
illnesses, and the good and bad omens associated with them.[21] If in spite
of all precautions, illness did occur, then a number of healing rituals could
be tried. Hali puts these words in the mouth of a woman instructing her
daughter about what *not* to do:

A woman whose children have all died young can try
various remedies. In some places, she is covered with ashes,
in other places, she is made to bathe. In still others, she is
forbidden to cook in a *karhai*, or to eat eggs, fish, *gur*, milk,
or curds. She should not attend funerals, nor the sixth day
bathing rites for new mothers . . . None of these women
realizes that God alone gives life or takes it away. If He has
not decreed something, none of these ill-founded proce-
dures will avail them anything. As for women who have
never given birth to a child, in some places fairies are
invoked for them, in other places, spirits are summoned.
Domnis come and sing all night before those who are
possessed by spirits, and they, in turn, shake their heads
wildly and demand whatever they like, as if the spirits were

gyrating and speaking within them . . . No one ever asks
which spirits bring children and points out that it is in God's
power alone to grant children or not.[22]

Hali here takes the scripturalist stance that God alone can grant life,
children, and health. He also implies that such rituals are worse than
useless, for they waste money, cure nothing and distract believers from
trust in God. Nevertheless, Hali betrays a lack of understanding of the
psychological stresses of purdah existence. Non-medical 'cures', belief in
the evil eye and exorcism were all part of an environment in which
hostilities often ran high but had to be repressed, and where professional
medical help was usually unavailable. Hakims or medical doctors were
men, and thus could not see their female patients. Feeling a pulse or having
symptoms described by a servant did not permit very accurate diagnoses.[23]
Ill women, or women with ill children, thus relied on household remedies
or on cures which at least led to the release of fears and nervous tensions.
The summoning of *domnis*, professional women entertainers and exorcists
who only performed before women, did not violate purdah and provided
a good evening's entertainment besides. A woman who was 'possessed'
could also vent her hostilities and frustrations in a socially approved
manner and feel better for it.[24] But quite aside from the scriptural or
scientific arguments against such all-female ceremonies, these were arenas
of ritual life over which men had no control. Such autonomy made
reformers like Hali uncomfortable.

Another arena of women's lives in which they were virtually independent of men was their domestic chores. Women did a lot of the cooking,
sewing, and mending, even where there were servants. Embroidery was a
valuable skill, passed down from mother to daughter. In addition, household maintenance was constant: One had to recover quilts, and restuff them
with cotton from time to time in order to keep warm in winter.
Clothes had to be aired, cooking pots sent out to be retinned
periodically, stoves replastered, roofs and walls checked for leaks, water
vessels maintained, and so on. The list of household skills and daily
concerns is endless. The literature indicates that women were busy from
dawn to dark, and that while much of their work was drudgery, it could
also be fulfilling when there was cooperation from others in the household.
Women helped one another, at least ideally, and the men, though
supportive, were not much involved. Men and women were dependent upon one another, but women had their own realm in which they
were supreme. It was a limited world, to be sure, but one in which

practicality and competence counted. Women were dependent upon men economically, but also remarkably self-sufficient. From the women's point of view, their world was central to life, and the other world of men peripheral.

This sense of competence, self-sufficiency and importance should not be discounted in assessing zenana life. Women were adept at getting things done tactfully by cooperation among themselves. Here, again in Hali's account, a mother gives her daughter good advice on household consumption:

> Now I am going to tell you how to get things from the bazaar day by day, so that [the servants] don't pilfer . . . You should ask all those who come to the house from outside (the water carrier, the potter, the miller women, the bangle-sellers) what the current market prices are. Ask them periodically, and when you detect a discrepancy between the reported price and what you paid, scold severely the servant who did the shopping. Get into the habit of buying those commodities for which there is no fear of spoilage, like oil, spices, *gur*, sugar, cardamoms, tobacco and lime for *paan*, etc., when they are in season . . . The remaining things, like fresh vegetables, meat, yoghurt, and milk have to be procured on a daily basis. For those, it is not good always to send the same person . . . Vary the person whom you send to do the shopping. That will keep the servants on their toes.[25]

A competent housekeeper had to be part spy and part diplomat, able to manage servants and keep the peace among a host of family members. This was the ideal. That it was not always so is evident from the variety of curse words noted earlier. Hali criticizes the women's tendency to quarrel as follows:

> [W]hen several [women] get together, they sit around and start complaining. Some complain about their mothers-in-law; others weep about their sisters-in-law. Some pour vitriol on their daughters-in-law; other retail their grievances against their husbands. Some find fault with X's marriage or joke about the amount of Y's dowry or cast aspersions on Z's ancestry. If anyone disagrees with anything another says, they quarrel. If anyone is the least bit

impetuous, she picks a fight with the sightest provocation.
Such women abuse and wound each other. They say taste-
less things to their husbands. They curse their children for
no reason. They grumble and argue with the servants, right
or wrong.[26]

One might dismiss this as just the standard male complaint that women
never talk about anything of substance. Hali's point, however, is that these
women, not having a proper education, lack self-control and decorum. If
they were educated, they might still talk about children and relationships,
and they might discuss matters like good health and child-rearing, or how
to bring literacy to the servants, as well. In addition—and this was
crucial—women would lead pious lives, control their tempers, and not
abuse one another, their children, nor their servants gratuitously.

Muslim women may or may not have viewed their isolation as a
problem. Indeed, even in its self-containment, zenana life was often very
satisfying, as the analysis of its language and customs has made clear. For
Muslim reformers such as Hali and Thanawi, however, women's realm
was problematic, for a number of reasons. Muslim men's preoccupation
with the status of women in their community around the turn of the century
is easily explained. As Muslims came to terms with British rule and took
up Western education, they found an increasing gap between their public
and private lives. Their women, whether educated at home in rudimentary
fashion or—more likely—totally uneducated, were the proverbial 'frogs
in a well'. The reformers complained that the women were backward,
superstitious and were moreover unable to provide intelligent companionship to their husbands or discipline to their sons in an increasingly
competitive political and economic environment. What was perhaps
worse, the women were ignorant of the basic tenets of their faith, tied to
customary rituals and observances that had little to do with scriptural
Islam: exorcism, saint worship of the most idolatrous sort, and expensive
life-cycle rituals that originated in the surrounding Hindu culture.[27]

The projected benefits of women's education, in this composite reformist view, were that women would be better companions to their husbands,
better mothers to their children, better homemakers and better Muslims.
Muslim social reform was comparable to Hindu social reform in that it was
tied to male visions of the need to stem religious and cultural decline, to
define their culture according to a universally recognizable standard, and
to preserve the family through raising the honour and dignity of its women.
This was a distinctly patriarchal form of social reform, with women the

beneficiaries of male concerns and action, again, very similar in character to much Hindu social reform.[28]

In one respect, however, reform was more problematic for Muslims than for Hindus; this involved the custom of purdah. Hindu reformers, whose women also observed a form of purdah, were willing to see the custom scrapped as an artifact of Muslim rule, whether that was a fair characterization or not.[29] But to Muslims, the custom had religious sanction and further served as a symbol of the distinctiveness of their culture. There was little or nothing in the writings and plans of Muslim reformers, therefore, that included tearing down the curtains of purdah. They eloquently criticized the effects of purdah: women's isolation, ignorance and detachment from externally-imposed standards of behaviour, but not the custom itself. Muslims reformers maintained that women could be educated, competent, free from superstition and backwardness, and still maintain purdah and all the respectability and status that veiling implied. They wanted to unveil women's minds, in other words, without unveiling their faces.

Within the group of Muslim social and educational reformers, there were men of the Western-educated, urban, service and professional classes, and others who were more traditionally-educated, or ulama. Hali and Maulana Thanawi are only two representative examples. Their views about women's education and legal rights obviously differed. The Western-educated tended to emphasize marital companionship and enlightened nurturing as ideal roles for the educated woman. The ulama tended to emphasize scriptural piety. Both contributed elements to the reformist vision of the way Muslim women ought to be. In their reactions to zenana life and its language, however, these differing emphases indicate very different ideological stances.

To the Western-educated reformer, the liberal philosophical adage would seem to be axiomatic: That which is separate is inherently unequal, and hence the culture of those that are segregated is necessarily inferior. Indeed, the discourse of inferiority applied by reformist men to their women was parallel to that visited upon the men by the colonial authorities. British rule was frequently justified in terms of the cultural inferiority of Indians, portrayed as passive and effeminate—and thus segregated from positions of power—in contrast to the masculine Anglo-Saxons. To break down their own ideological marginalization, reformers consequently had to break down their women's isolation. To do so involved imposing an externally-determined standard of behaviour, which also involved bringing women more under men's control. The self-sufficiency of the zenana was thus not only a practical difficulty for these men, but a philosophical one as well, and involved their own power relations with their colonial masters.[30]

For the ulama, however, women might inhabit a separate space, but according to the tenets of Islam, they were equal to men—as believers in God. Their inferior status, consequently, was not due to their isolation, but rather because of degenerate custom, falsely identified as religion. The ulama too wanted to impose a patriarchal standard of behaviour upon women, one determined by scripture. But in that scripture—at a certain ideal level at least—women and men were equal. The liberal discourse of separate but inferior and the Islamic discourse of separate but equal were in clear conflict. Ironically, the ideological stance of the ulama had a logical consistency, as well as a source from within their culture, which the liberals' position lacked.

While these debates raged, women could not help being affected by the social and political changes that were taking place. Women in purdah were so used to the system, not to mention the security and social prestige that it conferred, that their isolation was less a problem for them than it was for the men who were exposed to outside pressures. Women did have to cope with the practical problems posed by purdah: how to shop for vegetables, how to keep the servants from cheating, and so on. But again, these strategies were so much a part of the fabric of their existence, and the status that veiling implied was so valuable, that even these inconveniences did not seem very significant to women.

In seeking an education, however, girls had to overcome barriers to going out to school, something that their brothers did as a matter of course. If their families were sufficiently affluent, they might be taught at home by an *ustani* (women teacher), or by a grey-bearded *maulvi* who would come to the house to teach all the young children to read the Quran. Reading scripture was an honourable accomplishment, but to learn to read Urdu or—harder still—to write it, girls often had to resort to stratagems: getting a brother or male cousin to tutor them out of earshot of their elders, or surreptitiously practicing their *alif bey jims* using coal blacking from the stove.[31] The writing taboo was customary because if a girl learnt how to write, there was no telling to whom she might write letters, and this might jeopardize the honour of the family. Reformers in favour of women's education blamed false custom and misplaced notions of prestige for this taboo, but the fact remained that until girls started going out to school, it was virtually impossible for them to get an education in any way equivalent to that of their brothers. Thus in practical matters, and especially in the matter of education, isolation was a problem for women. Segregation was a barrier to equal education, and separate but equal schooling could take them only so far. The equality of all believers, which supplied the logical consistency in the ulama's reformist stance, was not in evidence when it came to actually achieving a higher education for bright young women, who were in other respects the equals of their brothers.

The women of reformist families followed the lead of their men in championing education for girls without demanding an end to purdah. The prestige of their status and the distinctiveness of Muslim culture were at stake, and in a society where Muslims felt threatened by their minority status, the pressure upon Muslim women not to break ranks with their community was overwhelming. Still, in agreeing with their men, Muslim women were obliged to follow their reasoning, and if women's separate existence was in fact inferior, then one possible response to a discourse of inferiority was a discourse of oppression. In order to claim the equality that should be theirs ideally, educated Muslim women could also blame custom for the excesses of the purdah system, and demand a mitigation of its practical effects as a way to the realization of their rights in Islam.

This, in fact, happened in 1918 in a meeting of Muslim women in Lahore, as reported in the Urdu women's magazine *Tahzib un-Niswan*. The women passed a resolution condemning 'the kind of polygamy practiced by certain sections of the Muslims'—note the qualifying phrase identifying the problem as customary practice—and went on to say that such polygamy was 'against the true spirit of the Quran and of Islam'. They further called upon educated women to 'exercise' their influence among their relations to put an end to this practice.[32] Some reformist men were scandalized by the fact that women had actually spoken out for their rights in this instance, and indeed, examples of such outspokenness on the part of Muslim women were rare in the early twentieth century. Still, such a resolution was only echoing what a number of liberal Muslim men had been saying for some time, and ironically, it paralleled their own growing desire for self-determination.

Aspects of the cultural critique by men, in particular their condemnation of false custom and evocation of the egalitarian nature of Islam, were beginning to make an impression. The men's motivation had been the imposition of a patriarchal standard upon, and some measure of control over, women's customary, 'corrupt', yet autonomous realm—not the liberation of women. And yet, in accepting this discourse of inferiority and an externally-imposed standard of behaviour as the norm, women could in turn blame the oppressiveness of custom and reclaim the egalitarian promise of idealized, scriptural Islam. Liberation from oppression for Muslim women is thus by no means a linear progression from reform, to education, to a realization of rights in the classic liberal pattern—but involves an ongoing dialogue with both male hegemony and the underlying religious authority, as variously interpreted.

Notes

An earlier version of this article was presented at the University of Hawaii's Ninth Annual South Asian Studies Spring Symposium, 1992. 'Other voices, other views: Anti-hegemonic discourse in South Asia', Honolulu, 5-7 March, with few apologies to Truman Capote for the title.

1. These generalizations are based on reading the biographies and autobiographies or reminiscences of women from the period, most notably Ahmadi Begam's biography (manuscript) of her sister, Muhammadi Begam, and Muhammadi Begam's biography of Ashrafunnissa, *Hayat-i-ashraf* (Lahore: Imambara Sayyida Mubarak Begam, n.d.). The latter has been excerpted and translated by C. M. Naim, 1987. How Bibi Ashraf learned to read and write. In *Annual of Urdu Studies* 6: 99-115.

2. For a fuller discussion of a variety of sources for the history of Muslim women in South Asia, see Gail Minault, 1986. Making invisible women visible: Studying the history of Muslim women in South Asia. *South Asia* (Australia), 9, 1: 1-13.

3. Just as the authors in the series *Subaltern Studies* must use government sources and other elite writings for their investigations of non-elites.

4. On Aligarh, see especially David Lelyveld, 1978. *Aligarh's first generation.* Princeton: Princeton University Press; on Deoband, see Barbara Metcalf, 1982. *Islamic revival in British India: Deoband 1860-1900.* Princeton: Princeton University Press.

5. Gail Minault, tr. 1986. *Voices of silence: English translation of Hali's Majalis un-nissa and Chup ki dad.* Delhi: Chanakya.

6. Barbara Metcalf has translated parts of it; see Metcalf, 1990. *Perfecting women: Maulana Ashraf Ali Thanawi's Bihishti zewar.* Berkeley: University of California Press.

7. Ibid,. pp. 110-11.

8. Minault, 1986. *Voices of silence*, p. 109.

9. For a list of various sources for the study of *begamati zuban*, see Gail Minault,

1984. *Begamati zuban* : Women's language and culture in nineteenth-century Delhi, *India International Centre Quarterly* 9, 2: 169, n.4.

10. Muhiyuddin Hasan, 1976. *Dilli ki begamati zuban*, pp. 79-80. New Delhi: Nayi Awaz.

11. These generalizations are derived from the texts discussed herein, as well as from Urdu novels such as those of Nazir Ahmad, *Mirat-ul-arus, Taubat un-nasuh*, and so on.

12. Wahida Nasim, 1968. *Urdu zuban aur aurat*, pp. 107-10. Karachi: Intikhab-i-Nau .

13. Metcalf, 1990. *Perfecting women*, pp. 79-83.

14. Nasim, 1968. *Urdu zuban aur aurat*, pp. 100-105.

15. Ibid, pp. 58-59.

16. Sayyid Ahmad Dehlawi, *Rasum-i-Dehli*; Hali, *Majalis un-nissa*; and Nazir Ahmad, *Mirat ul-arus* are all examples of this kind of reformist literature; see also Barbara Metcalf, 1982. Islam and custom in nineteenth-century India. *Contributions to Asian Studies* 17: 62-78.

17. Metcalfe, 1990. *Perfecting women*, p. 116.

18. Ibid., p. 118.

19. Minault, 1986. *Voices of silence*, pp. 59-61.

20. Christopher R. King's work on the Hindi-Urdu controversy makes a similar point, emphasizing their linguistic separation into Sanskritized Hindi and Persianized Urdu, as well as the differentiation of both from the 'surrounding ocean of popular culture'. See King, 1989. Forging a linguistic identity: The Hindi movement in Banaras, 1868-1914. In Sandria B. Freitag, ed., *Culture and power in Banaras*, pp 179-202. Berkeley: University of California Press.; the quote is from p. 188. Sanskritized Hindi also became symbolic of the righteous Hindu Golden Age, see King, 1992. Images of virtue and vice: The Hindi-Urdu controversy in two nineteenth-century Hindi plays. In Kenneth R. Jones, ed., *Religious controversy in British India*, pp. 123-48. Albany: State University of New York Press.

21. See Jaffur Shareef, 1973. *Qanoon-e-Islam or the customs of the Musalmans of India*, pp. 226-76. Tr. by G.A. Herklots, for a discussion of auspicious dates and directions. Reprint. Lahore: Al-Irshad.

22. Minault, 1986. *Voices of silence*, p. 65. A *karhai* is a cooking vessel, like a wok. *Gur* is a coarse brown sugar. A *domni* is a professional entertainer (masc. *dom*).

23. Compare this with the incident of the perforated sheet in Salman Rushdie, 1988. *Midnight's children*. London: Penguin.

24. For a psychological inquiry into indigenous healing practices concerning spirit possession, see Sudhir Kakar, 1982. *Shamans, mystics, and doctors*, pp. 15-88 Delhi: Oxford University Press .

25. Minault, 1986. *Voices of silence,* p. 71.

26. Ibid., p. 59.

27. It should be noted that Hindu reformers too objected to many such rituals and customs as 'superstitious' and 'decadent'. See Kenneth W. Jones, 1988. Socio-religious movements and changing gender relationships among Hindus of British India. In James W. Bjorkman, ed., *Fundamentalism, revivalists and violence in South Asia* pp. 40-56. New Delhi: Manohar.

28. Ibid.

29. For a discussion of the way that Hindu purdah differs structurally and functionally from that of Muslims, see Sylvia Vatuk, 1982. Purdah revisited: A comparison of Hindu and Muslim interpretations of the cultural meaning of purdah in South Asia. In Hanna Papanek and Gail Minault, eds., *Separate worlds: Studies of purdah in South Asia,* pp. 54-78. Delhi: Chanakya.

30. For a discussion of this point in a different (but congruent) Indian milieu, see Rosalind O'Hanlon, 1991. Issues of widowhood: Gender and resistance in colonial Western India. In Douglas Haynes and Gyan Prakash, eds., *Contesting power: Resistance and everyday social relations in South Asia* pp. 62-104, especially pp. 72-79. Berkeley: University of California.

31. C.M. Naim. 1987. How Bibi Ashraf learned to read and write, pp. 107-109.

32. *Tahzib un-niswan* (Lahore) 31, 20 April 1918, pp. 245-49. For further details see Gail Minault, 1981. Sisterhood or separatism? The All-India Muslim Ladies' Conference and the nationalist movement. In Gail Minault, ed., *The extended family: Women and political participation in India and Pakistan,* pp. 94-95. Delhi: Chanakya; and 1989. *Ismat*: Rashid ul-Khairi's novels and Urdu literary journalism for women. In C. Shackle, ed., Urdu and Muslim South Asia, pp. 135-36. London: School of Oriental and African Studies.

Killing My Heart's Desire:
Education and Female Autonomy
in Rural North India

PATRICIA JEFFERY AND ROGER JEFFERY

> Slower population growth has shown quite a strong correlation with faster income growth in the 1980s and better education is probably the key to both. The World Bank now proclaims women's education as one of the very best investments around, even in economic terms. (Harrison 1992)

> What's the benefit of being educated? If you study you have to make *roti* [bread, food] and if you don't study you have to make *roti*. So having studied, what is the benefit? (Santosh)

IF SOME WOMEN in rural North India express doubts about the significance of formal education for women, few demographers display any such caution. The current orthodoxy on how to reduce child mortality and increase the use of contraception in developing countries asserts that educating girls will have a dramatic effect, by raising women's status.[1] In this chapter we suggest a number of problems with this view. To begin with, although education and lower fertility clearly often go together in some way, there is little evidence that the linking mechanism is through the effect of female education on women's status or 'autonomy'. Furthermore, in any case, notions of autonomy and individual decision-making are of questionable value to understanding rural women in North India. We use our research among Jats in Bijnor district, Uttar Pradesh, to suggest that rural women do not experience education as something which liberates them, and that they do not necessarily see greater autonomy as desirable. We look at the meanings of education, and how it relates to changing fertility patterns, and conclude by suggesting an alternative way of conceptualizing women's agency.

The Demographic Paradigm

In the social demographic literature about North India, and in Indian government publications too, a central presumption is that the slow pace of fertility decline is a reflection of women's 'low status' in the area. Jain and Nag, for example, conclude that educational policies 'can reduce fertility and this effect can be enhanced by allocating disproportionately greater resources to female primary education' and they hypothesize that 'primary education, by providing basic functional literacy and numeracy, enhances women's status within and outside their family' (1986:1607). The basis for this argument is that the length of a woman's schooling is, in statistical terms, often a very good predictor of her completed family size, of her use of modern contraceptives, and of the mortality of her children, even when due account is taken of the influence of where she lives and her household's income or class position. Demographers interpret these correlations—sometimes jumping directly from *correlation* to *causality*—and *assume* that, for example, 'an educated woman can take greater responsibility for her children's health and is permitted to pursue appropriate strategies by other household members' (World Bank 1991:136). The argument is made most forcefully for mortality: 'There is overwhelmingly strong evidence that maternal education is almost everywhere a major *determinant*, if not the major determinant, of infant and child mortality in any locality' (Lockwood and Collier 1988:26). But very little is known about the content of education or about how it has these supposed effects on a woman's own attitudes and behaviour, let alone those of her significant others.

Clearly, longer schooling delays marriage, and thus educated girls are protected from giving birth before they are fully mature, when they and their children would tend to be at a higher risk. Beyond that, lengthy schooling is said to enhance a young woman's self-confidence, making her better able to confront doctors and minor government health workers, to deal with shopping, transport, and so on, and to manage relationships with her parents-in-law and her husband.[2] This is what Jain and Nag mean by 'enhancing women's status'. 'Women's status' is, however, a misleading conceptualization, since it tends to draw attention away from unequal gender relationships and power differentials, as well as homogenizing women and underplaying differences which stem from women's class positions, their marital status or their age. Furthermore, in the demographic literature, interpretations of women's status have been impeded by 'a lack of theory and a generally poor understanding of local cultural and institutional contexts' (Cain 1984). Dyson and Moore (1983) talk instead about women's autonomy, which they define as 'the capacity to manipulate one's personal environment' and 'the ability—technical, social and psychological—to obtain information and to use it as the basis for making decisions about one's private concerns and those of one's intimates' (Dyson and Moore 1983:45). We will discuss some problems raised by Dyson and Moore's approach, but we agree with their view (and that of many feminist writers) that indicators of autonomy should include who controls a woman's sexuality and fertility, and her role in the allocation of economic resources. What evidence is there that educated women enjoy more autonomy, defined in these terms, than uneducated women?

Demographers who have begun to address this issue have tended to use the standard tools of the trade—the social survey. For key demographic variables, this approach works tolerably well: it is possible in this way to collect seemingly simple data (age of marriage, educational level) and to subject it to numerical analysis. Indeed, we have collected such data ourselves. Like many previous writers, though, we hesitate to rely too heavily even on the more apparently uncontentious answers, such as number of live births or length of schooling, let alone the possibly more sensitive responses on age at marriage (especially when a woman has cohabited with more than one man) or infant deaths. Nonetheless, carefully conducted surveys can probably provide some meaningful correlations, provided non-sampling errors are recognized. Many survey analysts recognize that the survey is too blunt a tool to expose more subtle issues, but they continue to use questionnaires to collect material on social processes (like how children are defined as ill, and what determines what treatment they then receive). Their questions are often based on dubious assumptions, and they rely on intuition and plausible hypotheses when they try to make sense of any statistical correlations that emerge.[3] Alternative, more sensitive, styles of research are rarely taken on board; the work of Caldwell and his associates (1983) is a rare exception.

For South Asia, we know of only one study that used anthropological methods to address the question of how education affects women's autonomy, in this case with reference to child health (Lindenbaum 1990). Demographic theory tends to follow the modernization approach to social change, in which education is seen to have a common meaning throughout the world. By contrast, Lindenbaum treats schooling as an 'empty category'. Education has changing implications for her respondents in Bangladesh as 'a rapidly moving social counter' which 'defines a new aspect of [a woman's] status at the time of marriage' (ibid.: 358). Lindenbaum argues that her respondents do perceive psychological effects of schooling on women: educated women are thought to be capable of depending upon themselves, and to be braver and more open in discussions within their marital households. Schooling is also believed to lead to 'the genesis of manners and the emergence of a sense of companionship in marriage' (ibid.: 360). Educated women are economically more valuable: they cost less in marriage arrangement, can manage household finances, tutor their children (saving tuition fees) and be potential earners. According to Lindenbaum, schooling provides a form of 'assertiveness training' which results in women's higher self-esteem and relative freedom from dependency and constraint (ibid.: 363; see also Levine 1980). Lindenbaum concludes that education is 'an index of membership in a class culture that extends beyond the boundaries of the local village and a key to acquiring resources in newly forming systems of distribution' rather than 'an information "handout"', a body of knowledge that transforms the mind and the behaviour of the recipient along predictable lines' (ibid.:368).

Lindenbaum's work suggests that the implications of girls' education are locally specific, and may also vary along class and other lines. The differing strategies employed by parents as well as women's responses to their education are all in need of investigation. For example, some of Lindenbaum's respondents educate a first-born girl as if she were a son, and expect her to obtain employment and pay for the schooling of her siblings. In that part of Bangladesh, marriage expenses for educated girls are lower than for uneducated girls; and they are less likely to experience divorce or separation than uneducated women, for whom that is an increasingly common experience. These generalizations, however, contrast sharply with the situation in some other parts of Bangladesh (Amin 1993) and in other parts of rural North India (Das Gupta 1987; 1990). Thus, as we shall argue later, we cannot assume that female education leads to lower fertility because education enhances women's autonomy; this may be true in some places and at some times, but not universally.

Is 'Autonomy' an Appropriate Term in South Asia?

But we have other problems with the demographic paradigm. It is not just that the relationships between education and autonomy are variable. After all, it could just be that the absence of a simple relationship between female education and an increase in women's autonomy results from other aspects of the social structure. Dyson and Moore (1983), for example, establish regional typologies within India, looking at marriage systems, a woman's postmarital relationships with her natal kin, and property flows in marriage (including a wife's potential control over her dowry and other similar transfers) in their analysis. On all thcsc counts, North Indian women fare worse than those in South India. Although these factors may have an impact on women's autonomy, they may also operate directly in affecting fertility patterns.

More fundamental issues seem to be raised by a discourse which can accept at face value a description of North Indian women in which they appear to have little or no say in their everyday lives. Dyson and Moore (1983:46) describe the majority of these women—unschooled, married in their mid-teens to older men, working in the home or in family enter-prises—as 'socially almost powerless'. Cain (1984) focuses on women's almost total economic dependence on men. Amartya Sen, in one of the most sophisticated discussions of these issues, argues that a woman's bargaining power is enhanced by outsidc carnings because they improve her chances of survival should the marriage break down, as well as giving her a clearer perception of her individuality and well-being and providing her with a higher 'perceived contribution' to the family's economic position (1990: 144; see also Cain 1981). Like Ursula Sharma (1986), Sen sees negotiations within households as 'co-operative conflicts', in which perceptions—not simply the material value of men's and women's eco-nomic contributions—are crucial to defining people's entitlements to resources or health care, for example. Sen thus cautions that if female education does not lead to greater economic contributions, it can only affect a woman's marital position if it improves her situation should her marriage brcak down (through divorce, separation or widowhood) and if it changes people's perceptions—including those of women themselves—of women's rights.

But like Dyson and Moore, and others who provide 'externalist' ac-counts of women's position, Sen fails to show that education *per se* can change people's perceptions, without the changes in women's material conditions implied by female employment or changes in women's post-breakdown chances. His account still tends to leave uneducated, unem-ployed women in an analytic limbo. None of these authors addresses the issue of how women maintain a sense of self in such settings, nor deal with the intra-household relationships which may develop. In general, the empirical basis for exploring how women view themselves and their ability to influence their own lives is remarkably thin (Visaria 1985). The meaning of a woman's access to her natal kin, or of her 'ownership' (in legal terms) of property, for example, is only slowly being explored (Jeffery and Jeffery 1992; Vlassoff 1991).Yet these are the very women, as Gold and Raheja show in this volume, who speak through their songs and stories of very different worlds.

Many attempts to represent the situation of rural women in India, then, tend to produce an account in which women are seen as victims. Treating Indian women as victims typifies them as passive, demure, obedient and oppressed, and sets them up as people waiting to be saved. Such an approach leaves little scope for understanding how women negotiate and resist aspects of their situations. Yet one alternative—regarding women as agents—has its own problems, too, not least of which are elements of wishful thinking (Mani 1990: 36-38). Focusing on women's agency only in the form of struggle is to misunderstand the nature of women's agency within structures of domination. One attempt to avoid opting either to see women as 'victims' or as 'agents' is provided by the discussions in Haynes and Prakash (1991), who follow Scott (1990) in seeing power as always tenuous and in constant need of being secured because of resistance to it. But everyday forms of resistance are not very powerful (Adas 1991: 300-301). They are limited by an appraisal of the odds, by an understanding that the structures of power are not fundamentally alterable and that one must act within them. Resistance, then, is conditioned by the power structures to which it is a response—and it is more likely to be damage limitation than foolhardy bravado. Therefore a woman, as agent, may both resist her oppression and also be an agent in her own coercion. We need to find some better way of handling both structure and agency.

Resistance is also limited by the extent to which the ruling ideology controls people's consciousness. That control over consciousness may not be total, but nor is it totally lacking. Haynes and Prakash argue that subordinates make but partial critiques (or in Willis' terms 'partial penetrations': Willis 1977) of the situation in which they find themselves. Consequently, both at the level of the individual and the social group we can observe 'omnipresent tension and contradictions between hegemony and autonomy in consciousness, between submission and resistance in practice' (Haynes and Prakash 1991: 10-13). Or, to put it slightly differently, there is a 'complex mixture of deep-rooted commitment and reluctant compliance, of accepting things as they are and of undermining them through their questions and evasions' (P. Jeffery 1979 : 161).

It might clarify what we mean by 'cultural hegemony' if, for instance, we consider the connotations of the Hindi words that seem comparable to 'autonomy'. In English, the term 'autonomy' generally has a positive aura:

it is considered desirable and appropriate for people to be able to make decisions about their lives and act upon them. But the Hindi terms are often rather ambivalent, if not downright pejorative.

Perhaps the most neutral term that came up in discussions with women in the villages where we have worked is *mukhtiyar* (and other words connected with it, such as *mukhtiyari, ikhtiyar, ikhtiyari*). *Mukhtiyar* implies someone who is in control of her situation, someone who has authority to act as a free agent. Frequently, when we asked young married women about control over household finances, they would introduce the word in their adamant denials that they have such control, often seeming to be surprised that we thought it was possible. The word *azad* (free, independent) may have a positive resonance—for instance, in reference to a nation state—but it generally takes on a rather different colour when applied to women, when it is often used in the same breath as *besharm* (immodest, shameless). And the word *zimmadar* (responsible) was generally used by women commenting on the drawbacks and risks of being in a position that involves making decisions for which one is held liable. In other words, that which we might want to label 'autonomy' may not be valorized by women because it seems unattractive and frightening. Thus it is not simply that women *cannot* act autonomously.

In the rest of this chapter we explore the implications of this discussion for the material we have collected in Bijnor district, in fieldwork in several villages and among several caste groups, which now stretches over ten years.[4] In demographic terms, the most interesting features of the Jats on whom we particularly focus here is that, compared to other sizeable local caste groups, they have a higher contraceptive prevalence rate, lower fertility, and a higher proportion of young women who have been educated to secondary level or above.[5]

After briefly describing our fieldwork, we deal with three areas of women's lives: the arrangements of their marriages, control over economic resources within the household, and fertility decision-making. We describe how women not only perceive that they have very little scope for active involvement in marriage arrangements and in financial management, but also that they are often ambivalent about whether they want to take on the responsibilities that this would involve. Educated and uneducated women seem to be alike in their tentative response to these aspects of 'autonomy'. We ask what meaning female education has in this context, and how else we might understand the transition in fertility limitation which has taken

place. We conclude by discussing further the implications our account has
for wider issues of women's autonomy in North India.

CHOICE OF MARRIAGE PARTNER

This song represents a bride specifying to
her mother the type of groom that she would like:

O mother, I want to be married to a man in service,
I won't be married to a ploughman.
When a ploughman comes back from his ploughing,
A bad smell comes from afar,
When a man who works in an office comes from his work,
A lovely perfume comes from afar.
O Mother . . .

When a ploughman comes back from his ploughing,
He eats twelve-twelve thick *roti*,
When a man who works in an office comes from his work,
He eats two-two thin *phulka*.
O Mother . . .

When a ploughman comes back from his ploughing,
I can see his goad from afar,
When a man who works in an office comes from his work,
He brings wadges of hundred rupee banknotes.
O Mother . . .

mayya, kardey nowkerey-sang bahai-rey,
hal-jota bulam nahi bahai.

jub hal-jota hal pey sey aayey,
duro sey bad-bu aayey-rey,
Jub nowkerey nowkri sey aayey,
duro sey khush-bu aayey-rey.
mayya . . .

jub hal-jota hal pey sey aayey,
baara-baara roti khayey-rey,
jub nowkerey nowkri sey aayey,
do-do phulkian khayey-rey.
mayya . . .

jub hal-jota hal pey sey aayey,
duro sey peyna dikhai-rey,
Jub nowkerey nowkri sey aayey,
so-so ke gaddi dikhai-rey.
mayya . . .

A marriageable girl (whether educated or uneducated) who voices an opinion on her future marriage knows she is playing with fire. In the face of the potential wrath of her entire family, silence is prudent. But more commonly, women themselves endorse the ideas of family honour, of the shamelessness of displaying an interest in one's marriage (and by implication, one's sexuality), and of the appropriateness of leaving the whole business to their elders. Stepping out of line is dangerous—but not something that most women seek to do in any case. The small number of women who did assert their will became the focus of scandal and the objects of gossip in which other women were the key players.

In rural Bijnor in general, virtually all women are married and in the rural areas most are married in their mid to late teens; the only unmarried women over the age of 21 are a small number described as 'cracked' or 'weak-minded'. Basically, there is not a choice not to marry. Parents are expected to take charge and among Jats, the girl's parents initiate the enquiries about potential marriage partners; according to the Jat women in Nangal, parents would weigh up several factors in deciding for or against particular matches. The girl's own physical maturity was generally the key to the timing of her marriage, often because her parents fear being subjected to gossip and taunting if they fail to marry their daughters in a timely fashion. The Nangal women also outlined the considerations that their parents weighed up in evaluating potential matches, including the boy's occupation, age and physical appearance, his father's landholding, transport networks and the prospect of dowry demands. The educational levels of the girl and her potential groom were indeed generally salient and this is an important question to which we will return later. Here, the crucial point is that the girl's educational level bore no relation to whether she was consulted either about when or to whom she would be married.

The uneducated women to whom we spoke all said that they had not been asked for their opinion about their marriage: 'Who asked girls in those days' was a common retort. Arranging marriages is considered the responsibility of parents and their parents had simply done as they pleased in the matter.

Previously who asked a girl's opinion? I couldn't even have
uttered a word about it—I was too embarrassed. I just
silently overheard discussions about my marriage.
(Swati, uneducated middle peasant)

With us, no one asks a girl's opinion—and I was a girl and
also uneducated. My brother with a BA was not even asked
about his own marriage and he was very angry about that.
But with us, the parents do everything—they arrange their
children's marriages just as they wish.
(Shalu, uneducated middle peasant)

Shalu's comments might suggest that educated girls have more influence
over their own marriages, but according to the educated women in Nangal,
this was not so:

My opinion was not asked and nor did I say anything to
anyone about my marriage. Since my parents themselves
were looking for a good house to send me to, what need was
there for me to speak?
(Madho, 10th class pass, rich peasant)

Neither was my opinion asked about this boy, nor did
anyone take any notice of any opinion of mine. If I had
expressed my own wishes, my father would not have been
able to stand the shock. When my aunt forbade one possible
match he said that it was wrong of her to give that boy a bad
reputation. So for that reason I stayed silent. My father is
very old-fashioned and in this matter he considers it very
bad for a girl to speak.
(Ujala, 10th class pass, middle peasant)

Among the Nangal women, most had been aware that their marriage
was being arranged, but only one had voiced her opinion to her parents:

I was able to continue at school until 8th class as I was still
small but then my father stopped my schooling. He began
talking about getting me married but when I heard that I said
I would first study some more and then get married. My
schooling was stopped for a year, but then (as a result of my
obstinacy) my father filled out the forms and I studied up to
10th class at home privately. I still wanted to study some
more but my parents got me married. I managed to study

because of my obstinacy, otherwise who would have
educated me? My marriage was delayed for just 1-2
years—otherwise I would have been married at 16-17. As
it was I was married at 17, which is one year earlier than the
law permits. My parents looked for a boy in one other
place—he was my sister's husband's younger brother. I
myself said I did not want that match— it is not right to have
two sisters married into one house. Then my parents looked
here in Nangal—the go-between was my father's aunt's
son-in-law (FMZDH) who is my husband's uncle (HFyB).
(Nirmala, 10th class pass, middle peasant)

On the other hand, several women, including some educated ones, had
been unaware that their marriage was being arranged: the matter had been
taken in hand by the men of the household and was not discussed in the
girl's earshot.[6] It needs also to be noted that the bride's parents are
themselves not necessarily in full control of the arrangements. The father's
illness may mean that other relatives deputise, an elderly grandparent may
pressurize parents into an early marriage, the constraints of a large joint
family may remove decisions from the girl's parents:

My parents wanted a boy from a small family and they
wanted someone handsome for me. But it was not like that.
My father's father forced them to do this marriage—even
though my father and brother had seen the boy and did not
like him [his face is pock-marked]. My grandfather said that
he had given his word to the boy's people and he could not
break it. He told my father that he could get my sisters
married as he liked, but that I had to be married here.
(Kalavati, uneducated, middle peasant)

I was studying in 10th class when I was about 18-19 years
old and people in villages think that is rather old not to be
married. Then, too, it was my grandfather's (FF) wish that
I should be married. He is the most senior person in the
house, so his wishes have to be obeyed. In any case, my
father had lost both legs in a train accident some years
before, so he was not capable of arranging my marriage.
(Chaya, 10th class pass, rich peasant)

To admit that one's parents have arranged a bad match is something few women feel able to do. And most women do indeed re-

main married to the husband selected for them. Only one of the young women we interviewed in Nangal had been married previously—and her case sheds further light on the limits on women's ability to control access to their sexuality.[7]

Bhalla came from a family that owned only a small amount of land. She went only briefly to the local school. When she was about 18 her father married her about 30 kms away. But Bhalla was very unhappy because her mother-in-law and her husband used to beat her without any reason apparent to her. Eventually Bhalla ran away. She could not get to her parents' house because it was too distant, so she walked to the house where one of her cousins had been married. Her cousin's husband (*jija*) took her in, but within a few days he was visited by Harpal, a 50-year old bachelor from Nangal. They started talking about Bhalla, and Harpal offered to pay Rs. 2,000 for her. Bhalla was sent straight off with Harpal. Despite her act of defiance, she had been unable to decide her own future:

> I absolutely did not want this to happen. I said my jija should tell my parents but he didn't listen to a single thing I said. He just compelled me to go with this man. It was only 3-4 days after I had arrived at my jija's house. My husband's younger brother was married long ago, and my husband himself was very old and I'm much younger than him. I'm even younger than my sister-in-law [HyBW]. My sister-in-law's children are plenty big enough and even one of the girls has already been married. When my parents found out they were very angry with my jija and my mother came to meet me here.
> (Bhalla, uneducated, middle peasant)

Basically, the married women we talked to in Nangal—whether educated or not—had played no part in the arrangement of their own marriages. As one woman's sister-in-law (HeBW) commented, 'Previously, who used to ask a girl? Even if she's thrown into a well, she can't say anything!' Parents must arrange their daughter's marriage and the daughter should not question that either beforehand or afterwards. Songs often allow a little more licence, and this one (sung at the bride's house shortly before her departure to her husband's home) encapsulates some of the issues and feelings involved:

Listen-look, O my father, why have you married me
   so distantly?
Father, we are just like your tethered cows
Wherever you want to drive us, we have to go.
Listen-look . . .

Father, we are just like birds in your courtyard,
Having gleaned some grains we fly away,
Listen-look . . .

Your brothers' daughters have been married near about,
Why have you given me so far away?
Listen-look . . .

khaey-ko behai bedesh, sun-lukhey babul merey?
hum to rey, babul, khuntey key gaiey,
jiddar hank dey, hank jai.
khaey-ko behai . . .

hum to rey, babul, agana key chiriya
dana chug key, urh jai
khaey-ko behai . . .

tau-chacha key orey-dorey
humko to dena pardesh rey
khaey-ko behai . . .

Control over Economic Resources

Women's control over economic resources involves a coexistence of structures of subordination with a reluctance of women to seek 'autonomy'.On the one hand, a woman (whether educated or not) without employment outside the home, cannot manage substantial economic resources unless she is permitted to do so by her domestic authorities. On the other, there is widespread disapproval among women themselves of the employment of women outside the home, even for women whose educational level might make them employable in a range of respectable white collar jobs. Their proper place is as family workers based in their husbands' homes, engaged in a wide range of domestic labour, investing time in their children's education, household decoration and improvements and sewing, knitting and crocheting items for the home and their family. In that, the educated and uneducated women are hard to distinguish, at least those in the same class position.

Not one of the married women we interviewed was employed. They were all family workers, for the most part concentrating their work efforts in the house, and possibly around the cattle byre. What room, if any, do such women have for controlling the household's resources? If they do not control resources, how far can they be said to manage them, or do they merely implement subsistence budgetary strategies?[8] As we have discussed elsewhere, in the regulation of women's work and their visits to their natal kin, a key element is the structure of the household (*chulha*, or hearth) in which the woman lives.[9]

When a young married woman lives in a household with an older woman or women (generally her mother-in-law, and sometimes another woman such as her husband's older brother's wife), the senior woman normally takes charge of the domestic financial matters. If milk or ghi are sold by the household, the income is controlled by the older woman, she organizes the household's exchange (*len-den*) relationships when weddings and births take place, and she ensures that food and clothing for the immediate household are bought when necessary. The farming income is organized by the menfolk, her own husband and/or her son and this older woman must ask for spending money from them for routine expenses and for other expenditures incurred (as when a marriage takes place).

Young women in such households regard only the items they receive from their own parents as their own income (amdani), and even there, their control is not necessarily absolute. Generally, the daughter-in-law hands over foodstuffs and earmarked items of clothing to the mother-in-law who uses the food in the household at large and passes on the clothing to the individuals designated. The daughter-in-law retains the cash and clothing that her parents have presented specifically to her. What remains with the younger woman is clearly incapable of providing her with economic independence, a sari or two, maybe Rs. 10 or Rs. 50 will not go very far in that regard. She would normally need to ask her husband or other members of her household for money over and above what her parents provide. On the rare occasions when larger sums are given by her parents—generally because of specific requests for a loan to purchase a piece of agricultural equipment or provide for someone's medical expenses—the young woman is merely a conduit for the transfer of resources.

I don't have any income of my own. When there is spare
milk, we sell milk or ghi and that income remains in my
mother-in-law's pocket alone. Since she's still alive, she
keeps the income. Mother and son keep all the income and
they alone make the expenditures. I have no involvement
[*matlab*], whatever they do. I give the money that comes
from my parents to my husband. The things that are for
eating and drinking just get consumed in the house.
(Ujala, 10th class pass, middle peasant, joint household)

I have no special income of my own. My mother-in-law sells
ghi and that income remains in her pocket. Whatever money
comes from my parents, that alone is my income. The
clothes and the money from my parents remain with me.
When I bring foodstuffs from my parents' house, I just put
them in the house and they get eaten up. My mother-in-law
organizes the *len-den* for the house. My husband has also
set up a flour mill [*chakki*] separately from his father and its
income and expenses are his.
(Shalu, uneducated, middle peasant, joint household)

Once in a household in which she is the oldest or only adult woman
(because her mother-in-law has died, or because the households have
become separate at least for consumption purposes), a woman can gain
somewhat more control over the domestic finances. If milk or ghi are sold,
she will usually manage the income, she organizes the exchange relationships and retains control over virtually everything that she receives from
her parents.

But this situation should not be read as one in which she has much
economic independence. The incomes that she handles are small and the
bulk of the household finances will probably still rest with her husband.
The farming income is normally managed by him. Small sums may be
stored in the house for safekeeping, but that does not permit the woman to
spend it freely. Large sums will probably be deposited in the bank, under
the husband's name. Generally, he deals with larger-scale financial matters
(payment of school fees, agricultural equipment) and she requests spending money for smaller-scale purchases of foodstuffs. Her position as
supplicant is compounded by the need to spend these sums wisely, on
goods for the benefit of the household as a whole. Most women still rely
on their parents to provide some of their clothing (at the Holi and Tijo

festivals) and would not normally spend much household money on buying clothing for themselves. Nevertheless, women in such households generally consider that they have a degree of financial say-so that is denied them in joint households, since they have to express their priorities and negotiate their wants with their husband only, rather than with his male elders or his mother.

> My mother-in-law died when my husband was still a child, so at first I lived jointly with his older brother's wife. I became separate three years later. That was my decision, because I had to do all the work and my sister-in-law fought with me a lot. So to escape the fighting I became separate. He did not want to become separate but on my say-so we did. I don't sell milk, but if there is more ghi than we need, I sell that and keep the income. My husband also keeps the income from the land and grain with me. All the things that come from my parents remain with me and I do the ex-changes for the house. After we became separate, my father sent me an American [sic] cow for our own use. When we were joint, I had to do all the work for my sister-in-law's entire family. That was a lot of people and a lot of work. And I was not able to save up any money for ourselves separately. Now we are separate and we are saving for our own future—that will be useful for our children.
> (Dholi, uneducated, middle peasant, separate household)

There are many reasons—such as the power of the patriarch and landowner—why joint households remain joint over long periods of time. But one of the strongest reasons is that women married to only sons should remain joint with the mother-in-law until she dies, whereas women married into larger households are more likely to be able to separate.[10]

> There is only one mother-in-law and my husband is an only son. He has no older or younger brothers and his father is also dead. So from whom could I become separate? If there were sisters-in-law (HBW) then we'd see.
> (Ujala, 10th class pass, middle peasant, joint household)

Some of these women clearly find it irksome to have to continue to live in a household with their mother-in-law or others from their older affinal kin. A woman in her late 20s, with school-going children, may still need to ask the permission of her mother-in-law for major decisions, or in some cases even for minor ones.

> Everyone wants to live separately, me too. But it's inescapable [*majburi*] because I am the only daughter-in-law. I can't go anywhere on my own accord. I have to ask my mother-in-law and if she has said OK then that is fine but if she refuses I cannot go. I have to live killing my heart's desire [*mun mar kar rehna parta*].
> (Rita, 8th class pass, rich peasant household)

[handwritten margin note: ? ask permission from whom]

> There is this advantage when the household is joint, the house continues to be built up and make progress. A family should live in a joint household. But the damage for me is that I cannot buy anything for my children when I want to. Every single matter and every single thing has to be told to the elders. That's all, it's a bit difficult.
> (Anita, 8th class pass, middle peasant, complex joint household)

But several other women express countervailing views and emphasized what they considered to be advantages of living in a joint household. A particularly common refrain was that living jointly enabled them to escape the responsibilities that they would acquire if they were to live separately. In part this reflects women's weak positions, for if their judgement seems faulty and things go wrong, they are very vulnerable. To take a clear position is to enter unknown and perilous territory, and many women are unwilling to take such a step lightly:

> Living in a joint household, I have no worries about anything. All the responsibility is with my mother-in-law and nobody has to do all the work. Only my mother-in-law does the animal work, but if we were separate I would have to do that all myself. You get a thousand worries. Now, if someone comes to call me from my parents, I can go immediately. Being in a joint household is better.
> (Madho, 10th class, middle peasant, joint with mother-in-law and younger sister-in-law)

> Living in a joint household you just have to do a little work. And then there is no responsibility. There are no restrictions on coming and going. You can go and stay with your parents

for 1-2 months and then return. There are no worries about
the house.
(Swati, uneducated, middle peasant, separate)

Often, though, households do separate, and women do take on additional responsibilities. For some women, this entails more work, for
others less. But for all, it brings relief from day-to-day surveillance.

When the cooking is separate there is this benefit that there
is less work and also freedom [*azadi*].
(Shamo, MA [*Hindi*], rich peasant household)

But, as we have already indicated, the husband still controls expenditures, even if a woman is allowed to budget the daily distribution of
subsistence spending. Unless the husband seriously abuses his position
and fails to provide properly for his wife and children, this arrangement is
not the object of general disapproval by women. On the contrary, women
perceive their interests to be best served by binding their own with those
of their husbands. The very idea that husband and wife should organize
their finances separately from one another and that women should spend
money unilaterally is seen as a contravention of the ideal unity of the
married couple.

My husband alone meets all my expenses and he also gives
me money when I need it. He says, 'What would the two of
us do keeping our money separately?' What, are we separate
from one another [*alag*]? The matter is one only.
(Shalu, uneducated, middle peasant)

Only one of the Nangal women departs markedly from this picture,
in that she does control the income from the farm. She is from a village
near Bijnor town, and went to school and college there. After failing
her 7th class exams she wanted to stop, but her parents insisted that
she continue. She finally passed her 10th class exams. When she was
married to Kalyan in Nangal, he was a clerk in a ration shop in a
neighbouring village. Soon afterwards, he was accused of embezzlement
and suspended. He was thrown into jail, and his brother refused to bribe
the police to get him out. Money was lent by Kalyan's married sister,
and given by Satto's parents and by Satto herself from savings.

Kalyan and Satto became financially separate from his brother at that
point. But Kalyan had a 'fit' over his brother's attitude, and is incapable
of working their land. He earns a small income by acting as clerk for the

local bus-owner's union. He said it was up to Satto whether they keep the land or sell it, and Satto decided to farm the land herself. As a woman, she cannot plough, so she hires a servant; and Kalyan helps with some of the heaviest labour—lifting and loading cane for example. But she manages all the farm income herself, which she says would have been impossible if she were not educated.

Even so, she remains unusually dependent upon her parents. They give to her partly out of love and partly because she is living in straitened circumstances (*patli halat*). They have told her not to bother Kalyan with financial worries but to turn to them instead if she needs anything. This she does. She has never bought clothing for herself and her children in all the time she has been married and her father has given her quite substantial sums of money on several occasions, not just the token Rs20 or Rs50 that a visiting daughter would normally expect to receive. She intends to send her son to live with her parents, as pressure of work prevents her from delivering him to school in Nangal. She is keen to see him educated and teaches him a little at home when she has time. She leaves her baby daughter asleep at home while she collects fodder and does other farm work. She also wants the girl to be educated, at least a little solid education is necessary, though beyond that (she says) it is a matter of destiny.

> Even though the educated don't get jobs either these days, I still want my children to be able to do their own household accounts. Education never causes damage. I now think I should have gone further in school. Education's good for everyone, whether they get a white-collar job or not. My own education was at least of this much benefit, that I can teach my children something and I can keep my accounts.
> (Satto, 10th class pass, middle peasant)

It will not do, however, to romanticize Satto, or see her as a role model for other women. Her solution to the situation was the only plausible way of averting the financial disaster of leaving the farm untended or selling the land. She is coping but only with considerable financial help from her parents. And she feels overburdened by her responsibilities. Unlike other women who listed in loving detail the jewellery and other items they had received when they married, Satto could not recall anything. Her mind is filled with her work around the home and the farm. Since her cohabitation, she has never been to stay at her parents' home—not even when her younger sister was married—because of her work in Nangal. She only goes for the day or at most overnight.[11] She compares herself unfavourably with her mother, whom she describes as 'never having seen what direction my father's fields are in'. And in relation to family planning, she is adamant:

> I absolutely don't want any more children. For one thing I
> have a son and a daughter. We have both 'things' so what
> else needs to be done? Secondly, all the work is on my
> shoulders.No one comes to help me out, so who could I
> make responsible for the care of my children?

Even Satto's rather extraordinary situation, then, lends little support to the notion that education is a route to autonomy for women. In general, indeed, our discussions with women in Nangal do not point to any differences between the educated and uneducated with respect to the norms they articulate about joint and separate living, and the financial implications that those living arrangements entail. What is more, because the more educated are, in general, in wealthier households, they are more likely to be in a joint household than the uneducated are. For example, considering only women aged under 45, only eight of the 38 landlord or rich peasant women in Nangal are living in households where they are the only married woman, compared with 21 of the 32 poor peasant or landless women. In other words, the more educated women are normally in the kind of domestic situation in which they have the least control over financial resources, the reverse of what might perhaps be expected from the supposed links between education and autonomy that we have just outlined.

Reproductive Choice

The demographic literature that we have just reviewed draws explicit connections between female autonomy, education and levels of fertility.[12] Here we want to explore what differences (if any) we can discern in the fertility behaviour of the educated and uneducated Jat women married into Nangal, and ask what evidence there is for their exercising 'autonomy' with regard to contraceptive decision-making. Because access to secondary and tertiary education is quite recent, we shall consider only those 206 women in Nangal who were married after 1960. Even so, the 44 rather better-educated women (to class 6 or above) have only been married for an average of 9 years, whereas the uneducated have been married for an average of 16 years. Moreover, education is closely linked to class, and the numbers are small, so our conclusions are tentative (see Table 5.1). Nevertheless, after allowing for the length of time that women have been married, there is no evidence that educated women are having fewer children than the others. Further, it does not seem possible to link educational differences to differences in contraceptive behaviour. Of the couples married after 1960, 54 have been sterilized (either the husband or the wife). The mean number of children of the seven educated women (class 6 or above) who have been sterilized is 3.7 children. The equivalent figure for the 47 uneducated women who have been sterilized is 3.6 children. These differences are not statistically significant.[13]

Table 5.1 : Live-born children to Jat women married 1960 or later, by year of marriage, length of schooling and class

Marriage Year	Schooling			
	0	1-5 years	6+ years	All
1960-69	5.24	4.67	4.5	5.07
(Std dev	2.19	1.72	2.12	2.06)
N of women	41	15	2	58
Mean marriage length	26.5	26.5	28.5	26.6 yrs
1970-79	3.21	3.54	3.56	3.34
(Std dev	1.72	0.88	1.33	1.49)
N of women	34	13	9	56
Mean marriage length	16.5	17.2	17.0	16.9 yrs
1980 and after	1.58	1.39	1.39	1.47
(Std dev	1.18	1.27	0.97	1.12)
N of women	36	23	33	92
Mean marriage length	6.2	5.6	5.6	5.8 yrs
	Class			
	Rich Peasant	Middle Peasant	Poor Peasant and landless	All
1960-69	4.08	4.97	6.60	5.07
(Std dev	2.07	1.80	2.27	2.06)
N of women	12	36	10	58
Mean marriage length	25.9	26.5	27.6	26.6
1970-79	3.11	3.44	3.23	3.34
(Std dev	0.93	1.67	1.36	1.49)
N of women	9	34	13	56
Mean marriage length	17.5	16.5	17.5	16.9
1980 and after	1.52	1.40	1.73	1.46
(Std dev	0.87	1.11	1.62	1.12)
N of women	21	60	11	92
Mean marriage length	6.2	5.7	5.7	5.8

Source: From maternity history data collected by the authors,
October-December 1990.

To focus on couples for whom contraception would be a salient issue, the 23 women we interviewed were in the age band 25-34 and all had at least one living son. The educated women were slightly younger (27 on average, versus 29), were married 2.5 years later (19.2 versus 16.75 years old) and had thus been married for shorter periods (8 years as against 12). Only two of the women (both uneducated) had as many as four children; four had three children, thirteen had two children, and four had one child. Six (five of them uneducated) had already been sterilized and a further seven (two uneducated) were using the contraceptive pill or an IUCD.It is clearly hard to unearth the decision-making that results in contraception. Nevertheless, a cautious reading of our discussions with the Nangal women indicates that they rarely made a decision to contracept by themselves.

Just one woman (Sudha, uneducated) said that she was sterilized without consulting her in-laws. She had three children and had taken pills for several years after her second delivery. She again took pills after the third child but became pregnant. She obtained an abortion and was sterilized at the same time. She said she was often unwell and wanted no more children. Her mother-in-law, however, had wanted her to have more children, and her husband had opposed sterilization because he was afraid of the operation itself. When she suffered no adverse symptoms, he accepted the situation, saying that two boys and a girl were right, as he was worried about rising costs and did not have enough land for more children. Another woman (Madho, 10th class), whose husband and parents-in-law want her to have just the one son she already has, reported using the Copper-T for a while. When she found it did not suit her, she resorted to pills, which she had stopped taking when we interviewed her, partly because she felt they had disrupted her menstruation. But, unlike her in-laws, she wants a second child—after which she would be sterilized. By contrast, Seema (uneducated) reported that she had been sterilized while under the anaesthetic after a caesarean delivery of a stillborn girl. According to her sister-in-law (HeBW), Seema had narrowly escaped death during the labour. Having seen her problems, Seema's husband had willingly agreed to the operation, although the two of them had not previously discussed the matter and their only son had polio in one leg.

Far more common, however, is for the husband and wife to report reaching the decision about family planning together, sometimes even in the face of opposition from their elders.

I have a Copper-T but would like to have the operation. That's what my husband also thinks. But his mother will never agree—she wants me to continue having children. But we shall get the operation done. She'll be angry for a few days and then she'll be silent. I wanted the operation when I gave birth the second time but the doctor said that I was weak and should wait for a couple of years.
(Shalu, uneducated, middle peasant)

My husband would have liked a girl, but the healer who has been treating me for ghost possession said there was no girl in my destiny. When my husband heard that he asked what was the point in having any more children and he had my operation done. His mother did not want that but we did not listen to her. When my mother found out, she was very angry. She said that my uncle would be upset, and that we should have one girl at least, that we'd had the operation done after only two children.
(Primod, uneducated, middle peasant)

Between the two children, I used various methods, sometimes condoms, sometimes pills. I did not have a Copper-T. Since the second child I've also been using condoms and pills. I haven't had the operation and nor am I going to. None of us want that, not myself or my husband, nor his parents. You see, no one knows what God's intentions may be from one second to the next. And if a child dies, what then? Because of that fear, I haven't had the operation, but I'm making other arrangements to stop having children and that is something decided by my husband and me alone.
(Shamo, MA, rich peasant)

Between the boy and the girl I had had a stillborn boy so my husband wanted to have another son. But then I had another girl. So I had the operation done at the time I gave birth. I'd had a Copper-T after my first girl but that did not suit so I had it taken out. The two of us took the decision about the Copper-T and the operation—we didn't ask anyone's advice.
(Nirmala, 10th class, middle peasant)

Whether educated or not, all these couples have decided that two or three children are enough, as long as one (and preferably two) are boys. In most instances, this was with the support of the man's parents.

The two women with four children are both using modern contraception; Shanti has been sterilized and Ombati has an IUCD. Ombati, in particular, is insistent that her four are too many; she (and her father-in-law) wanted to stop at three, but she was frightened of the sterilization operation and her fourth child was unwanted. Nearly all the women who are not currently contracepting plan to do so soon. The major difference between the uneducated and educated women is that the educated are more likely to use spacing methods — the pill or IUCD—whereas the uneducated are mainly favouring sterilization.

The only couples apparently hesitating about actively limiting their families are those with only one child; one woman whose husband refuses to allow her to be sterilized (apparently believing the operation would be a threat to her health); and another woman (N131) who believes she is infertile because she has not conceived for so long. Only one woman said that it was up to God if she was to have more children; but she too wanted to stop at the three she had, and said that she would be sterilized when her husband said so. What we know about the decision-making surrounding family limitation gives no support to the argument that 'female autonomy' is a key intervening variable. There is also little evidence of female autonomy in relation to marriage choice and control over economic resources and women's accounts of contraceptive decision making reinforce that conclusion. And crucially, there are no straightforward differences between educated and uneducated women on any of these counts.

In these examples of marriage choice, household structure and fertility limitation, then, we can see the complexity and interplay between facets of control over women and their lack of power, and their acceptance of key elements of their situation. This potent combination of power and ideological hegemony make it rather unsurprising that we have little evidence of women acting autonomously or even seeking to do so. Fear or disapproval of autonomy would be a better characterization of their condition.

Education for Girls

The preceding discussion suggests that the connections postulated in the demographic literature between female education and female autonomy are rather problematic. What, then, should we make of the expanding educational opportunities for girls in rural Bijnor? And, if education does not seem to make women more autonomous, what is its significance in this part of North India?

Secular education is certainly widely respected—by men and women alike—in rural Bijnor. Uneducated people are defensive about their inability to read and write, and they frequently comment that they have been damaged in every way (*sara nuqsan*) by their illiteracy. Illiterate people sometimes describe themselves as 'thumbprint people' (*angutha-wala*), or as 'blind'; they say that others treat them as if they were animals. Several women described differences in style and demeanor between an illiterate person and one who has been educated: some of the uneducated women described themselves as 'just like a beast' or '*pashu ke saman*' (*pashu* means beast, with connotations of being brutish or simple). One colourful assertion was that an uneducated person given his death sentence written on a piece of paper would wander around happily with it because of ignorance of its contents.

Most people agree, then, that education has a value in itself, a unique value for any individual who has been educated. As one woman put it, 'education is not something that another person can snatch away, but all other things can be taken away or divided'. Beyond that, people often found it difficult to articulate the benefits of education; it gives 'just every advantage' (*sara faida*).

For boys, education seemingly offers some specific advantages, especially the chance to escape from the daily grind of wage labour or own-account farming. Certainly this ambition is central in discussions about education for sons—though people are also painfully aware that good jobs are not easily obtained without a substantial bribe in addition. Education is sometimes—but by no means universally—considered essential for a farmer these days, especially in enabling him to keep proper accounts. Unschooled men also talk about their daily experience of humiliation at the hands of petty officials, in their dealings with banks, the sugarcane society and sugar mills, or with shopkeepers and moneylenders.

Local opinions on the value of education for girls are diverse. The conventional perspective—mainly held by the older generation, and increasingly on the retreat in Nangal—is that lengthy education for girls is a costly and rather pointless exercise. In this view, education is valued primarily as a route to employment, but girls are not going to be sent out to service and will do the same work in the house after marriage, whether educated or not.

What would have been the advantage of being educated? I
suppose that if I were educated, I might have been married
into a better house or to a man in service. But beyond
education is destiny [*qismat*]. Even some educated girls are
not getting men in service or good houses, and some uneducated girls are going into good houses. That's a matter of
one's own destiny. In any case, whether you are educated
or not, there is no difference in the housework.
(Seema, uneducated, middle peasant)

Only a few of the young women in Nangal indicated that they intended
to educate their daughter with employment as an end: for most, employment was simply not a consideration (as it had not been for themselves).
One of the two Jat women with MA in Nangal, indeed, decided not to
pursue her studies further because she would not be permitted to work
outside the home:

After doing my BA I was married, and then I did my MA
alongside my husband. I wanted to study even further, but
my husband does not like service. He said that even if I
studied further I would have to take charge of the house and
would not be sent out for service. So what is the point of
studying any more since I shall have to stay in the house?
(Shamo, MA Hindi, rich peasant)

Employment for a girl is just a possibility to be activated in
dire circumstances, a residual ambition at most: 'in a calamity [i.e. widowhood], an educated girl could live in her
in-laws' house without being a burden on anyone. She will
stand on her own feet'.
(Nirmala, 10th class pass, middle peasant)

These days, however, education for girls is widely seen as a key counter
in the marriage (not the labour) market. People often talked about the
responsibility to try to marry one's daughter into a 'good house' (*achcha
ghar*). This is something of a catch-all term, for people in different
economic circumstances have different expectations and options. Apart
from pertaining to the physical structure of the house and to its social
atmosphere, the term implies a family that is at least moderately well to
do (preferably owning a lot of land or in a flourishing business, public
sector employment or professional occupation). Such economic security
can usually be taken to mean that the women of the house need not work

outside, be it in the family fields or in paid employment. Sustaining such an economic position requires young men of the family to be educated if they are to have any hope of obtaining employment that will reduce the drain they make on the family land, and ensure that they will be able to support their parents as well as their wife and children well in the future. And these days, an educated groom is likely to insist on being married to an educated bride.

The marriage system has, of course, long been competitive; the main recent change has been to add the girl's education to the other issues which parents consider: landholding, subcaste or family (*khandan*) and appearance. The Jat marriage system—as in much of North India—is hypergamous. While a bride may be married to someone of equal education, it is far more common for a bride to be married to a man with some years more education than herself: in Nangal, for instance, that gap is anywhere up to a dozen years. A woman is highly unlikely to be married to someone with less education. This puts an upper limit on how far parents are prepared to educate a girl. Even though the sex ratio is highly adverse to women, parents of girls with a wide range of educational achievement are in competition for matches with smaller numbers of highly educated men. Clearly, everyone cannot succeed in their aims to marry their daughter into a 'good house'. Parents of girls have to look in places where they think they will be accepted:

> Everybody wants a good boy and a good family for their girl. My father wanted there to be land and that the boy should be a little bit educated, and that there should be no demands, that the boy's people should be straightforward and that they should not live too far away. He didn't want a boy in service because I am not educated.
> (Dholi, 3rd class, middle peasant, husband 2nd class)

Dholi's brother had wanted her married to an educated groom but their father had retorted, 'What sort of education has our girl got that we should go looking for an educated boy? This boy is straightforward, what else is necessary?'

The key advantage educated girls are considered to enjoy, and the reason most women give for wanting their daughters to be educated, is precisely this enhancement of their marriage chances. The fear that they will find it hard to marry their daughter into a good house is an important reason for trying to ensure that she is well educated:

It would be good if my son could stand on his own feet—I'd
like him to get service. The girls will study just a little—
what service do farmers' girls do? But I do want them to
study. Everyone wants an educated girl, so if they aren't
educated there'll be worries over getting them married.
(Karuna, uneducated, middle peasant)

My father-in-law says that my daughter should just be sent
to school until she is capable of some work [*kam laiq,* i.e.
housework], say to 8th or 10th class, for she is to be married
and not sent out for service. But I want to get her properly
educated, because boys generally want to be married to an
educated girl.
(Chaya, 10th class pass, rich peasant)

The motor behind girls' education is the place of young educated men
in a rapidly changing economic situation; as more boys are educated to
higher and higher levels, girls' education is dragged up behind them. With
increasing problems of obtaining employment, the stakes for young men
are rising all the time. The dilemma besetting parents is that the marriage
market is very fluid and a seemingly sensible strategy during the girl's
childhood may be out of kilter with the marriage market by the time she
reaches marriageable age. Levels of education for girls that would have
been considered more than adequate just a few years ago now seem
incapable of ensuring a good match for them. How can they calculate what
is best for their daughter? How much can they afford to spend on educating
her? How much education will she need to ensure a good match? What is
the pool of well-educated young men from whom her husband can be
chosen and could she be over-educated and unmarriagable?

Something of these shifting sands can be captured in the Nangal
women's educational experiences. Several had faced obstacles in being
educated. Some never went to school, or had their schooling stopped
because their labour was needed at home, especially if they were the oldest
daughter or if their mother was ill. Others were spoilt by their grandparents
and kept at home (rather than exposed to the harsh discipline of school life)
because of the special love felt for them. Some had been prevented from
attending school because there was no school in their natal village. But the
more general picture is one of parents' not exerting much pressure on their
daughters: the uneducated women often look back regretfully, commenting 'what parents paid attention to girls' education in those days?' Even
girls whose parents did attend to their schooling may find their education

curtailed because relatives considered no more was necessary for marriage:

> My parents stopped my education in order to get me married. I had come to an age to be married and they said that I had enough education for marriage. They said my in-laws could let me study further if they wished, but my parents had fulfilled their own wishes on that.
>
> (Shamo, MA Hindi completed after marriage, rich peasant)

The overall diversity of experiences is echoed within the sibling groups of the Nangal women, educated and uneducated alike. There are uneducated sisters alongside educated ones, and girls who had never been to school with brothers who had completed tertiary education. Sometimes the building of a school in the village enabled younger sisters to become more educated than older ones. But, equally, girls attending school were not always encouraged to continue if they wavered, preferred to play or feared the teacher's beatings; and older sisters were sometimes more educated than younger ones. There seems no clear trend even within families.

Then again, the importance of marriage is linked to a range of tactics as parents weigh up the importance of educating a girl against the problems of doing so. Many villages with primary schools do not boast secondary ones and girls often stop attending school after completing 5th class. Partly this is because parents will not allow their near pubertal daughters to travel beyond their village. In addition, girls are often taken out of school because their parents judge them sufficiently educated for marriage and now in need of being taught domestic skills without the distractions of schoolwork. In villages with schools just up to class 8, similar considerations come into play at that stage. Girls living in peri-urban villages have more chance of being educated to higher levels because schools are more accessible. Moreover, girls who have completed 8th class can continue their studies by enrolling as 'private' rather than 'regular' students. The private student studies at home and from private tutors, a neat way of ensuring that she acquires the desired accreditation while learning domestic skills and being protected from gossip that might affect her marriage chances. Unlike the 'regular' student, she rarely faces challenges to her self-confidence from negotiating the vagaries of travelling alone or meeting people outside her kin network.

Not surprisingly, parents who feel they have misjudged the effort they should have put into educating their daughters may resort to deceit in order to achieve a successful marriage for them.[14] Sometimes this involves

showing falsified school certificates; in other cases parents just assert that
their daughter is educated when she is not.

> When my marriage was being arranged, my brother lied and
> said I was 5th class pass. My husband found out afterwards
> and was very angry. He would not speak to me properly.
> Then he went to my parents' house and asked why he had
> not been told in the first place, for then he could have
> married me or not as he pleased. Then my brother asked my
> husband what service he was doing, and if he was going to
> send me out for service. What can I tell you about what I
> have had to endure because of being uneducated?
> (Primod, uneducated, middle peasant)

Her husband put a brave face on the situation:

> If the boy is educated, the girl also should be educated. An
> uneducated girl can't remember things so well, she can't
> make sure the children go to school properly. It wasn't my
> choice to have an uneducated bride, but we had to take what
> we could get. I didn't have any service so what could we
> expect?
> (Om Pal, 10th class, middle peasant)

Education is not simply an important counter in marriage negotiations,
however. Most of the women consider that education has important
practical benefits within marriage, even for those women who will not be
in service or compelled to deal with bank officials and the like.

> Previously I thought, what, would I get a job after being
> educated? Now I realize that being able to read is also
> essential for all household affairs. But what can I do now?
> (Brijesh, uneducated, middle peasant)

Discussions with the men about why they want educated brides indicate
considerable consonance between men's and women's views of the importance of education for a woman's domestic roles. One asset is that an
educated wife has good manners and is no longer a rustic:

> Writing-reading is never useless because it increases your
> knowledge. Your education stays with you. If I need to make
> a calculation, then I can do so. I can also read books. And
> an educated person looks different, their style of dress is

different. An unlettered person is uncouth [*ganwar*] and
does not even know how to make conversation properly.
(Chaya, 10th class pass, rich peasant)

Consequently, educated women are considered better able to fulfil the
'status production' aspects of their domestic obligations.[15] While this
includes being socially competent and knowing how to treat guests properly, it most especially concerns childrearing (*palan-poshan*). An educated
mother will be able to teach her children good manners and good habits:
as one man put it, 'if the wife is educated, the children will turn out all
right' [*agar gharwali ki talim hai, bachche sahe ho jaenge*]. Central to the
child-rearing roles of educated women is the task of supervising children's
school work, ensuring that the children apply themselves to their studies
(rather than running around the village out of control) and saving money
that might otherwise be spent on tuition fees.[16] Uneducated women not
only cannot help with their children's school work but have to contend
with their children's querulous and disrespectful comments: as one women
put it, 'if I were educated, my child wouldn't call me stupid [*baoli*].'

> If I'd been educated, I would have to do the same house-
> work. But being educated is another matter. If I had studied,
> it would have been good—I realize that now. I'm very upset
> that my parents did not compel me. A human being without
> education is just like a beast. I can't teach the children, nor
> can I do accounts. There is nothing but damage from being
> uneducated.
> (Swati, uneducated, middle peasant)

> I don't get any great benefit from being educated. I'm 10th
> class pass and have to cook *roti* [food, bread]. If I were more
> educated, I would still have to cook *roti*. And if I were
> completely uneducated, there would still be this very house-
> work to do. It's not that my in-laws send out for service or
> don't make me cook *roti* because I'm educated.But there is
> this benefit, that I can teach my children, or deal with
> essential papers, and I can read books if I ever have spare
> time.There's never any disadvantage in being educated.
> (Madho, 10th class pass, rich peasant)

Some women also talked of being able to help with household accounts
[*hisab-kitab*] and keeping records of gift exchanges in the wider kinship
network. Men also welcome those social skills of educated women that

might save them time or effort. An educated woman can go shopping or visit her natal village without difficulty. The one certain disadvantage of a totally uneducated wife is that she cannot read or write letters; but, then, as a few men cheerfully acknowledged, this might usefully keep their parents-in-law ignorant of their daughter's domestic disputes. The only man who considered his wife's education had economic benefits outside the domestic sphere was Kalyan, whose wife Satto we discussed earlier. According to Kalyan, Satto's education has helped not only with the childcare and the general atmosphere of the house, but it has made her able to think carefully and make the right decisions in the farm work.

While some men said that an uneducated wife is not necessarily unintelligent, and is just as likely to see to the housework and the children properly, most would concur with one uneducated woman's comment, 'this is not an era to be without education'. Women's education is thus valued, but not for any increase in autonomy which education might give a woman. The motivation is to get girls better married. The crucial point here is that—barring Kalyan—those who advocate female education, just as much as those who consider it unnecessary, are framing their arguments within the same idiom. Whether a woman should be primarily a wife and mother is not at issue. What is being contested is whether and to what extent education can enhance a girl's marriage chances and make her a better mother. Thus it would be hard, if not impossible, to connect people's reasons for favouring female education to the enhancement of 'female autonomy'.

Some of the unintended consequences of education for girls may, indeed, lead them to *lose* autonomy rather than to experience more of it. Female education has slotted in as a modern lynchpin of a particular sort of patriarchal system. Where education and service for sons is at a premium, education for daughters reinforces a pattern of dependence and subordination. At least in part, this results from the hierarchical nature of North Indian society: a gender analysis which is blind to issues of class can only be misleading. Class competition becomes most obvious in the escalation of dowry demands. Only the relatively wealthy can succeed in paying the school fees to educate their daughters to BA or MA level; having done so, they must also provide a larger dowry. Very highly educated girls need a massive dowry in order to 'catch' one of the few Jat men as well or better educated. One of the two Nangal boys studying for a medical degree, for example, was given Rs. 100,000 in cash, as well as a refrigerator and a colour television, cloth and jewellery, at his engagement to a girl from Bijnor town who was studying for an MSc. Examples like this at the top of the scale fuel the demands made by the parents of boys lower down the pecking order. As dowry demands increase, and more pressure is put on parents to protect their married daughters by making adequate financial provision for them, young women—whether educated or not—become more vulnerable to their husbands and their parents-in-law.

Amongst rich peasant and landlord households, there is a greater stress on status production work and seclusion for women. Young women in these classes are also more likely to live in joint households, since the economic reasons for maintaining unity are more compelling. As a result of a general trend towards single sons, or because one son may be working away from home, most women in these classes are likely to spend the first fifteen or more years of their married life having to share their hearths with their mothers-in-law. There is no evidence as yet that they will be able to turn their education into work outside the house. The only trend which might change this situation is that these families are beginning to set up satellite households in town for providing their children with the superior schooling experiences that the towns can offer. Women who run such households may have more independence of action, though at the cost of becoming isolated housewives.

This possibility is out of bounds for middle and poor peasants, but they struggle to keep up in whatever ways they can. In so far as they try to emulate their wealthier neighbours, and are following similar demographic and educational strategies, the effects on women are likely to be similar, if more partial and incomplete. Education can be seen as a way of domesticating women into new forms of patriarchy, rather than offering them new horizons.[17] We would not want to be read as arguing that education for girls should be abandoned. What we are, however, trying to do is to warn against the complacency which suggests that it is a panacea.

Fertility Limitation

We have argued so far, very much on a terrain determined by the demographic literature, that educated and uneducated Jat women in Nangal display very few differences in attitudes or behaviour with respect to key areas of their lives—choice of marriage partner, access to economic resources, and fertility limitation. We have also argued that the meanings of female education are largely framed in terms of its implications for a girl's position in the marriage market. Among the Jats of Nangal, then, neither the intended nor the unintended consequences of female education seem to bear any relation to female autonomy. But if female autonomy is not rising, why is fertility among the Jats so low and contraceptive use so widespread compared with other populations in western Uttar Pradesh?

In our view, low fertility among the Jats of Nangal is more comprehensibly connected with wider economic processes than with female autonomy. Essentially, virtually all the Jats we interviewed seem convinced that there are potent economic reasons for limiting their families:

> I wanted just the two children and I'm happy with that. Why would I want to have more than that in these times? We don't have that much land and there is no other income, so how could we meet the expenses of more children? There are just two children and we want to bring them up properly.
> (Primod, uneducated, middle peasant) N246

> I want just two children, because with more children you can't pay proper attention to them. With few children you can rear them well. For two children you can provide for their schooling and their clothing as you wish. You can clothe them well and feed them well. With more children all that is very difficult, in these expensive times. And also, we have one boy and one girl, so what is the point in our making a third?
> (Shamo, MA, rich peasant) N159

These days, nearly all Jat boys in Nangal are being educated to class 10 (age 16) and many to class 11 or 12 (age 18). To the costs of their schooling and tuition must be added the bribes necessary to try to obtain jobs. People baulk at having to do this for more than one or at the most two sons. Moreover, if the sons fail to obtain employment, they will have to support themselves and their families from land that would become progressively more divided. And, although a daughter might be less costly to educate, the burden of providing her dowry is enough of a nightmare. No one voiced the contrary view that there are benefits from a large family.

Jats may be unusual in taking such a narrowly economic approach to fertility decision-making. There is evidence from the colonial period, as well as from the Nangal village census we did in 1990, that the Jats have a marriage system that tends both to limit fertility and to disadvantage women and girls in ways that are distinguishable from other local landowning groups.

Female infanticide in the nineteenth century (for which, in Bijnor the Jats were particularly notorious) and female neglect in the more recent past are probably the keys to the considerable surplus of Jat males over females in the distict. Associated with that, it was common in some families for only one or two of a set of brothers to be married. Unmarried brothers are widely rumoured to have sexual access to their brother's wife. While most married Jat men have Jat wives from the district, another feature of the shortage of Jat women is the greater recourse made by Jat men than by men of other caste groups to buying wives [*bahu mol lena*], from the foothills of the Himalayas, from neighbouring districts, or from further east in Bihar. Such bought brides usually have no say over their marital destiny; and they are generally so cut off from their natal kin that they benefit neither from the social nor financial support that natal kin normally provide their out-married women. In their husband's village, they are derogatively described as 'mountain person' *(paharan)* or 'easterner' *(purabi)*.

Given the shortage of marriageable Jat women, men with many brothers may have been disadvantaged in the marriage market and never have received any offers of marriage; and poorer Jat men may have been unable to buy a bride. Thus, we cannot be absolutely sure that the significant numbers of adult Jat bachelors reflects an explicit intention of preventing land fragmentation from one generation to the next. But it clearly had that effect, as many Jats themselves are aware, and contributed to the ability of the Jats as a whole to retain their dominant position in the local economy. As such, Jats are better placed than other social groups both to afford education for their sons and to reap substantial benefits from that education, through mobilization of kinship and other political networks and bribes to obtain employment in the rapidly expanding public sector. Connected with this, Jats of all social classes may have been more likely than most other landholding caste groups in the locality to adopt modern contraceptive techniques.

During our research elsewhere in rural Bijnor (Jeffery, Jeffery and Lyon 1989) many women talked of wanting to limit their fertility because incessant childbearing was damaging their health. This is not an argument that we heard in Nangal, possibly because low fertility has already been widely established and women's health issues are much less salient. On the whole, the men in our earlier research were less favourably disposed to family limitation than the women, who generally lacked the capacity to put their wishes into practice. Fertility levels remain high in those villages.

We should not, however, rush to conclude that declines in fertility are symptomatic of higher levels of female autonomy. The Jats in Nangal provide us with no evidence that family limitation is fuelled by autonomous women or motivated by women's desire to increase their autonomy. On the contrary, in this case, fertility limitation and educational strategies seem to go hand-in-hand with a particular form of control over women. Given this structural context, we should add, it is also by no means inevitable that declining fertility will enable women to wrest more control over their own lives: if women now engage in higher quality mothering than before, putting more effort into overseeing their children's school work, investing more time in domestic hygiene, food preparation and so forth, they may have little or no time for more freedom of action. In other words, in order to explain the transition to low fertility among the Jats, we see no need to put female education (nor any presumed effects of increased female autonomy) into the equation at all.

Conclusion: 'Autonomy' or 'Weapons of The Weak'

In conclusion, we want to change tack and ask whether there are serious problems with the overall framework within which we have been present-ing our material here. In the terms we have adopted from social demogra-phers, the Jat women in Nangal seem to have little autonomy. But would alternative approaches to women's agency be more fruitful?

At the beginning of this paper we referred to the work of James Scott and of others who have been influenced by his perspective on everyday forms of resistance. Granted that social and political structures oppress and control the subordinates within the system, these authors argue that to portray subordinates as passive is to provide a woefully lop-sided account of social reality. For example, in the discussions in Haynes and Prakash (1991), power is always tenuous and in constant need of being secured because of resistance to it. Such challenges are not necessarily spectacular or revolutionary in nature, like outright peasant rebellions. They can be 'everyday resistance', the mundane and ordinary 'weapons of the weak' (such as dissimulation, sabotage, slander). They are typically rather un-planned individual attempts at self-help rather than larger-scale coordi-nated resistance. And they generally avoid overt confrontations that would bring out the full forces of repression. They are what the peasantry does 'to defend its interests as best it can' (Scott 1990: 29). We find this approach a valuable corrective, but it is still vulnerable to exaggerating the extent to which people are controlled in the flesh but not in the spirit, people with an autonomous consciousness, free from determination from above.

In the light of this formulation, taking our lead from the demographic literature has hampered our approach to female autonomy in rural Bijnor, because of a very limited notion of agency as well as a failure to take seriously the structures in which women are located. How can sending girls to school for a number of years empower them if the structures of domination in which they are embedded remain unchanged? But it is not merely a question of power. The notion of agency is bound up with what people want to do and ideas about that relate not only to their assessment of what they can do but of what they *ought* to do. Women themselves may be crucial actors in reinforcing the normative limits to autonomy in other women. For example, one Jat woman in another of our research villages (originally a resident of Bijnor with a BA) had made a 'love marriage'. She was rumoured by her neighbours to have had a previous affair with a Muslim, and was said to have made her husband's three brothers 'happy' (by implication, sexually) before being admitted to his house to live. She is now socially virtually isolated (except for one of her three sisters-in-law) and plans to move back to Bijnor, ostensibly to oversee the children's education. In this and other cases of pre- and postmarital affairs, the gossip hardly touched on the men involved.

Such ideas are part of the fabric of social givens and it is not at all obvious that girls' schooling seriously exposes them to the sorts of alternatives that would permit them to challenge this hegemony in the realm of ideas. As we have shown, not even educated women are demanding to be consulted on the timing of their marriages or the choice of a spouse, but they are all aware that some women have been consulted. Similarly, they are not demanding to be able to control their household finances, and there is ambivalence about whether it is worth taking on the responsibilities and risks which would come with even the limited management of day-to-day expenditures. On the other hand, as we indicate as well, some women are deploying everyday forms of resistance—and not just among educated women. The educated and uneducated Jat women in Nangal are deploying essentially similar resources to manipulate selected aspects of the system of which they are part.

Yet this is not to say that there is nothing besides power and the power of ideas over women's minds. Like other women, those we know in rural Bijnor 'acquiesce yet protest, reproduce yet seek to transform their lives' (Comaroff 1985:1); they work the system 'to their minimum disadvantage' (Hobsbawm 1973). In the interviews in Nangal, and even more forcefully in the more anthropological phases of our work in rural Bijnor, we have many instances of women struggling against their situations. The manner in which they do so, however, does not necessarily rely on the resources generally assumed to be crucial by demographers.

Paraphrasing Scott (1990: 337) we can suggest that the system of male privilege, status and property operates not only in the interests of men but also of women. Women are promised benefits, so they too have a stake in the prevailing social order, and some at least of these promises material-ize—largely the economic ones of providing an income and life-long support. The strains in the system show up in the demands being made for larger dowries and further gifts after the marriage has taken place; and cases of deceit during marriage arrangements. But in Bijnor, few men—whether rich or poor—are abandoning their wives or making multiple marriages in order to maximize receipts from their in-laws.[18] Thus the woman who seriously and conspicuously challenges her lot has much to lose.

Moreover, a woman who steps too far out of line will find that her in-laws punish her insurrection, and her parents may fail to back her up. For the most part, woman's struggles are more likely to be indi-vidualistic attempts to ameliorate their situation within the system, rather than confrontational insubordination that challenges the very basis of the system. Generally, women's resistance is severely channeled by the structures in which women are located. Often, it entails using resources that are (in principle at least) available to all, whether educated or not.It generally occupies the 'middle ground between violent struggle and mere submission to authority' (Haynes and Prakash 1991: vij), cautious and undramatic forms of resistance working within the system. The resistance often (but by no means always) involves concealment and secrecy, using techniques that might seem devious and underhand to those against whom they are used, and which are often hard for the transitory researcher to uncover.

One type of resistance that can illustrate this is the use women make of their links with their natal kin to circumvent or avoid constraints and problems in their affinal village. Crucially, it is appropriate for a married woman to maintain contacts with her natal kin, and they do, in general, offer her the best ways to ameliorate her position in relation to her in-laws, or to enhance her influence in some spheres of her life. Thus, resistance based on such ties can usually be more readily legitimated than actions that are more openly defiant. Apart from those Muslim women married within their natal village, and those women married into the same village as their sisters or cousins, the typical married woman in Bijnor has links to her natal kin that are both outside her affinal village and unique to her. This provides a relatively secret space for building on the social and economic resources that her parents can provide.

A woman's parents, for instance, normally send grain, clothing and cash to her and people often say that lavish gift-giving is one way in which a woman's position in her husband's household can be enhanced. Most parents need little prompting to provide for their daughter's well-being in this way. Sometimes, though, women may be more pro-active in their relationships with their parents, seeking financial help or the space to do things that they cannot do in their marital home.

From our earlier research, we have examples of women seeking an abortion or contraception while staying in their parents' house, with the explicit intent to take control over their fertility without the permission or knowledge of their husband and his relatives. Other acts of resistance can be less secretive: in Nangal, for instance, two women whose parents live on the outskirts of Bijnor have sent their children there for their schooling. Publically, this can be justified in terms of providing better quality schooling for them than is available in Nangal—but, in both cases, the women provided a more nuanced account:

> My girl is the darling pet [*lad-piyar*] of her father and grandparents and she did not study here. That's why I've sent her to live with my parents. They also pet her but they pay attention to her schooling too. I certainly want my girl to be educated. These days, people are only asking for educated girls.
> (Shalu, uneducated, middle peasant) N075

> I have no income of my own. Just the money and clothes from my parents, that's my only income. The foodstuffs from my parents are eaten by everyone in the house and the cloth that comes for particular people goes to them. The *len-den* for the house is done by my husband's aunts (HFBW). I'm very worried. My husband's grandfather controls all the family money and he considers money spent on education an extravagence [*fuzool kharch*]. According to the calculations of the old days, education seems very expensive, so he does not give enough money and he gets angry when he sees how much it costs. For that reason alone, I am worried. That's why I have sent my older boy to live with my parents in Bijnor. I don't know how my children's education will turn out if this state of affairs continues.
> (Anita, 8th class pass, rich peasant, joint household) N080

In another instance, the threat that the daughter would be repudiated by her husband impelled her natal kin to foot the bill for her medical treatment:

> After I was married, I began to suffer from possession *[kuch oopar]* and some people in my in-laws' village began saying that he [Samar Singh] would make another marriage. Several people there, especially my oldest brother's wife, said that I was entitled to a share there and so I should be helped. My father and brother also thought that if he abandoned me, all the expenses of my marriage and the dowry would have been wasted and my life would have been spoilt too. So, fearing that, my parents paid out Rs. 2,000-3,000 on my illness. I had become so weak that my first child was born only after seven or eight years. My mother was still paying for my treatment when I was pregnant for the first time. I was very weak and she said she would feed me up but the doctor said that I had to have treatment, so my mother paid for that. Every month, Rs100 of medicines came for me. My mother-in-law is very miserly, so when my first son was born, my people did not send many gifts [*chuchaq*]. They were angry with my husband's parents because they had been taunting me about my illness and then about my treatment. My brother asked why they should give much and said that he would help only me in future. While I was joint with my mother-in-law, all the things from my parents remained with her, but now that I'm separate I keep everything myself.
>
> (Primod, uneducated, middle peasant) N246

We need, however, to note that there are various ways in which these and other examples of resistance recounted by the women in Nangal and our other research villages are limited. For one thing, as our earlier research indicated, the fear that women will marshall support for their resistance surfaces in men's comments about the need to control the wife's contacts with her natal kin (Jeffery et al. 1989:31-6). Then, again, women in Nangal—in line with women we talked to in our earlier research—commented that one significant drawback to separating cooking hearths is that a woman's access to her parents is compromised, because her responsibilities tie her more comprehensively to her affinal village (ibid.:49-54).

Beyond that, women's acts of resistance are limited by what their parents (or possibly the mother alone) will agree to. While parents continue to be concerned for their daughter's welfare after she is married, they will not readily intervene if trouble arises. Their daughter's marital difficulties are not supposed to be their business. Consequently, such interventions often come quite late in the day, in part because daughters themselves are inhibited from saying anything until their position becomes unbearable. Once involved, parents generally try to keep the marriage together rather than help their daughter to escape it, and if it fails they will almost certainly try to ensure that their daughter is remarried. A mother may help her daughter to obtain the contraception denied her in her in-laws' village, but mothers also pay for infertility treatments for their daughters. Excessive wife-beating may persuade parents to provide their daughter with refuge and to criticize their son-in-law and set conditions for their daughter's return—but too tough a stand may generate a backlash. Indeed, parents often tell daughters to bear their problems silently rather than break the expectations of demure wifely behaviour and of non-intervention by her parents. Since the woman is dependent on her parents' agreement to help her, her negotiating position in relation to them is not very strong—while her parents themselves cannot exert much pressure on her in-laws.

At the individual level, then, there are clear limitations to the 'everyday resistance' that women can activate through their parents. At a structural level, too, such strategies do not sow the seeds of concerted action. Resisting problems by going outside the affinal village has a scatter effect on women's struggles. Rather than focussing their efforts within their affinal village and perhaps developing more corporate and confrontational forms of struggle, women engage in largely covert and individualistic attempts to ameliorate their situation.

Beyond that, too, there are other general features of women's position that should make us cautious of assuming that women's forms of resistance will be like those characteristic of class-based or ethnic underclass groupings. For one thing, women are dispersed through the class hierarchy and women in higher class positions are often directly exploiting other women, which undermines women's organizational potential. Again, as has been implicit in much of the foregoing, at any one time women within the household are divided from one another by age and seniority. But perhaps more crucially than that, the passage of time produces a new mother-in-law from the old daughter-in-law, a process that is not paralleled for Harijans, for instance. Such prospects for promotion affect the nature of women's partial penetrations and resistance.[19]

But we should not underestimate the significance of women's relatively minor requests. Such demands are not revolutionary—but as Scott reminds us, even those who take part in revolutionary situations are mostly fighting for 'rather mundane, if vital, objectives that could—in principle if not in practice—be accommodated within the prevailing social order' (1990: 341)'. Since many other features of the system itself in rural Bijnor are rapidly changing, however, it becomes even more difficult to predict how significant these changes might become. What will happen when almost all Jat girls are educated? What will happen when their own two or possibly three children no longer demand much care and attention, and the woman herself is still only 35 or 40? When educated women in their turn acquire a daughter-in-law, will they still enforce norms of co-residence? Or will the norm of 'not leaving parents-in-law on their own' break down as off-farm employment (maybe at some distance) replaces the family farm and social and economic mobility increases?

Some of the answers to these questions depend on overall changes in the Indian economy—the rate at which jobs are created, government policy towards agriculture and so on. All we can say is that the present signs suggest that change in several spheres of life may have considerable significance for women's autonomy. Education for girls, for example, seems to be about the inculcation of manners and middle class morality, of newer forms of respectable behaviour. This may have the effect of subduing women even further. Alternatively, it may just make them less likely to engage in crass and overt resistance, but give them new ways to operate in more quiet backstage resistance, within their relationships with their husbands—about which we still know very little.

Notes

1. The newspaper coverage in the UK of the 1992 *State of the world's* population, of a speech by Prince Charles, and of the preparations for the Rio 'Earth Summit' all reiterate this argument; see the *Guardian*, London, 1 May 1992, p. 25. Examples of the argument that raising female education is also one of the most feasible ways of reducing fertility and child mortality can be found in Jain and Nag 1986; Sathar et al. 1989; and Lockwood and Collier 1988.
2. Lindenbaum (1990) and Caldwell et al. (1983) both suggest that a later age at marriage also increases a young married woman's ability to deal with her marital kin.
3. For more specific discussion of the demographic literature, see Basu and R. Jeffery (forthcoming).

4. This fieldwork consisted of two extended periods (February 1982 to April 1983, and August 1990 to July 1991) and several shorter visits, one of two months in August-September 1985. We are grateful to the Economic and Social Research Council, who funded the 1982-83 and 1985 trips; and to the Overseas Development Administration, who funded our research in 1990-91. All the views presented in this paper are our own, and should not be attributed to either funding body. For more detail on our research methods and background to the villages of Dharmnagri and Jhakri, see P. Jeffery et al. (1989).

5. In rural Uttar Pradesh as a whole, the crude birth rate in 1987-89 was 38.7 per 1000 population, compared to the all-India rural figure of 33.0 (*Sample Registration Bulletin* 25, no.1, June 1991). Female literacy (literate women as a percentage of all females) in rural Bijnor in the 1991-62 census was 17.5%; in rural Uttar Pradesh the figure was 16%, and the all-India figure was 25.2% (*Census of India 1991: Provisional Population Totals*, Paper-2 of 1991).

6. This compares with comments from our other research villages where several women responded to our question by saying that since their own mothers had not been consulted how did we imagine that their opinions would have been sought.

7. The vulnerability of women who have been abandoned, divorced or widowed is clearly analysed in Dreze 1990; see also Cain 1986.

8. Pahl (1983) usefully distinguishes these three aspects of domestic finance. See also the discussion in Standing (1991).

9. We discuss the ways in which women's work patterns vary according to class and household composition, in P. Jeffery et al. 1989: 43-54.

10. The reasons why peasant joint households in North India break down are discussed in many places: see, for example, Mandelbaum 1988.

11. Marriage in Bijnor involves two ceremonies, one at the wedding itself and the second to mark cohabitation (*gauna*). In the past these two events may have been separated by several years, when child marriages were common; now the normal gap is six months, and the two ceremonies are sometimes carried out simultaneously.

12. This list does not, of course, exhaust the matters which demographers consider.

13. Numbers of infant and child deaths to the educated women are too small for statistical analysis to be reliable; the raw figures show that about 11% of the children of educated women died before the age of 5, but 18% of the children of uneducated women did so.

14. Deceit on the boy's side also occurs, of course, driven by attempts to maximize the dowry that is offered. In general, power in marriage negotiations lies in the hands of the boy's side.

15. The work done by Indian women in maintaining the status of the family is discussed in Papanek (1979) and Sharma (1986).

16. Tuition is usually regarded as essential for getting good grades; stories abound of teachers who do little teaching in class but only help the children who pay

for after-hours tuition. In Bijnor in 1990-91, tuition for children aged 11-13 might cost Rs. 50 per month; for older children, tuition could cost that much for each of several school subjects.

17. We are not here engaging with the effects of the curriculum, classroom context of schooling, quality, or kind of schooling (single-sex vs co-education) which, it has been argued, also tend to help create demure 'Sita-like' schooled women; for example, see the articles in Chanana, ed. 1988.

18. In parts of Bangladesh, men do seem to be increasingly denying their economic obligations to their wives: see Cain et al. 1979.

19. These issues—of the bases of women's unity and divisions—have been well discussed in many places; see for example Caplan and Bujra (1978). Surprisingly, this problem is not confronted in the collection edited by Haynes and Prakash (1991)—perhaps because the gender chapters focus on 'post-marital breakdown' situations of a small minority of women. These are interesting in their own right and can maybe act as a foil to see the normal situation of women; nonetheless, this is left implicit and the possibilities and options for resistance that are open to the more typical woman are not explored—yet the book is supposedly talking about *everyday* resistance.

References

Adas, Michael. 1991. South Asian resistance in comparative perspective. In Douglas Haynes and Gyan Prakash, eds., *Contesting power: Resistance and everyday social relations in South Asia, 290-305. New Delhi: Oxford University Press.*

Amin, Sajeda. Forthcoming. Female education and fertility in Bangladesh: The influence of marriage and the family. In Alaka Basu and Roger Jeffery, eds., *Education, autonomy, and fertility in South Asia.* New Delhi: Sage.

Basu, Alaka, and Roger Jeffery. Forthcoming. *Education, autonomy, and fertility in South Asia.* New Delhi: Sage.

Cain, Mead. 1981. Risk and insurance: Perspectives on fertility and agrarian change in India and Bangladesh. *Population and Development Review* 7,7: 435-74.

——.1984. Women's status and fertility in developing countries: Son preference and economic security. World Bank Staff Working Papers no. 682, Population and Development Series no. 7.

——. 1986. The consequences of reproductive failure: Dependence, mobility and mortality among the elderly in South Asia. *Population Studies* 40: 375-88.

——, S.K. Khonam, and S. Nahar. 1979. Class, patriarchy and the structure of women's work in rural Bangladesh. Centre for Policy Studies Working Paper, Population Council, New York.

Caldwell, John C., P.H. Reddy, and Pat Caldwell. 1983. The causes of marriage change in South India. *Population Studies* 37: 343-61.

Caplan, Pat, and Janet Bujra. 1978. *Women united, women divided: Cross-cultural perspectives on female solidarity.* London: Tavistock.

Chanana, Karuna, ed. 1988. *Socialisation, education and women.* New Delhi: Orient Longman.

Comaroff, Jean. 1985. *Social bodies and natural ideologies.* Chicago: Chicago University Press.

Das Gupta, Monica. 1987. Selective discrimination against female children in rural Punjab, India. *Population and Development Review* 13: 77-100.

——.1990. Death clustering, mothers' education and the determinants of child mortality in rural Punjab, India. *Population Studies* 44, 3: 489-505.

Dreze, Jean. 1990. Widows in rural India. Development Economics Research Programme Discussion Paper 26, London School of Economics, London.

Dyson, Tim, and Mick P. Moore. 1983. On kinship structure, female autonomy and demographic behaviour in India. *Population and Development Review* 9: 35-60.

Harrison, Paul. 1992. Battle of the Bulge. *The Guardian* (London) 1 May, p. 25.

Haynes, Douglas, and Gyan Prakash, eds. 1991. *Contesting power: Resistance and everyday social relations in South Asia.* New Delhi: Oxford University Press.

Hobsbawm, Eric. 1973. Peasants and politics. *Journal of Peasant Studies* 1, 1: 3-22.

Jain, Anirudh K., and Moni Nag. 1986. Importance of female primary education for fertility reduction in India. *Economic and Political Weekly* 21, 36: 1602-1607.

Jeffery, Patricia M. 1979. *Frogs in a well: Indian women in purdah.* London: Zed Books.

Jeffery, Patricia M., Roger Jeffery, and Andrew Lyon. 1989. *Labour pains and labour power: Women and childbearing in India.* London: Zed Books.

Jeffery, Roger, and Patricia M. Jeffery. 1992. A woman belongs to her husband: Female autonomy, women's work and childbearing in Bijnor. In Alice Clark, ed., *Gender and political economy.* New Delhi: Oxford University Press.

Levine, Robert A. 1980. Influences of women's schooling on maternal behaviour in the Third World. *Comparative Education Review* 24, 2/2: 53-105.

Lindenbaum, Shirley. 1990. The education of women and the mortality of children in Bangladesh. In Alan C. Swedlund and George J. Armelagos, eds., *Disease in populations in transition: Anthropological and epidemiological perspectives*, 353-70. New York: Bergin and Garvey.

Lockwood, Matthew, and Paul Collier. 1988. Maternal education and the vicious cycle of high fertility and malnutrition. Policy, Planning and Research Working Papers (WPS 130) in Women in Development, Population and Human Resources Department, The World Bank, Washington D.C.

Mandelbaum, David. 1988. *Women's seclusion and men's honor.* Tucson: University of Arizona Press.

Mani, Lata. 1990. Multiple mediations: Feminist scholarship in the age of multinational reception. *Feminist Review* 35: 24-41.

Mohanty, C. 1988. Under Western eyes: Feminist scholarship and colonial discourses. *Feminist Review* 30:61-88.

Pahl, Jan. 1983. The allocation of money and the structuring of inequality within marriage. *Sociological Review* 31:237-62.

Papanek, Hanna. 1979. Family status production: The 'work' and 'non-work' of women. *Signs* 1.4:775-81.

Sathar, Zeba, Nigel Crook, Christine Callum, and Shahnaz Kazi. 1988.Women's status and fertility change in Pakistan. *Population and Development Review* 14, 3: 415-32.

Scott, James. 1990. *Weapons of the weak: Everyday forms of peasant resistance.* New Delhi: Oxford University Press.

Sen, Amartya. 1990. Gender and co-operative conflicts. In Irene Tinker, ed., *Persistent inequalities: women and world development, 123-49.* New York: Oxford University Press.

—, and Jean Dreze eds., 1990. *The political economy of hunger* New Delhi: Oxford University Press.

Sharma, Ursula. 1986. *Women's work, class and the urban household.* London: Tavistock.

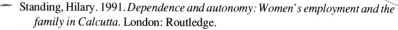 Standing, Hilary. 1991. *Dependence and autonomy: Women's employment and the family in Calcutta*. London: Routledge.

Visaria, Leela. 1985. Infant mortality in India: Level, trends and determinants. *Economic Economic and Political Weekly* 20, 32-34:1352-59, 1399-1405, and 1447-50.

Vlassoff, Carol. 1991. Progress and stagnation: changes in fertility and women's position in an Indian village. *Population Studies* 46, 2 :195-212.

Willis, Paul. 1977. *Learning to labour*. Farnborough: Saxon House.

World Bank. 1991. *Gender and poverty in India: A World Bank country study*. Washington, D.C.

6

Gender and Politics in Garhwal

WILLIAM SAX

When we did the goddess Nanda's special worship in
1922, five hundred goats were sacrificed. One goat for
each out-married daughter, and one for each house. It
came to a total of five hundred, counting all the neighbouring villages. But in 1927 animal sacrifice (*bali*) was
stopped. Since then the girls give coconuts, cash, and the
other materials for worship. One coconut for fire ritual
(*yajna*), and one to take home. In 1928, the year after
animal sacrifice was stopped, thirty-five children died
from whooping cough, and four or five homes were left
childless, with no sons.

Nevertheless, when Nanda's annual festival came round,
people said, 'We may die, all five-hundred of us, but then
what will happen? What will she do? We're all ready to
die.' The goddess had to believe them, when they said,
'We'll all die, but we won't give animal sacrifice.' Those
who had been left childless said, 'We've already been
destroyed: take us first.'

Then, in 1951, came her big pilgrimage. The royal prince
[patron of the event] came and said, 'Start the animal sacrifice.' We said, 'OK brother, you make some slips of
paper. Make twelve of them. Six will say 'animal sacrifice', and six will say 'fire ritual' (*yajna*). We got a platter
from the bazaar and said, 'Honoured prince, you hold the
platter, and our goddess Nanda will select the paper. None
of us: either a child or the deity.' She picked out three.
Two said 'fire ritual' and one said 'animal sacrifice'. Then
she possessed her oracle and said, 'I will take animal sacrifice, but if I take it in your house, I will live there as

[the terrible goddess] Chandika. I will take your sacrifice, but in the form of Chandika, not as Nandadevi.'[1]

HINDU GODDESSES ARE notoriously changeable. I shall recount a number of songs and stories of the Hindu goddess Nanda which depict her as alternatively griefstricken creatrix, dependent child, nubile maiden, frenzied warrior, demonic monster, and peaceful goddess. Scholars have typically construed one of these contrasts—between those forms of the goddess who accept only vegetarian offerings and those who accept bloody sacrifices—as a problem in need of an explanation.[2] Thus Dumont poses himself the question: How can a goddess who accepts bloody sacrifice coexist with the Brahmanical, vegetarian theory which she 'contradicts'? His answer is that 'Brahmanism, unable to rationalize the presence of complementary opposites, sifts and substantializes Hinduism. Shall we say that the place occupied by the goddess is the result of a 'compromise', that she is 'tolerated'? Is it not better to state that she is present but that the system cannot account for her presence?' (1960:40 n. 13).

Dumont's theory is undermined by Hindu practice, which offers many examples, not only of goddesses who accept both bloody and vegetarian sacrifices, but also of goddesses who alternate between the two types. For example, buffaloes are sometimes sacrificed to the goddess Nanda, and sometimes they are not, and this variation is characteristic of Hindu goddesses throughout South Asia. Should we say, with Dumont, that 'the system cannot account for [the] presence' of such goddesses? Should we do so, we will in the end find ourselves excluding one of the most salient religions of South Asia—the *shakta sampradaya* or 'tradition of the worshippers of the goddess'—from the 'system' of Hinduism.

Beck also has difficulty with the multiformity of the goddess. She first suggests that the South Indian goddess Mariyamman be considered a form of Durga. There is some evidence to that effect, but 'if we select the Durga myth, then the marriage ritual [in Mariyamman's cult] becomes an anomaly'. So, she suggests, the associations with Kali might be more apposite, since 'the young, mild tempered Sati [daughter of Daksha] . . . becomes the fierce Bhadrakali . . . [and] in this context Mariyamman's alternating, two-sided character portrayal makes more sense' (1981:108).

Obeyesekere (1984) propounds a psychological theory of the projective formation of 'bipolar goddesses' in the Hindu pantheon (McGilvary 1988), as does Gatwood (1985). O'Flaherty (1980) and Ramanujan (1986) both perceive a dichotomy in images of the goddess, contrasting benevolent, nurturing 'breast mothers' with malevolent, punishing 'tooth mothers'. To

make matters worse, the goddesses Durga and Kali are often conflated:
Bennett confuses them in her description of Nepali myth (1983:262), and
Beck asserts that most devotees do not distinguish the two: she herself
writes of the goddess's 'violent underside as punisher and angry death
dealer (Durga-Kali)' (1981:86-87). In his discussion of the 'internal seg-
mentation' of Hindu deities, Fuller clarifies several of the issues involved
by distinguishing among goddesses who accept vegetarian offerings (*nai-
vedya*), those who accept bloody sacrifice (*bali*), and certain intermediate
forms (1988:25-27). Bennett assets that with the Hindu view of women so
strongly characterized by contradiction, it is not surprising that the nature
of the Hindu goddess Devi should also be contradictory (1983:261).[3] She
goes on to argue that both 'destructive' and 'gentle' aspects alike 'are
fraught with contradiction, and therein lies the Devi's power as a symbol'
(ibid.:262). Contradiction upon contradiction, which Bennett ultimately
resolves by asserting that 'in some respects Durga embodies a predominantly male perception of women' and Parvati, a female view (ibid.:269).

While it does seem that some versions of the songs of Nandadevi
represent a female perspective, and others a male perspective, I think that
for both theoretical and methodological reasons it would be a mistake to
let the matter rest there. Theoretically, specification of the differences
between male and female powers, experiences and perspectives is helpful
and indeed imperative in analysing the social construction of gender. But
such differences must be derived from the shared social and cultural field
within which they are mutually determined. Until we can account for the
social production of the distinctions of gender, we shall be limited to
formally reproducing those distinctions, whereas our goal ought to be to
empower ourselves to change them.

Methodologically, uncritical acceptance of the 'contradictions' of
Hindu goddesses as noted by Western scholars does violence to the Hindu
point of view, according to which the goddess is one. Bennett herself
admits that, despite the hundreds of forms taken by the goddess, 'to the
villagers they are all one' (1983:261; cf. n. 1 p. 307; also Dimock
1984:194). Rather than reifying our own, external apprehension of contradiction, we should ask the more interesting question: Why do we perceive
an opposition where Hindus insist on a unity?[4]

The Songs of Nandadevi

The Hindu goddess (*devi*) named Nanda is worshipped in upper Garhwal
and Kumaon, at the trijunction of India, Nepal and Tibet in the North Indian
state of Uttar Pradesh. For more than a thousand years, she was the royal

goddess of local kings (Atkinson 1974 [1882], vol. 2 part 2: 813; Dabaral
1965-78, vol. 4: 250; Kielhorn 1896; Sircar 1956), and today she remains
popular among members of all castes, male and female, young and old.
Her songs[5] are known and sung throughout the region, especially by local
women who, like Nandadevi herself, are *dhiyanis* or 'out-married daughters'.[6]

Attitudes toward the songs vary, especially between men and women.
Although nearly everyone thinks of them as a kind of history (*itihas*),
nevertheless some people (primarily men) say that they have less 'credibility' or 'respect' (*manyata*) than a printed text because they are thought
to be less permanent. And since they are less permanent, the songs are also
inferior. Written texts are associated with male, Brahmin priests, and oral
literature with lower-ranked ritual[7] specialists and women. These differences are evident when one compares male with female versions of the
songs of Nandadevi, or priestly with low-caste versions. Male and priestly
versions of the songs tend more closely to approximate classical, Sanskrit
versions of the goddess's story—especially the *Devi Mahatmyam*[8]—while
female and low-caste versions provide an alternative perspective that
stresses fertility and the powers of the weak, especially females. That such
an alternative perspective was characteristic of nearly all of the songs of
Nandadevi I collected was rather striking, given the fact that they were
gathered from several distinct areas where separate dialects were spoken,
and that they were all transmitted orally, having to the best of my knowledge never been written down in their entirety before I did so.

I collected several versions of the songs of Nandadevi during fieldwork
in 1983-86. The most complete version came from Nauti village in the
Chamoli district of Garhwal, and it is from that version that the cosmogony
that follows is excerpted. Nauti is one of the major centres of the cult of
Nandadevi: it contains a small temple to Nanda's brother Hit and two
yantras or geometrical representations of the goddess. (Bloody sacrifices
were formerly offered to the older of these *yantras*; the new one has never
received such a sacrifice.) The Nautiyals of Nauti, highest-ranked Brahmins in Garhwal, were in former times goddess priests (*shakta purohita*)
of the kings of Garhwal. Every year during Nanda's festival in the month
of Bhado (Hindi *bhadrapad*), in August-September at the end of the rainy
seaon, up to a dozen women from Nauti sing her epic song. The performance lasts several nights, and the song is not sung in its entirety at any other
time. Recording and translating the song were joint endeavours. Shekhavati Nautiyal and Janaki Singh of Nauti village graciously sang it for me
over the course of several weeks in October 1984, and I later transcribed

it and translated it from archaic Garhwali into Hindi with the indispensable
aid of Dabar Singh Ravat of Toli village, and from Hindi to English almost
entirely on my own. The following excerpted portion of Nandadevi's song
begins after a primordial goddess named Adishakti has given birth to the
goddess Parvati, who was given birth to the woman Nalina, who has given
birth, in turn, to the bird Pankhina.

CREATION

Adishakti was very happy.
'I created the sky above, I created the earth below.
I created the eastern kingdom, I created the western kingdom.
I created the southern kingdom, I created the northern kingdom.
I created the forests and mountains, I created the trees
    and plants.
I created the rocks and cliffs, I created the pebbles
    and boulders.
I created the Ganga and the Yamuna, I created the wishing cow.
I created the bards and Brahmans, I created the five high gods.
I created the tall and the spreading trees, I created
    the kings of the earth.
I created the faithful earth.

'But how can I live without a man?
Without a man, for whom shall I live?
Without a man, there is no wealth.[9]
Without a tree, there can be no shade.
How shall I give birth to that shade-giving tree?
Or must I remain a sad little girl?
How can I give birth to a man?'

Shakti incarnated as Maya,[10]
She gave the incarnation of *Mahamaya*.
'How can I give birth to a man?
How can I live without a man?'

Maya enveloped the ocean.
The blood began to flow from her womb.
Maya's blood began to flow,
And from it the god Brahma was born.
Now Maya was very happy:
'I created my man from my own body!'

The god Brahma stood with his hands humbly folded.
'Mother,' he said, 'you should not say such things!
I am a son of the blood from your womb;
Your "man" can't be born of your own womb's blood!'
The god Brahma stood with his hands humbly folded.
'Mother, assign to me my daily work.
O Mother, why have you given me birth?
Mother, assign to me my daily work.'

'Go to the world of Brahma, my son.
Go there and build a house for yourself.'
Then she created the world of Brahma.
She established the world of Brahma.
'Rely on our God Narayana, my son.'

Now Maya became very sad.
'How can I give birth to a man?
I will give birth to a man from my own body.
I will produce a tree from my own body.'
Maya again enveloped the ocean.
The blood began to flow from her womb.
Jatilo Bagyelo[11] was born.

'O Mother, why did you give birth to me?
Mother, assign to me my daily work.'

'My son, in the wilderness you'll be a king.
My son, I will make a cave for you there.
And when my day of difficulties arrives,
On that day, my son, I will surely summon you.'

Then Maya again enveloped the ocean.
Kaliya Lohar[12] was found in her blood,
Kaliya Lohar was born
Kaliya Lohar stood with hands humbly folded.

'Assign to me, Mother, my daily work.'
'Go, my son, to Kalangiri mountain . . .'[13]
Rely on God, my son.
And when my day of difficulties arrives,
On that day, my son, I will surely summon you . . .'

'You must make the slicing-knife, my son,
To eliminate my suffering.
How can I live without a man?
How can I live without my tree?
You must forge the seven knives,
You must forge nine slicing knives.'

Then the Lohar made the seven slicing knives.
He gave them to Maya; 'May you live lakhs of years.
You have erased my troubles, my son.'

Then Maya bathed and washed herself;
She bathed and washed the seven slicing knives.
Then Maya worshipped the seven iron knives.
She worshipped the knives with milk and with rice.
She offered them incense of *masi* and *gugul*.[14]
Then she embraced the seven iron knives.

Maya moved on from Kalangiri mountain.
The burning lamp[15] went up to Pamwali meadow.
She stopped at Pamwali and looked all around.
At Pamwali meadow she bathed all the knives.
She offered them incense of *masi* and *gugul*.
She worshipped the knives with milk and then rice.
Then she embraced the seven iron knives.
Maya moved on from Pamwali meadow.
The burning lamp went to the Stairway of Heaven.
At the Stairway of Heaven, she bathed and she washed.
She bathed and washed the seven slicing knives.

Then Maya worshipped the seven iron knives.
She worshipped the knives with milk and with rice.
Then she embraced the seven slicing knives.
Maya moved on from the cold Steps of Heaven.
The burning lamp reached the high Path of Bhrigu.
On the high Path of Bhrigu, she bathed and she washed.
She bathed and then washed the seven slicing knives.
Then Maya worshipped the seven iron knives.
She worshipped the knives with milk and with rice.
Then she embraced the seven slicing knives.

'Now become present, O seven slicing knives!
I am alone, a broken-hearted girl,
And who will rid me of my sorrow?'
Maya recited the seven-sound mantra.
'Now become present, O seven slicing knives!
She struck with the knives, and her head took a tumble.
Then Maya leapt from the high Path of Bhrigu.[16]
Now Maya's one body has become two;
Maya's head flew up to high Mount Kailash,
And her trunk, it fell down into Rishasau town.
The goddess's head became Bhola Sambhu Nath,
Bhola Sambhu Nath on high Mount Kailash.
In Rishasau town was old Hemant the Sage.
In that Sage's home, Gauradevi[17] was born.

What is the evidence for my assertion that the songs of Nandadevi represent a 'female perspective'? To begin with, our text gives an account of creation as female emanation. In contrast to the popular Hindu theory of conception, in which the woman is regarded as a 'field' or passive receptacle for the male's fertile seed (Manu ix. 31 ff. in O'Flaherty and Smith 1991; Marriott 1976; O'Flaherty 1980:29-30), the Adishakti of our song reproduces offspring from her menstrual or uterine blood (Gwli *pasyou* = Skt *pushpa*), the generative equivalent of semen, her 'female seed' (O'Flaherty 1980:33-34; Shulman 1980:104-108). The image of a female as the creatrix or emanator of the world clashes with the myths and stories most often encountered by students of the Sanskrit tradition: within Hindu mythology, 'the instances of unilateral female creation are by far outnumbered by unilateral male creation' (O'Flaherty 1980:39; also 28, 55-56). However, this may be truer of written Sanskrit myths than of vernacular and oral ones. Cosmogonies in which a goddess has the primary creative role have been reported throughout India, and they tend to be associated with oral rather than written texts (Gold n.d. and Ramanujan n.d.). And oral cosmogonies are often transmitted by women in the home, while the written texts of the classical tradition are associated with male transmission in school and temple. Women's versions of the songs of Nandadevi present an image of a powerful, autonomous creator-goddess, but this image is not generally accepted by men. In fact, few of them are even aware of it. Why is this so? In large part, it is precisely because the songs of Nandadevi are orally transmitted. They are therefore regarded as less

permanent, less accurate, than the written scriptures of classical Hinduism.

There is of course another and perhaps more obvious reason why
village men were largely unfamiliar with the image of the powerful
creator-goddess in this song: it was sung by women, and women's songs
are rarely taken seriously by men. Even a local schoolteacher who was
one of the most sensitive and intelligent men in the village had quite
simply never paid any attention to their content until his interest was
sparked by my own. For most men, the songs were merely 'folktales'
(*dant katha*, literally 'tooth stories'), esoteric women's songs that could
easily be dismissed, while the veracity of written scripture was seldom
questioned. One of the most effective ways to support male domination
was simply to ignore the oral literature of women. And even if the men
were to become aware of the contents of the cosmogony just reproduced
here, with its explicit themes of blood and sexuality and its temporary
inversion of male and female roles, they would be confirmed in their
belief that it was not a fit subject for serious attention.

For the women of Nauti, the situation was different. They regarded
the songs as holy 'waking-songs' (*jagar*) or 'meditations' (*dhyan*). Because of the sanctity of the songs, the women who sang the most complete version for me insisted that our recording sessions take place in
the village temple, and they bathed before each session. Like men,
women learn the songs from their mothers, and elderly women who
have known the songs longest, sung them year after year for decades,
reflected upon and 'internalized' them to the greatest degree, seem to
have few doubts about their veracity. Most of this lengthy folk epic
concerns the birth, childhood, marriage, departure and return of the goddess Nanda, who is thought of as an 'out-married village daughter', in
other words, as a female who, like most human females, is compelled
upon marriage to leave the village of her birth to reside elsewhere with
her husband. Nearly all women—singers and listeners—are moved to
tears by certain parts of the songs, especially those that describe the
young bride's departure from her natal village. I have argued elsewhere
that the story of the goddess Nanda closely parallels the life courses of
local females, that a bride's compulsory change of residence after marriage (from her natal place to her husband's place) is the source of some
of the most pervasive tensions and anxieties of local peasant women,
and that the songs and spectacular pilgrimages of the goddess Nanda
directly address this problem (Sax 1990; 1991). For these and other
reasons, it may fairly be said that her songs exemplify a female per-

spective, and it is only in female and low-caste cosmogonies that the goddess is given such a prominent and creative role. By contrast, I recorded a high-caste, male version of this song (reproduced in the following pages) that omitted the cosmogony altogether, substituting for it a description of a female slave proceeding from pilgrimage place to pilgrimage place throughout the subcontinent, lighting temple lamps at the behest of her male masters.

While the inordinate fecundity of the goddess Adishakti may strike the Sanskrit scholar as unusual, it should come as no surprise to students of Indian folklore. Women provide agricultural as well as domestic labour throughout India; on them depends the reproduction of children and lineages as well as crops, and their fertility is often the subject of myths. Female labour is particularly important in Garhwal, where women are responsibile for the lion's share of agricultural as well as household production. In addition to cooking, raising children and caring for livestock, they are also responsible for planting, weeding, and harvesting crops, processing grain, gathering firewood, and cutting grass for fodder. Men generally do the marketing, tend the livestock if no children are available for the task and perform needed repairs of the house, terraces, or irrigation canals. They are also very fond of cards. Ploughing is the only specifically 'male' task. The life of a Garhwali woman is often one of unrelieved hardship, and the men are surprisingly candid about this.[18] As my neighbour once said,

> Here in the hills, a man without a woman will die of
> starvation or become a yogi. Why? Because women do all
> the work. From feeding the children to milking the buffalo
> to cutting the wood to weeding to harvesting to raising a
> family. What do we men have to do? Plough. It's not like
> that in the plains—there the men work and the women don't.
> But it's like that here, and on Kumaon side, and in Pauri.

Whenever I interviewed Garhwali women, I always asked them what the most important aspect of a woman's life was. Almost without exception, they replied 'work' or 'the fields', and when I would ask what a young bride could do if she was mistreated in her husband's home, the answer too was nearly always the same: 'She can flee to her parents' home. She can become a female ascetic (*mai/jogin*). Or she can kill herself.' Most Garhwalis believe that female suicide is very common in their region, and the same opinion was voiced over a hundred and fifty years ago by the first British Commissioner:

Suicide is very prevalent among females of the lower classes. The commission of this act is rarely found to have arisen from an immediate cause of quarrel, but is commonly ascribable to the disgust of life generally prevalent among these persons. The hardships and neglect to which the females in this province are subjected, will sufficiently account for their distaste of life, as with a trifling exception, the whole labour of the agricultural and domestic economy is left to them, while food and clothing are dealt out to them with a sparing hand. Suicide is never committed by males, except in cases of leprosy, when, as in other parts of India, the leper sometimes buries himself alive. (Traill 1828: 197-98)

No statistics are available on this subject, and it cannot be determined whether this widespread notion actually represents the facts. But it is certainly believed that mistreated women resort to suicide, and the threat of it is commonly and effectively employed by frustrated village women to obtain concessions from their husbands and others. A local scholar paints the situation in grim colours:

the sequence of events leads the woman to her personal limit. The husband must make money to pay off his debts from 'the sale of a virgin'.[19] The young wife continually hears the scolding of her husband's mother and sisters. No particular aid or empathy is obtained from her parents. Thus tortured by familial and personal problems, she is compelled to commit suicide [*atmahatya*]. When her husband fails to return for many years, she becomes another man's lover. She becomes a female ascetic, and takes refuge in some convent. Murder and suicide are thus not only personal tragedies, but also the causes of social problems. (K. Nautiyal 1982: 40)

Garhwali women's problems are compounded by the frequent absence of their husbands. As in many regions of India, Garhwal's is a 'money-order economy', dependent for anything more than a bare subsistence upon the remittances of men employed elsewhere. Garhwal also has one of the proudest regiments in the Indian Army, and military service is among the most sought-after careers. For most men, any outside career, even one with low prestige and wages, is preferable to remaining in the village. Over 70 per cent of the adult men in Nauti were employed outside the village, leaving their wives to manage family affairs, either by themselves or under their mother-in-law's watchful eye. Many observers have commented on the tension in the relationship between husband's mother and son's wife in India (Bennett 1983:180 ff., Davis 1983: chap 4; Inden and Nicholas 1977:87 ff; Jacobson 1977), and this theme need not be rehearsed again. Garhwali women's troubles are aggravated by the absence of husbands, who are often their main or only protectors; thus women included absent males in a set of related problems leading to flight, world renunciation and suicide.

Given such a context, the goddess Maya's solution to her lack of a husband parallels that of Garhwali women in similar situations. Incomplete because lacking a spouse, she solves her dilemma by cutting off her own head. The rest of the myth recounts the process of reuniting the disjoined parts of the goddess's body. Hence in a fundamental sense, the songs of Nandadevi constitute a meditation on the theme of unity and disunity, primordial wholeness and historical fragmentation—a theme with both sociological and mythological referents. Originally a single being, Adishakti desired to create a second. Unable to unite with that second, she created yet another by dividing herself in two. Fragmentation succeeds fragmentation. It is the ominous cancer-theory of Indian society as uncontrolled fission.[20] But fragmentation is followed by reunion, and again by fragmentation, in an endless cycle of forms that is *samsara*, the conditioned world.

The inordinate fecundity of the goddess—her tendency to multiply forms—is related to her nature as *maya*. Maya is the first epithet to be employed in the *Devi Mahatmyam*, the main ritual text of Nanda's priests from Kurud,[21] and the most popular goddess liturgy in North India—possibly in all of India. The term *maya* is 'as old as the Rig Veda, where it means "wile" or "magic power", a power that belongs primarily to Varuna' (Coburn 1984:125). It comes from the root *ma*, 'to measure or divide', but is perhaps best rendered in English as 'the power of multiformity'. Like the Advaitic notion of *avidya* (ignorance), *maya* is the 'fiction of separation' of objects in the real world (Heimann 1937, 51,93). As Mahamaya in the *Devi Mahatmyam*, the goddess 'entices humans into taking themselves, i.e., their egos, seriously, thereby perpetuating the pain of life in *samsara*' (Coburn 1984: 125). In other words, given the radically un-Cartesian assumption that governs much of Indian thought—that the world is fundamentally one—apparent duality must be illusory. Note the further characteristics of *maya*:

all *mayas*, all measurable definite things, are then inferior
to the Avyaktam, to the presumed primeval chaotic and
ever-producing mass, as is taught by the Sankhyam. To
begin with: all *mayas* . . . are smaller . . . subordinate
. . . emanations from [matter]; thus all *mayas* are inferior,
because secondary in Time . . . [and] liable to destruction'.
(Heimann 1937: 51)

Although the word *maya* is conveniently translated as 'illusion' in
English, it should be remembered that at the empirical, everyday level,
these separate, created *mayas* are real enough. They are 'illusory'—and
the force that produces them is called 'illusion'—only because they are
less real, and more changeful, than ultimate reality. Maya is pure, evanes-
cent form, and the fecundity of the goddess thus reflects her nature as *maya*,
the 'power of multiformity' in general, here a named goddess who emanates the various forms and beings of the empirical world.

The creative activity of Maya depends on her power of multiformity,
but it is motivated by desire. Earlier, as the bird Pankhina, she emanated
the world, and was 'very happy' when she saw the results. But the
presence of others soon gives rise to desire. 'How can I live without a
man?' she asks,

'Without a man, for whom shall I live?
Without a man, there is no wealth.
Without a tree, there can be no shade.
How shall I give birth to that shade-giving tree?
Or must I remain a sad little girl?'

All of Maya's troubles, leading finally to her self-decapitation, could have
been avoided were it not for the power of desire which, as elsewhere in
Hinduism, quite literally makes the world go round. While the enjoyment
or fulfillment of desire is encouraged as *kama*, one of the four 'aims of
man' (*purushartha*), it is generally considered a hindrance to ultimate
goals:

On the one hand, ethnographic evidence indicates that un-
satisfied desires are believed to produce deleterious results
and that a prerequisite for physical and psychological health
is the gratification of desire. On the other hand, following
the Sanskritic tradition, passion hinders liberation and thus
a prerequisite of salvation is freedom from passion. (Bhattacharyya 1984: 81; cf. Shulman 1980:349)

As Maya, the goddess's desire for a man is explicity sexual: she is dissatisfied, incomplete, remorseful; a 'sad little girl' (*dukhyari bali*) unable to live without a man (*purush*) and the comfort and protection he offers, the shade (*chaya*) he provides as a metaphorical tree. To be married is to be whole and complete, and a human being is not regarded as a full, adult member of society until he or she has undergone this most important of life-cycle rites (*samskara*). I have seen unmarried Garhwali youths sit down to eat with adult men, only to be asked, 'Have you tied the string?'— a reference to the so-called 'sacred-thread ceremony' (*upanayana samskara*, Gwli. *bart bandh*, 'tying the string'), which is a prerequisite to marriage. Those who had not undergone this rite were not allowed to eat in the company of adult males.

The goddess Maya, however, cannot achieve marital completion because there are no suitable mates. Her child Brahma will not accede to her overtures: she is his mother, and sexual union would be inappropriate. Such a sexually aggressive mother is relatively rare, though by no means absent, in Hindu mythology. A.K. Ramanujan and Ann Grodzins Gold have collected folk Puranas from Karnataka and Rajasthan, respectively, in which a primordial goddess begets and then attempts to seduce Brahma and Vishnu, whose fate is much harsher than that of the reluctant gods in our tale: when they refuse, she destroys them. The sexually aggressive mother is supremely dangerous, a fusion of the erotic woman and the subordinate wife, who drains the male of his power. Such a dominant goddess 'violates the basic Hindu categories of male-female relationships' (O'Flaherty 1980: 77, 99), since according to Hindu assumptions and theories, female sexuality is a powerful force that must be subordinated to male control.

> The benevolent goddesses in the Hindu pantheon are those who are properly married and who have transferred control of their sexuality (power/nature) to their husbands. Symbolically, a woman is 'a part of her husband, his half-body'. Rules for proper conduct mandate that she transfer her powers, as they accumulate, to her husband for his use (Wadley 1977: 118).

The same goes for human females. In Tamil Nadu, it is believed that women have more *shakti* than men, that men must control the dangerous and excessive sexuality of women, and that all kinds of bad things may happen if they do not (Daniel 1980: 65-66, 78-79). Similarly in North India, 'The daughter obeys her father and the sister is under the protection of her brother (and fervently desires his protection as he is her primary link with her natal home . . .)' (Wadley 1977: 25). Babb writes that women's powerful and dangerous sexuality must be bound in and through marriage, that uncontrolled female sexuality is characteristic of witches and of fierce and bloodthirsty goddesses, while controlled sexuality and the auspicious power associated with it is characteristic of chaste wives and benign goddesses (1975: chap 7). Women's desires are potentially insatiable, and threaten the physical vitality of men, which is dependent upon their supply of semen: such notions are very widespread in India (see, for instance, Beck 1981; Bennett 1983; Brubaker 1978; Hiltebeitel 1980; Leslie 1983; Liddle and Joshi 1986; O'Flaherty 1973, 1980, 1984; Wadley 1975). What has been less frequently noticed is that these horrific images are (probably much) more representative of male perspectives and concerns than of female ones. In the women's songs, the goddess's only violence is not directed at men or even at other creatures, but rather at herself. The anthropologist Ann Gold has collected a number of women's folk songs from Rajasthan, and these songs present us with a believable, earthy female self-conception, one in which women's sexuality is associated with their birth-giving capacities. According to Gold, these women do not imagine themselves as sexually insatiable creatures seeking to draw the life-force from men; rather

> the more persuasive image of female nature offered by the folklore includes a sexuality not rampantly destructive but seeking mutuality with males. The erotic imagination suggests a relish for sexual encounter on both sides that is more human than demonic . . . the sexual and maternal aspects of female nature seem fused rather than split, and generative rather than destructive images of female power emerge. (1988: 33)

Recall that Maya created the male gods from a relatively low, hot and 'polluting' substance—her menstrual blood, her 'female seed'. Parthenogenetically extruded, these gods were not sufficiently differentiated from her to be appropriate mates. As Brahma says in the song, 'Your "man" can't be born of your own womb's blood!' Moreover this initial relationship of Maya to her offspring inverts the classical, hegemonic paradigm of a good marriage, which is explicitly directional: prescribed marriages, wherein the male is sexually and politically dominant, giving commands as well as semen downward to the subordinate female, are 'with the hair' (*anuloma*), while bad marriages, in which a superior female weds an inferior male, are 'against the hair' (*pratiloma*). Maya's offspring were unacceptable as mates for two reasons: they were not sufficiently differentiated from her, and they were liberally and figuratively 'beneath her'.

Nothing in the Hindu world, however, lasts forever: Indian mythology abounds in stories of persons related as husband and wife in one birth, parent and child in the next, and so on (O'Flaherty 1980: 105-107). After death and rebirth, the self (*atma*) remains 'unchanged' in some mysterious way, but the body is different. Maya makes a marital re-union possible in one fell stroke, by dividing her head from her body. The head is reborn as Shiva on Mount Kailash, and the body as Gaura in Rishasau. He is superior, high, and cool relative to her, while she is subordinate, low, and hot relative to him. In this way, asymmetries in the earlier relationship of Maya to her offspring are reversed, and a once-disbalanced pair is balanced; to use Marriott's terms, a mismatched couple is 'matched'.

Yet the new relationship is hardly symmetrical. It is just as unbalanced as the one that preceded it, only this time it is culturally sanctioned, 'appropriate' because the male is literally and figuratively on top. The culturally subversive image of a divine creatrix is incorporated within a story that valorizes male dominance; myth provides a model that serves male interests, and is thus an example of gender politics. In effect, myth here declares that female autonomy is untenable, that the goddess Maya, powerful and creative though she is, can achieve fulfillment only by uniting with and subordinating herself to a male. Although female power and fertility are thinkable, female independence is not.[22] To put it in other terms, the counter-hegemonic tendencies of the first part of the song are neutralized by being absorbed into and contained by the hegemonic, male-dominated discourse on gender. In this connection, it is revealing that the only version of Nandadevi's songs that I recorded from a high-caste male replaces the subversive cosmogony with this story of a female slave:

> Now is the time for the gods to light their lamps.
> The five gods summoned their obedient slave girl.
> The obedient slave girl came and she said,
> 'Tell me, O gods, what work must I do?'
> The gods said, 'O slave girl, now is the time
> To light all the lamps and the fires in our temples.'
>
> Whence came the lamp? From an earthen quarry.
> Who are your parents, O lamp made of earth?
> My mother is earth and my father, the sky.

> She tore a white cloth and she rolled out the wicks.
> She melted some ghi and then filled all the lamps.
>
>
> 'Obedient slave girl, now don your jewellery.'
> The slave girl began to put on her twelve garments.
> 'Wear these twelve ornaments, obedient slave.
> Even the sun is shamed by your beauty.
> Your bosom enchanting, your back covered in silver.'
>
>
> In one hand she took a flaming firebrand.
> In the other she grasped a cup of pure ghi.

After this, the obedient slave girl travels the length and breadth of India, sweeping temples and lighting lamps at many famous temples and other places of pilgrimage. Finally, when morning arrives, she returns to Mount Kailash in the Himalayas.

> 'Listen, O gods, to my faltering voice.
> Please concentrate on what I am saying.
> O gods, I have travelled in many far lands!
> O gods, I have travelled among many strange men!
> O gods, I have travelled to all the gods' houses!
> O gods, I have travelled to all the gods' temples!
> I have gone to the temples, the large and the small!
> I HAVE LIGHTED THE LAMPS IN ALL OF THE TEMPLES!'
> Listen, all of you who are singing and listening:
> This didn't just happen today, but instead
> In the time of the gods.
> It is not a recent affair.

At this point the lead singer stopped, and asked for a smoke.[23] A break in the song was clearly signalled, after which the narrative of Nandadevi and her husband, Shiva, was resumed. In this all-male version of the song, there was no reference to female creation, nor to any powerful or autonomous goddess. The entire section had been excised, replaced by the simple description of an obedient slave girl who sweeps temples and lights lamps at her male masters' command. It would be difficult to imagine a greater contrast.

Immediately following her auto-decapitation, the goddess Maya seeks a new home in which to take birth. She settles on the home of Hemant the sage and his wife, Mainuli, who are old, wealthy and childless, and are performing a fire sacrifice (*yajna*) in order to obtain progeny. The goddess's birth is the answer to their prayers:

> A daughter was born to old Hemant the sage.
> In the old sage's home there was shouting for joy . . .
> A daughter was born like a star in the sky.
> A daughter was born like a fish in a lake.
> A daughter was born who shone like the sun.
> A daughter was born like the moon at night.
> A daughter was born, an incomparable virgin.

Even as an infant, Gaura's actions anticipate her eventual destiny, which is to marry Shiva. When she is only eleven days old, she climbs up to the ridge of the house and announces, 'This is my Kailash', to which her mother replies, 'What are you doing? You're only eleven days old! What will the neighbours say?' When she reaches adolescence, Gaura retires to a holy place to practice asceticism, in an attempt to please Shiva. When Narada the sage visits her in the hope of arranging her marriage, she says,

> 'Listen to my feeble voice, O my uncle.
> Let me be without home, but not without husband.
> If you let me be without husband, I'll curse you.'

Confident of the girl-goddess's acquiescence, Narada must still convince her parents and Shiva to assent to the union. In some versions, Narada arranges the marriage of Shiva and Nanda at the instigation of the other gods, who are distressed at Shiva's power and implore Narada to 'break' his asceticism; elsewhere no specific motive is given other than his desire for the culinary delights of Rishasau.

Narada's main device in arranging the marriage is a kind of religious blackmail. He refuses to take food from Shiva's hand because the god is unmarried, hence incomplete, less than fully adult. When Shiva asks Narada why he will not accept food, the sage replies

> 'Can there be laughter without any teeth?
> Can there be speech without any tongue?
> Can there be man without any woman?'

> Swamiji then seized his sharp fire-tongs.
> 'You sinful bhat! I'll not leave you alive!

You wish to destroy my *tapasya*, you *bhado*![24]
Ahead sprinted Narada, Swami close behind:
Shouting and cursing, they ran to Cow Pass.

Swamiji Shankar returned to Kailash,
But Narada followed him, stayed close behind.
The petrified Narada hid in a corner,
And Swamiji's anger subsided a bit.
'Listen to what I will say, Narada:
In all the three worlds there's no woman for me.'
'But I've seen a woman who's just right for you.
A sage's young daughter's the woman for you.
She's of the right age, plays the 'game of limbs' well!'
(version three)

Narada plays the same trick on Hemant and Mainuli when he goes to
visit them, saying,

'Sage, I won't eat the food of your home,
Because in your home is an unmarried virgin.
The ancestors, also, will not drink the water
That comes from the hand of an unmarried person.
Brahmins, as well, will not eat the food
That comes from the hand of an unmarried person.
The calf of a cow will not eat the food[25]
That comes from the hand of an unmarried person.
Crows as well[26] will not eat the food
That comes from the hand of an unmarried person.
You have an unmarried girl in your home.'

In version number seven, Narada tells Hemant that

after twelve years, a girl pollutes the land. If an unmarried
girl stays in the house after twelve years, the earth is
polluted. Her father goes to hell. You have a fourteen-year-
old girl here. Your golden land has been polluted. That's why
I purified it. Don't be angry with me, but this land is defiled.
You have to marry Gaura somewhere or other.

And in version number three he elaborates on the dangers of keeping a
nubile, unmarried female in the house, saying,

'A tender young maiden's the source of much sin.[27]
Some call her your daughter, some call her your wife.
Who knows or has heard will call her your daughter,
Those who don't know will call her your wife.'

Here our songs depict a very common North Indian attitude, one that helps explain part of the anxiety with which parents anticipate the marriages of their daughters. The young woman's burgeoning sexuality is clearly regarded as a threat. She must be properly married and placed under the control of a male, if the old Brahmin and his wife are to maintain the purity of their home; otherwise shame or disaster may follow. Another incentive for the early marriage of daughters is the belief that every time an unmarried girl menstruates an embryo dies, and that the sin lies on the head of her father.

The tale of Narada's religious blackmail is found in nearly all versions of the song, male and female, high and low caste. What women emphasize in their versions (and men do not) is the departure of the young bride from her familiar home in the valley to the home of Shiva, her husband, on high Mount Kailash. Below there is milk and rice in abundance; above is only 'snow to wear and snow to eat'. Much tension and anxiety is associated with the new brides' obligatory change of residence after they are married. Not only the young woman, but her village friends and family all feel great sorrow (see Narayan 1986). Indeed, the best known and most loved of all the parts of the song is when the young goddess-bride leaves her natal village. And this departure is itself the event that is spectacularly represented during Nandadevi's periodic ritual processions. Local women's issues are thus of central importance in the cult. When women sing this part of the song their eyes fill with tears and they are sometimes unable to continue. Members of the audience (especially young brides newly arrived, or girls about to be married) are often overcome by emotion.

'I look about and all I see is high Kailash Mountain.
I look in all directions, but see only the realm of darkness.
How, O how, will I ever live on high Kailash Mountain?
Where, O where, did he come from, this old
    dope-smoking yogi?
What an evil thing they did, my mother and my father!
Those sinful sages married me to high Kailash Mountain!'

The Devi's body filled with anger like froth from a boiling pot.
A rivulet of blood-red tears fell from Nanda's eyes.

The goddess shed red tears of blood: 'Oh, widow that I am!
My fortune has been ruined! Even birds can't live on Kailash!
There is no mouse's squeaking; no pleasant, sweet birdsong.
The birds don't ever sing here, and there are no buzzing flies.
For sleeping, only rough mats and for wearing, only leaves.
Shiva's ten-ton fire belches poison to the skies.
Sitting in my hut of leaves, I envy all the world.
How, O how, can I ever live on high Kailash Mountain?
How, O how, can I ever live in high Himanchala?'
(version five)

Nandadevi shows her destructive power when she is neglected. Her
tears result in a 'curse' (*dosa*): drought, epidemic disease and catastrophe
afflict her natal place, so that Hemant and the other sages are obliged to
perform a buffalo sacrifice in her honour. She is invited back to her natal
place, fed, honoured and worshipped, and then escorted back to her marital
residence atop Mount Kailash, and this is the mythical origin of her ritual
processions.[28]

Finally, we come to the story of Nanda's battle with the buffalo demon.
Like the cosmogony with which we began, it posits a reversed, disordered
state of affairs: the sexual desire of a low-caste son for his high-caste
mother; and like the cosmogony, appropriate relations are re-established
by a violent act of decapitation. The following is my synthesis of several
versions collected in 1984-86.

DEVI AND THE BUFFALO DEMON

Parvati was the daughter of Daksha; she was also a goddess,
and King Daksha had given her to Shiva. Once upon a time,
Shiva went wandering in the world, and she wanted to go with
him, though he warned her against it. But she was of the
stubborn caste of women, and insisted on going along.
As they were wandering, they came across a deep jungle
where wild men [*jangali manush*] raised buffaloes. A small
male buffalo had been born and they threw it in the jungle
just as Parvati and Shiva were strolling by.

Parvati said, 'Shiva, I will take this buffalo to Kailash,' but
Shiva replied, 'If we take him it will result in our misfortune.'
Parvati said 'No, he's just a small boy [*chota balak*].
I will rescue him and raise him.'

'Listen, Devi, you're being foolish!
He's neither pure nor very smart.
You never do a thing I tell you.
His caste is of a line of demons.
Tomorrow, Devi, having raised him,
He'll become a virile youth
He will be death's messenger!'

'Don't take such a bad road,' he told her.
'He is of a demonic caste; after we raise him,
he'll become our enemy. He will betray you.'

She said, 'Swami, I'll raise him myself.'
He said, 'How will you raise him? He needs milk.
I've said no.
Why do you insist on raising this buffalo calf?
You haven't any milk.'

Devi cuts her little finger,
And the milk comes flowing out.
Shiva says, 'Why should I raise him?'
Devi cuts her little finger,
Puts it in the young calf's mouth.
Devi says, 'How fine he is!
What a lovely, loyal child.
He's drinking milk. Be off, my Swami!
From my little finger, milk is flowing!'

On the way back to Kailash, Parvati had labour pains.
Now she was a mother. On the third day she had her
third-day bath; on the fifth day she had her fifth-day bath.
On the eleventh day she bathed again, called the Brahmins,
and had the calf's horoscope read.[29] They began his horoscope,
and said, 'Oho! He has quite a fiery name! His name will be
Madan Singh. His mother and father are of a demonic lineage.
He will marry his mother, and be his father's enemy. He will
be his mother's groom and his father's adversary.'

Then they had a great feast and worship.They fed the
buffalo calf, and he grew very large. He kept growing and
growing and growing, and when he was two years old,
he became infatuated with Parvati. He began to 'go to' her.

He said, 'Give me Devi Parvati in marriage.'
Shiva said, 'Parvati, I told you that day I wouldn't take
this child to Kailash, I wouldn't take him to my ashram,
that he would cause us grief and do something criminal.'

Parvati fell at his feet and said,
'O Swami, you spoke the truth.'

What did this buffalo calf do? He chased Parvati.
Parvati went ahead, and the buffalo went behind.
Running and running through all the jungles,
he shook Shiva's seat. He said to Shiva,
'I will sleep with[30] Parvati. I will make her my Lakshmi.
I will make her my woman.' Shiva became afraid.
He said to the demon, 'Listen, I will give Parvati to you.'
All the gods said, 'This goddess will be given to you.
She will be married to you, O demon Madan Singh.'[31]

Parvati was embarrassed.
She began crying, but the demon was happy
because the gods had given her to him.

The gods took out an ascetic's water-gourd along with
sixty-four swords, and make a *chakkar*[32] with sixty-four arms,
nine eyes and eight arms. They took Parvati into it, and then
they said to Madan Singh,

'O calf, you will do seven circumambulations of this altar
along with Parvati.'[33]
Then what did they do?
They bound him hand and foot with a rope.
The demon said, 'What are you putting on my body?'
They answered, 'We're putting on your wedding clothes.'

The calf became very happy, and
began to circumambulate the altar.
Devi was very embarrassed.

The gods conspired and plotted that there
would be seven circumambulations of this altar.[34]
The demon took Parvati's hand,
and they began to give her to him.
On that day, Parvati took incarnation as Mahakali.

She has sixty-four limbs, a sword in one hand,
skull in one hand, nine eyes, and eight arms.
From that day, Kali drinks the blood of this male buffalo.
From that day, in the form of Kali and the *puja* of Kali,
from that day the demon is killed, he is killed.[35]

In other versions, the buffalo demon is not tricked into being sacrificed,
but instead is destroyed by the goddess in battle. Here is a characteristic
example:

One day Narada went to Kailash. Gaura asked,
'Narada, where have
you come from today?'
He said, 'I've come from Andhapuri.'

She said, 'Did you go to my adopted son's
[the buffalo demon's] house? Is he well?'

Narada answered, 'Ha! You're calling him
your adopted son and
he is saying he wants to marry you!'
Narada went to Kailash from Andhapuri.

The demon said, 'Narada, where have
you come from today?'
Narada said, 'I've come from Kailash.'
He said, 'Did you see my mother Gaura? Is she well?'

Narada said, 'Ha! You call her
"mother" and she says,
"I sleep with that demon."'

The demon got angry and said,
'It's a dark thing, a cruel thing!
I am of the caste of demons—
I'll bring her here right now, on my shoulders!'
He headed straight for Kailash.

Gaura saw him from far, far off.
She said, 'Oh, God, is this Narada's scheme?'

She cooked a gecko and set it on the road
along which the demon was coming. She said,
'When he stops to eat it, I'll explain everything to him.'

She took down her pounding staff and began to pound rice.
When the demon finally reached there,
he saw the lizard on the road and said,
'Oho, I thought maybe Narada was lying, but he was
definitely telling the truth. This token is right in the path.'

He got even angrier.
He went over to where Gaura was pounding rice.
Just as he reached there, Gaura fled into her palace.
She said, 'Look, demon, don't come in here!
What are you trying to do?
Listen, O demon, what are you doing?
Listen, O demon, I speak from the heart.
I speak from my mind, O son I have raised . . .
Be quiet, son! You've become my enemy?
 Listen! Think! Understand!
I raised you! How have you become my enemy?
Stop! Don't do it! Don't believe those lies!'

She tried to calm him down but he went on into the house.
She said 'Don't come inside—this golden palace will be
ruined! Listen, think!'

He didn't pay attention to a word she said.
She warned him, 'I'll break your horn with this
pounding staff if you don't do as I say.
Do as I say! Why are you behaving like this,
because of what others say? Don't do it, don't do it!'

He didn't obey; he squeezed inside and
she struck him with the pounding staff.
One of his horns was knocked off.
New demons were born from every drop of blood that fell . . .
She girded her loins and rolled up her sleeves.
She bound her waist with a cloth and took the form of Chandi!
She was surrounded by demons.
She had a sword in one hand, a discus in another,
a trident in another, a pot of liquor in another,
and a skull in another.
She kept striking tens of thousands of their platoons,
kept striking and striking them. (version four)

The story of Nanda and the buffalo demon has a great deal in common with the *Devi Mahatmyam*, which is probably the most popular goddess-liturgy in India, and is the chief liturgy of Nanda's priests from Kurud. But similarities go only so far. In the *Devi Mahatmyam*, the goddess defeats lustful demons. She also defeats a buffalo demon, but the buffalo demon is not lustful, and the threat of sexual union between mother and son is not invoked. The latter theme does, however, occur in the myth of Andhaka, and the sheer number of Puranas—*Kurma, Linga, Matsya, Padma, Saura, Shiva, Skanda, Vamana, Varaha, and Vishnudharmottara*—in which the myth is found (O'Flaherty 1973: 360 n. 75), suggests its wide distribution and textual 'popularity'. However, Andhaka has a human and not an animal body, he has no substantial kin relationship with Parvati (who is his mother only because she is Shiva's wife), he is destroyed by Shiva rather than Parvati, there is no false wedding ceremony, and his death is his means to enlightenment, which is not so for Madan Singh.

So although they are similar to some Sanskrit myths, the vernacular songs of Nandadevi relate to a different set of concerns, one of which is to provide a mythical charter for the buffalo sacrifice, the central ritual of the cult. Taken together, myth and ritual address the same issues as did the comogonic story of Maya and her children. Like them, the goddess and the buffalo demon are mismatched in nearly every respect: she is mother and he, son; she is divine, he demonic; she is a Brahmin, he is of low caste; she is a person and he is an animal. The sexual longing of both Madan Singh and the goddess Maya is solved in the same manner: decapitation of the inferior. Told that he is to have his desires fulfilled and marry his mother, the demon is led to what he foolishly believes to be a wedding altar, tormented, and beheaded. Both Madan Singh and Maya seek unity, but what is required is division. Division is necessary in order to re-establish proper relationships, that is, to keep subordinated and separate that which is either demonic or female, and hence low.

In a literal and substantial sense, Gaura becomes the mother of the buffalo demon: she experiences labour pains after adopting it, and she nurses it on the milk from her finger. The relationship of giver to receiver of maternal milk is an emotionally charged one in Garhwal, and provides the rationale for local food taboos: people say that it is sinful to consume the flesh of a cow because cows are like mothers since people drink their milk. Local mutton-eaters are horrifed at the thought of drinking goat's milk, and the same reasoning accounts for the absolute prohibition against consuming the flesh of buffaloes, which, along with cows, are classified as 'big animals' and are therefore inedible.

With the exception of bears (which are thought to be the most 'like humans' of this group), wild animals such as deer, pigs, and mountain goats are not considered 'big'. Neither are domesticated goats and sheep which, as 'small animals', are regularly consumed—unless some person drinks their milk, in which case he would never eat their flesh. At bottom, these prohibitions depend upon the great value placed upon milk, both as a pure food and as a source of the mother-child relationship.[36] So strong is the relationship between givers and receivers of milk thought to be, that men abhor the thought of erotically fonding their wives' breasts. When I told them that men in my culture often do so, they were aghast, saying that this was like making love to one's own mother.

Although most local Harijans (Untouchables/Dalits) flatly deny that they or their ancestors ever consumed the flesh of sacrificed buffaloes, others maintain that they do or did. In fact, when one asks simply, 'Why are Harijans low?' one nearly always receives the same answer: 'Because they eat (or their ancestors ate) the buffalo.' Though I doubted such statements at first, eventually I came to believe them. My most reliable informants claimed to have seen it with their own eyes during childhood, and some Harijans confirmed that it was true. It seems likely that until the last generation, Harijans were trapped in a vicious circle: rarely able to afford meat, they were allowed and even expected to consume the flesh of the sacrificed buffalo. But this consumption was itself the reason for their untouchability, producing and reproducing it in the eyes of their higher-caste neighbours.

All this has now changed. Garhwali Harijans no longer consume buffalo flesh, and most of them vehemently deny that they ever did so. The change is probably the result of the Harijans' own efforts to alter their customs and attributes, and hence their ranking, a process that has been well-documented elsewhere in India (Marriott 1968: 164-66; Moffatt 1979: 54-55). But even if customs have changed, presuppositions have not. Whether the accusations are untrue and the Harijans never consumed buffalo flesh, or true and the Harijans changed their customs, the underlying assumptions are the same: You are what you eat; consumption of mother's milk establishes an asymmetrical, substantial relationship of mother over child; and to sexually or gustatively 'enjoy' (*bhogna*) a milk-giver's body is a sin characteristic of hot, backward, 'demonic' beings, vegetarianism being characteristic of cooler, *dharmik*, 'refined' beings. Thus the external change in food habits was structured or determined by a set of underlying and interrelated principles.

The Many Forms of Nanda Devi

Thus far our songs have depicted Nandadevi as a gentle young girl and supremely powerful goddess, as a modest wife and as a drunken, naked warrioress. Her military attributes are shared by innumerable Hindu goddesses, for instance, Mariyamman more than a thousand miles away to the south, who is challenged by several gods and a demon, none of whom can defeat her despite the fact that she is a young girl (Beck 1981: 94). But Nandadevi and Mariyamman are only two of many forms (*rupa*) taken by the goddess. One of her most virulent forms is that of disease, especially smallpox (Egnor 1984; Nicholas 1982), and measles (Garhwali *dadara*, Hindi *khasara* or *choti mata* [little mother]), which are regarded as her sign, and are hence considered auspicious. Even mental disorders are attributed to Kali, though never to major male deities such as Vishnu, Shiva or Krishna.[37] One villager said that each of the skulls on Kali's garland represents one of the forms she has taken.

In her songs, Nandadevi's *maya* is strategic: she creates hundreds of replicas of herself in order to deceive the buffalo demon, and these forms are increasingly terrible, sheer horror being another weapon in her arsenal. Her horrific aspect is illustrated by the experience of a neighbour of mine, a rather down-to-earth veterinarian. He told me that he did not go in much for fairs and spectacles, and from my knowledge of the man I would say that this was probably so. But a few years ago, he said, he heard of an oracle of Kali who actually drank the blood of the buffalo, so he went to the spectacle to see for himself.

> The buffalo's head was severed just over the *yantra*, as it is supposed to be. And the oracle laid down with his face right next to the gaping wound, and drank the fountain of blood gushing from it. It seemed to me that he drank gallons of it. Now, that may or may not be so, but when I saw his face smeared with blood, and the demon's eyes, my whole body trembled. I was entranced—I couldn't move.

Two aspects of this sceptic's commentary are quite illuminating. He points out that the sacrifice took place precisely over the *yantra*: from his perspective, a guarantee of its authenticity. And he refers to the goddess' eyes as those of a demon (*daint*), suggesting that there is a little to distinguish divine from demonic blood-drinkers.[38]

Such multiformity is characteristic of Hindu writing about goddesses, and to some extent of devotees' perceptions of them. In the *Devi Mahat-*

myam, Parvati emanates the fair-complexioned and beautiful Gauri, and
herself is left black and hence (by the usual Indian prejudice) ugly.
Discussing this episode at length, Coburn (1984: 154) concludes that the
text 'appreciates . . . the symbiotic relationship between these forms of
the goddess [and], her enormous metamorphic potential.' The goddess
may quickly change her attitude as well as her form: from kind and
benevolent to cruel and punishing. For instance, Nanda is said to have
become jealous when a village elder in Nauti established a new, vegetarian
yantra in her temple: villagers attributed a drought the following year to
her anger. Commenting on the same incident, one man said that the elder

> thought he was a real big-shot, bringing it in front of
> Nandadevi—he thought he could oppress [*dabana*] her, but
> she oppressed him. Since he stopped animal sacrifice, she
> has given him many difficulties—his wife died, he had a
> lousy son, and so forth. And he had been a great devotee!
> But you can't play with Devi's anger . . .

How can we account for the multiformity of the goddess? I suggest that
instead of regarding her many forms as 'contradictory', we think of them
instead as embodiments of different points in a female life cycle. She is
most benign as an unmarried, virgin girl, but with her sexual maturity, an
element of danger enters (particularly from a male perspective). So Nanda
is married, and her potentially dangerous sexuality and its attendant
energies are subordinated to her husband, Shiva. As a properly married
wife, she is much less volatile. The rituals of the wedding and the symbols
of wifehood strongly emphasize the 'binding' of her female energies. The
one proper, socially sanctioned outlet for them is the bearing of children.
Wife and mother together constitute the proper, auspicious forms of
womanhood in Hindu culture; together they constitute the overt, conscious
paradigm of the ideal female for most Hindus.[39]

Now, goddesses are never called 'wife', though fierce goddesses tend
to be called 'mothers' (*ma* or *mai* in Hindi). Thus when Nandadevi is called
Nanda Mai, as she often is, it is a clue that she is being considered in her
fierce aspect, as a threatening mother. This is the form she takes in our
songs, when she destroys her lustful son Madan Singh. Thinking that she
has been deserted by her husband, Shiva, Nanda voices her distress at being
a 'widow' before killing the demon. We can identify a third aspect of the
goddess here: a demonic, threatening, bloodthirsty aspect, uncontrolled by
a male and thus unable to contain her inherent *shakti*. Perhaps this accounts
for the anomaly that fierce goddesses who are called 'mother' (Durga, Kali,

Nanda) are often childless (Ramanujan 1986: 56). And just to add to the confusion, let us add one more paradoxical element: the erotic nature of these 'mothers'. Nicholas notes that the goddess Durga in Bengal 'is as sexually desirable to a man as only a greatly idealized woman could be—and, as his mother, she is sexually forbidden. Thus, the figure of Durga embodies elements of strong ambivalence' (1982: 198). Who is this seductive, threatening, childless 'mother'? Friedrich has pointed out that sexuality and maternity tend to be kept apart in most cultures, and suggested that this is because conjoining them would entail 'too great a concentration of power' (1978:187). This is a fair representation of the Hindu situation, where the very name of the goddess—*shakti*—means 'power'.

From grief-stricken creatrix to dependent child to dangerous adolescent to obedient wife to warrior-goddess, Nandadevi seems to represent all women at once; the sum of all female life cycles and possibilities; the union of male and female perspectives on femaleness, the synchronic apotheosis of countless diachronic histories. Her shifting forms are transitory and diverse manifestations of an underlying unity. Much the same is implied by a proverb frequently uttered by Garhwali men, that a woman is

Mother when giving food	*khate samay ma*
Genetrix during sex	*bhogte samay janani*
'Prosperity' when worshipping	*pujte samay lakshmi*
'Death' when quarrelling	*ladte samay kali*

In our songs, the 'illusory' and shifting nature of the goddess's *maya*, that is, her power of multiformity, is dramatically illustrated. According to version six, when she was about to fight the buffalo demon, she noticed a lot of liquor in Kubera's storehouse.

> She was tired and thirsty, and drank a large amount. She wiped off her sweat with her nails, and her entire skin came off along with the blood. This became many forms. Nandadevi became Chandika. Nandadevi cut off the demons' heads, and Chandika drank the blood from their necks. When only one demon was left, he begged for mercy. They wrapped him in a sari and tossed him over a cliff.

Here the distinctions between the goddess and the demon whom she opposes grow tenuous. She shows no mercy, and is black and ugly, literally bloodthirsty. Moreover, her *maya* is shared by the demon: every time he sheds a drop of blood a new, equally powerful demon springs from it. This episode is of course closely modelled on the story found in the *Devi Mahatmyam* (8:40 ff.); we also note that in that scripture, the chief of demons, Mahishasura, takes the forms of a buffalo, lion and elephant before Durga finally destroys him (3.29-33). At the beginning of this essay, I defined the goddess's *maya* as 'the power of multiformity'. Now we have come half circle, and are confronted with a demonic as well as a divine *maya*. There is little to.distinguish them as powers: the numerous replicas of Kali, created to drink the blood of the demon, are every bit as horrifying as the demon himself.[40] However, *maya* has to do with illusion and truth; our myth does not ascribe divinity to the most beautiful being, but rather to the most truthful, that is, the least changeful. In the end, and in response to the taunts and challenges of Nishumbha, the goddess resumes all forms into herself, saying, 'I am all alone in the world here. Who else is there besides me? See, O vile one, these goddesses, who are but my own powers, entering into my own self!' (*Devi Mahatmyam* 10.4-5).

Recall that in the *Devi Mahatmyam* Durga was created out of the 'powers' (*shakti*) or the 'lustre' (*tejas*) of all the gods. She used these powers separately, caused herself to become many in order to fight the demon's army, and, finally, in response to his taunts, resumed all the forms into herself. Out of diversity was constituted a unit, the goddess Durga. Now the name *Mahamaya* or 'Great Maya' is not only found in the songs of Nandadevi, but is also the first epithet employed in the *Devi Mahatmyam*, and is used to introduce this text in the *Markandeya Purana*, from which it is excerpted. This clue suggests that in some sense, the scripture takes the nature of *maya* as its central problematic. It concludes that the goddess Durga is *maya*, is herself the origin and end of all *mayas*. Note that as Chandika, she literally re-absorbs the dangerously fecund demon by consuming him. Again our text confirms a more general ontology: apparent opposition is illusory, only unity is true and real (*sat*). Coburn writes that it 'is precisely this point—the essential homogeneity of apparently heterogeneous forms—that lies at the very heart of the *Devi Mahatmyam*' (1984: 100).

The same point was once made by several of Nandadevi's priests, who explained to me that Kali and Nanda were the same goddess. I asked them how this could be so if—as they maintained—Kali accepted bloody sacrifice and Nanda did not. Three of them answered:

(first priest):

Form after form after form——she indeed is the one
who takes on forms
(*anek ruparupaya—rup dharan karne wali vahi hai*).

(second priest):

It's just like Brahma, Vishnu and Shiva are one being (*murti*),
but three gods. Here we sit at the temple, blabbermouths
(*baknewale*). If we go to get wood, we are wood-carriers
(*lakadihar*). If we go to the mill, we are millers (*ghatwal*).
If we carry the god's things, we are bearers (*dyobari*).

(third priest):

But each has his own inherent capabilities (*adhikar*).

    The idea is that form is not fixed and determinate, but rather fluid and
changing. Neither is it 'given' transcendentally by the gods, nor is it
specifiable once-and-for-all by mortal persons; rather, it is determined by
the actions of both divine and human beings. This is how the priests of
Nandadevi account for one goddess with multiple forms. At different
times, in different places and situations, she is called upon to perform
different tasks, and her various forms are the result of these shifting
contexts.

    But this is where theological and sociological interpretations collide. If
there is any sociological significance to the gender of a deity, as I think
there must be, then one cannot fail to note that whereas (mostly male)
theologians find it easy to collapse multiple goddesses into a single
goddess, it is not quite so easy with regard to the major gods of the
pantheon, whose cults have been for the most part historically distinct and
even mutually hostile.[41] If it is true that various forms of the goddess
represent different parts of the female life cycle, then the effect of conflat-
ing them is to deny the autonomy of the stages, to 'flatten out' and
essentialize an important culture representation of femaleness. Meanwhile,
a multiplicity of male gods is more generally accepted, thereby enriching
the representation of maleness. This is of course just what one would
expect in any male-dominated society. Just as the voices of the women
who sing Nandadevi's songs are ignored, so the multiplicity of female
experience is denied.

Notes

I would like to thank the Fulbright-Hays Commission and the National Science Foundation for generously funding my doctoral research in 1983-86, the Charlotte W. Newcombe Foundation for supporting the dissertation writeup, the Center for the Study of World Religions, and the Harvard Academy for International and Area Studies, under whose aegis I have written this essay. Parts of this essay have previously been published (Sax 1991). I am grateful to Oxford University Press to reprint them here.

1. From a tape-recorded interview with Devaram Nautiyal, a kind of publicist (*mahamantri*) for the goddess Nandadevi. The presumption is that most people would cease offering animal sacrifice before allowing such a cruel, blood-thirsty goddess as Chandika to enter one's home.
2. An important exception is Egnor (1984), who has explained the multiformity of Mariyamman according to Sanskrit and Tamil etymologies, where *mari* means 'death' or 'rain'. However, by a folk etymology, *mari* means 'to change', and *amman* means 'lady' or 'mother', so that the goddess is in fact recognized as the 'changing lady'.
3. This statement complements Bennett's argument about the 'filiafocal' and 'patrifocal' models of women, which she claims are opposed yet simultaneously extant in Nepali culture.
4. Fuller tries to skirt this problem by arguing that 'distinctions which are clear in ritual practice are not necessarily so clear in the thinking of ordinary people, who may be ambiguous about the identity of the deity who receives sacrifice' and cites Reiniche (1979:119) in support of his position. However this comes dangerously close to asserting that the outside observer knows what the natives are doing better then they do themselves.
5. In 1984-86, Dabar Singh Ravat and I recorded and translated eight versions of the songs of Nandadevi. Version number one was the most complete version recorded. It is sung annually by six or eight women of Nauti village for nine nights during Nandadevi's annual festival. The version translated here was about six hours in length, and was sung in the *Chandpuri* dialect of Garhwali by Shekhavati Nautiyal and Janaki Singh in October 1984. Version number two was sung at my request by Ghanashyam Gaud, a Brahmin priest of Nandadevi, in November 1984. Version number three was sung through the night during an annual pilgrimage in August 1985. In place of the cosmogony, it describes the rising and setting of the sun over the Himalayas. Singing was led by Subedar Sureshanand Gairi, a Brahmin. Version number four was related at my request by Bir Ram Jagariya, in Ghenti village about Garuda in Kumaon. Version number five was sung at my request by Lilavati Gaud. Version number six was partly sung, partly spoken, at my request by a professional *jagariya* of the Bhall caste of Bhotiyas, who performs it for patrons of the Tolcha and Marccha (commonly called Bhotiya) communities

of former nomadic traders with Tibet, now settled in the upper reaches of the Niti valley on the Tibetan border. Version number seven was recounted by a Tolcha from Lata village, in the Niti valley. Like the singer of version six, he requested that he not be named. It differs in several respects from all the other versions.

6. See Sax 1990 and 1991 for fuller discussions of the *dhiyani* in Garhwal.
7. The English word 'ritual' is meant as a translation of the Garhwali word *devakarya*, literally 'the work of the gods'.
8. The *Devi Mahatmyam* is also known as the *Durga Saptashati* or the *Chandi*, probably the most popular Sanskrit story concerning the goddess.
9. *maya*, 'wealth'. In Garhwali, *maya* means 'wealth' or 'material object(s)' as well as 'magical power'.
10. Here the term *Maya* is a female name. A pun seems to be intended, playing upon the several meanings of the word *maya*.
11. '[The one with] matted locks [who sits upon] a tiger skin', evidently a form of the great Hindu god Shiva.
12. Kaliya Lohar, an important mythological figure; ancestor of the ironworking Lohar caste; weaponsmith for the Pandava brothers.
13. The mountain (*giri*) of time/death (*kala*).
14. *Masi* is a root and *gigul*, a flower. Monier-Williams gives 'bdellimum or the exudation of *Amyris agallochum*' for gugulla/guggulu (1976 [1889]):356. My thanks to David White for pointing this out.
15. *Jagani jyoto*, a formulaic phrase used to refer to deities when they are moving across the landscape.
16. Bhrigupanth above Kedarnath was traditionally associated with suicide. See Dabaral (1965-78 vol. 4:413-414; vol. 3:476; Krsnadas 1957; Oakley 1905:150; Sax 1983; Sharma 1977:48.
17. Garhwali people of all castes know the songs of Nandadevi. When they are asked to sing her songs, or tell her story, they invariably sing about Gauradevi. As one of Nandadevi's priests put it,

> 'They join them together in many places in the songs:
> [*gitom mem anek jagah mila dete haim*]
> They're one and the same. They say "Gaura" in the waking-songs,
> and "Parvati" in the scripture. In the *Chandi* [*Devi Mahatmyam*]
> they call her Gauri, Navadurga, and so on.
> In our motherland [*matribhumi*], we say Bhagavati . . . There's a difference
> in language, but the main thing [*mul chiz*] is one. The image is in the temple;
> we fold our hands and go to see it. There are two or three doors, windows,
> and so on. There are lots of doors, but they all lead to the same place.'

18. The scientists at an agricultural research station in Almora reported that one of their greatest priorities was to determine ways in which local men could be induced to contribute to agricultural labour (Joan Erdmann, personal communication).

19. The term is a pun. The neologism 'sale of a virgin (*kanya vikray*)' refers to the traditional Garhwali brideprice wedding, which is the opposite of the normative wedding of the plains, *kanya dana* or 'the gift of a virgin' associated with dowry.
20. Uncontrolled fecundity seems to have had a major impact on the Hindu mythological imagination. See also n.40.
21. The village of Kurud is one of the most active centres in Garhwal for the worship of Nandadevi.
22. Compare Gatwood's (1985) theory of the 'spousification' of Hindu goddesses.
23. Interestingly, he addressed his small audience as the 'divine assembly of gods', echoing the slave girl's term of address.
24. *Bhat and bhado* are both terms of abuse for Brahmins.
25. *Pinda*, fine foods such as *pakora, dal-bhat,* and so on, are traditionally fed to livestock on the Garhwali festival of Bhagwali (Hindi *Deepavali*).
26. Feeding crows is auspicious, and is done on the festival of Makar Sankranti while reciting this verse:

> *le khava lagado mede bhalo dagado.*
> *le khava mashu, mede bhali sasu.*

(Crow, take this flat *pakora*, and give me a welcome companion (spouse). Crow, take this meat, and give me a welcome mother-in-law.)
Crows are also fed on Parvan Shraddha. On the festival day, people offer water (*tarpan*) and food to the ancestors. Food is offered to dogs and crows from two other containers.
27. *Patik*, from Sanskrit *pat*, 'to fall' (into hell).
28. According to another story, Nanda cursed the kingdom of Kanauj where her sister Vallabha resided, and Vallabha's husband, King Yashdhaval, was obliged to perform a pilgrimage to Nandadevi in order to obviate the curse (see Sax 1990 and 1991).
29. The sequence of purificatory baths and the summoning of a Brahmin to read the horoscope are all standard post-partum rituals.
30. *Gaman karunga*, lit. '[I] will go to.'
31. Mekhasur in the original. The demon is sometimes called Madan Singh, sometimes Mekhasur. This indicates that he was born in the month of Magh, and even now, Garhwali farmers take great care to ensure that no calf is born in that month. If by chance a male buffalo calf if born in Magh, it is immediately destroyed.
32. *Chakkar* (Sanskrit *chakra*), literally 'circle'. The *chakkar* is a circular *yantra* or geometrical representation of the goddess over which animal sacrifice is performed. During the ritual, the goddess is invoked and is believed to temporarily inhabit it.
33. These actions parallel the seven steps of the Hindu wedding ceremony. The demon is being tricked into thinking that he is to be married to Parvati.

34. Most Hindus believe that the seven circumambulations of the fire altar in the orthoprax wedding rite are the crucial act joining husband and wife.

35. Parts of this composite story were narrated by Ummid Singh, a professional storyteller, in response to my question regarding the origins of the buffalo sacrifice.

36. A Hindu calendar I once saw depicted a white cow labelled 'India' standing in the middle of the picture, from whose teats gushed several streams of milk, into the mouths of a Hindu, a Sikh, a Muslim, and a Christian. Equally the 'children' of Mother India, all gladly partook of her nourishing substance.

37. South Asia Seminar lecture presented by Mitchell Weiss at the University of Chicago, June 1986.

38. In Gujarat as well, to drink the blood of a sacrificed buffalo is to be filled with divine presence (Jain n.d.: 22).

39. Wadley characterizes the Hindu ideal of the wife as 'good, benevolent, dutiful, controlled', and of the mother as 'fertile, but dangerous, uncontrolled' (1977: 12, 125).

40. The idea of extreme, uncontrolled fecundity seems to constitute a particular nightmare for the Hindu mythological imagination. This is particularly interesting in light of the well-known propensity of Indian social forms—joint households, castes, political parties, religious sects, village power cliques, and so on—to cancer-like, uncontrolled multiplication.

41. I do not wish to ignore a certain monistic tendency in Indian religious thought, which often asserts that all forms of divinity are ultimately one. My argument is rather that on the level of specific deities, it is much more natural, easier and more common to assert the unity of the multiple forms of the goddess than it is to assert the unity of, say, Shiva and Vishnu.

References

Atkinson, Edwin T. 1974. *Kumaun hills: Its history, geography and anthropology with reference to Garhwal and Nepal*. Delhi: Cosmo Publications. First published in Allahabad in 1882 as *The Himalayan districts of the North-Western Provinces of India*.

Babb, Lawrence A. 1975. *The divine hierarchy: Popular Hinduism in central India*. New York and London: Columbia University Press.

Beck, Brenda E.F. 1981. The goddess and the demon. *Purusartha* 5:112-44.

Bennett, Lynn. 1983. *Dangerous wives and sacred sisters: social and symbolic roles of high-caste women in Nepal*. New York: Columbia University Press.

Bhattacharyya, Deborah P. 1984. Desire in Bengali ethnopsychology. *Contributions to Asian Studies* 18:73-84.

Brubaker, Richard Lee. 1978. The ambivalent mistress: A study of South Indian village goddesses and their religious meaning. PhD diss. Divinity School, University of Chicago.

Coburn, Thomas. 1984. *Devi Mahatmya*n: The crystallization of the goddess tradition. Delhi and Varanasi: Motilal Banarsidass.

Dabaral, Sivaprasad. 1965-78 (2022-2035 V) (eight vols.). *Uttarkhand ka itihas* [History of Uttarakhand]. Dogada, Garhwal: Vir Gatha Prakashan.

Daniel, Sheryl B. 1980. Marriage in Tamil culture: The problem of conflicting models. In Susan S. Wadley, ed., *The powers of Tamil women*. Syracuse: Syracuse University Press.

Davis, Marvin. 1983. *Rank and rivalry: The politics of inequality in rural West Bengal*. Cambridge: Cambridge University Press.

Dimock, Edward C. Jr. 1984. A theology of the repulsive: The myth of the goddess Sitala. In John Stratton Hawley and Donna Marie Wulff, eds. *The divine consort: Radha and the goddesses of India*. Delhi: Motilal Banarsidass.

Dumont, Louis. 1960. World renunciation in Indian religion. *Contributions to Indian Sociology* 4:33-62.

Egnor, Margaret (née Trawick). 1984. The changed mother, or what the smallpox goddess did when there was no more smallpox. *Contributions to Indian Sociology* 18.24-45.

Friedrich, Paul. 1978. *The meaning of Aphrodite*. Chicago: University of Chicago Press.

Fuller, Christopher J. 1988. The Hindu pantheon and the legitimation of hierarchy. *Man* 23:19-39.

Gatwood, Lynn E. 1985. *Devi and the spouse-goddess: Women, sexuality, and marriage in India*. Delhi: Manohar.

Gold, Ann Grodzins. 1988. Sexuality, fertility, and erotic imagination in Rajasthani women's songs. Unpublished manuscript.

—-.n.d. Story of creation (*arthav* given by *gujar barava*, Amar Singh, following reading out of *poti*). Unpublished manuscript.

Heimann, Betty. 1937. *Indian and Western philosophy: A study in contrasts.* London: George Allen.

Hiltebeitel, Alf. 1980. Rama and *Gilgamesh*: The sacrifices of the water buffalo and the bull of heaven. *History of Religions* 19.3:16-44.

Inden, Ronald, and Ralph W. Nicholas. 1977. *Kinship in Bengali culture.* Chicago: University of Chicago Press.

Jacobson, Doranne. 1977. Flexibility in Central Indian kinship and residence. In Kenneth David ed., *The new wind: Changing identities in South Asia.* The Hague: Mouton.

Jain, Jyotindra. n.d. Myths and rituals of the goddess and the buffalo in Gujarat. Unpublished manuscript.

Kielhorn, F. 1986. Pandukesvar plate of Lalitasuradeva. *Indian Antiquary* 25:177-84.

Krsnadas, Sri Gangavisnu, ed. 1957. *Kedarakalpa.* Bombay: Laksmivenkatesvara Steam Press.

Leslie, I. Julia. 1983. Essence and existence: Women and religion in Ancient Indian texts. In Pat Holden, ed., *Women's religious experience*, pp. 89-112. London: Croom Helm.

Liddle, Joanna, and Rama Joshi. 1986. *Daughters of independence: gender, caste and class in India.* London: Zed Books.

Marriott, McKim. 1968. Caste ranking and food transactions: A matrix analysis. In Milton Singer and B. S. Cohn, eds., *Structure and change in Indian society.* Chicago: Aldine.

——.1976. Hindu transactions: Diversity without dualism. In Bruce Kapferer, ed., *Transaction and meaning.* Philadelphia: ISHI.

McGilvray, Dennis. 1988. The 1987 Stirling Award Essay. Sex, repression and Sanskritization in Sri Lanka? *Ethos* 16 (2): 99-127.

Moffatt, Michael. 1979. *An untouchable community in South India.* Princeton, NJ.: Princeton University Press.

Monier-Williams, Monier. 1976 [1889]. *A Sanskrit-English dictionary.* Berkeley: Shambala.

Narayan, Kirin, 1986. Birds on a branch: Girlfriends and wedding songs in Kangra. *Ethos* 14(1): 47-75.

Nautiyal, Kusum. 1982. *Garhwali nari: ek lokgitatmak pahachan* ('Garhwali women: An Introduction from folksongs'). New Delhi: Sanmarg Prakashan.

Nicholas, Ralph W. 1982. The village mother in Bengal. In James J. Preston, ed., *Mother worship:Theme and variation.* Chapel Hill: University of North Carolina Press.

Oakley, E. Sherman. 1905. *Holy Himalaya: The religion, traditions and scenary of a Himalayan province (Kumaon and Garhwal).* Edinburgh: Oliphant, Anderson, and Ferrier.

Obeyesekere, Gananath. 1984. *The cult of the goddess Pattini.* Chicago: University of Chicago Press.

O'Flaherty, Wendy Doniger. 1973. *Ascetism and eroticism in the mythology of Shiva*. London: Oxford University Press.

—. 1980. *Women, androgynes, and other mystical beasts*. Chicago: University of Chicago Press.

—. 1984. The shifting balance of power in the marriage of Shiva and Parvati. In John Stratton Hawley and Donna Marie Wulff, eds., *The divine consort: Radha and the goddesses of India*. Delhi: Motilal Banarsidass.

—, and Brian K. Smith. 1991. *The laws of Manu*. London: Penguin

Ramanujan, A.K. 1986. Two realms of Kannada folklore. In Stuart A. Blackburn, and A.K. Ramanujan, eds., *Another harmony: New essays on the folklore of India*. Berkeley: University of California Press.

—. n.d. A creation myth in a folk Purana. Unpublished manuscript translated from the Kannada in July 1985.

Reiniche, M.L. 1979. Les dieux et les hommes; Etude des cultes d'un village du Tirunelveli, Inde du sud. *Cahiers de L'homme Ethnologique-Geographique-Linguistique*. n.s. 18. Paris: Mouton.

Sax, William S. 1983. The great departure. Paper presented to the International Conference of Anthropological and Ethnological Sciences, Vancouver, B.C., August 1983.

—.1990. Village daughter, village goddess: Residence, gender, and politics in a Himalayan pilgrimage. *American Ethnologist* 17 (3): 491-512.

—. 1991. *Mountain goddess: Myth, ritual, and politics in the Central Himalayas*. New York: Oxford University Press.

Sharma, Man Mohan. 1977. *Through the valley of the gods, travels in the central Himalayas*. New Delhi: Vision Books.

Shulman, David Dean. 1980. *Tamil temple myths: Sacrifice and marriage in the South Indian Saiva tradition*. Princeton: Princeton University Press.

Sircar, D.C. 1956. Three plates from Pandukesvar. *Epigraphica Indica* 31: 277-98.

Trail, George William. 1828. Statistical sketch of Kumaon. *Asiatic Researches* 16. Reprinted 1979, in Delhi by Cosmo Publcations.

Wadley, Susan S. 1975. Shakti: Power in the conceptual structure of Karimpur religion. Chicago: Department of Anthropology, University of Chicago.

—. 1977. Women and the Hindu Tradition. In Doranne Jacobson and Susan Wadley, eds., *Women in India: Two perspectives*. Columbia, MO: South Asia Books.

7

Oranges for the Girls,
or, the Half-Known Story
of the Education of Girls in
Twentieth-Century Banaras

NITA KUMAR

IN 1933 EACH girl in the Agrawal Samaj School was charged one anna as *chana shulk* ('fees for grams'), and was given, as convenient, chana and fruits at recess. Kind-hearted people like *deshratna* Babu Shivprasad Gupta's garden yielded oranges and other fruits that were also occasionally distributed.

The statement, tucked away in one of the many thick Agrawal Samaj magazines[1] I had been perusing, made me smile. Not because the fruit distribution was not an excellent idea; but because the pompousness of the declaration (*deshratna*—'jewel of the nation'—and 'kind-hearted' in this context) is in inverse proportion to the interest displayed in the first teachers of the school, the women's conference organized annually by them for the Samaj, and the school curricula and the response of teachers, students and guardians to it. The fact of the girls receiving oranges from a rich and patriotic man being more significant than most other facts about the students was an amusing comment on what is considered important in women's history, and also an indicator of the problems in trying to recover any section of this history.

I am interested in understanding how and what girls studied in early twentieth-century Banaras, and here I will carry out a partial investigation through the medium of three girls' schools. In Part 1, I look at Agrawal Samaj School, not so much to give a complete history of the institution as to outline some broad facts and alternative narratives. In Part 2, I look at Arya Mahila School, which had a woman founder who wrote voluminously, leaving no room for complaint of dearth of records. But she has been deified into a saint, a goddess, supposedly above 'worldly' concerns, and this represents the pattern of accommodation of many female activists within mainstream Banaras culture.

In Part 3, I look at Durga Charan Girls' School, reverting again to the 'problem of oranges', the question of what is being repressed when certain statements are made, and how that repression is actually a wielding of power, to construct, define, re-tell and authenticate. An additional theme that arises from the case of Durga Charan concerns the nature of the new curriculum chosen by the people of Banaras in the twentieth century. This new discourse of modernity itself succeeded, if not exactly in fashioning new individuals, at least in preventing a reproduction of the old. The plans of the founders and managers of all three schools regarding the socialization of their girl students were unsuccessful partly because of these larger changes in discursive formations. Men did not achieve the Indian-Western synthesis they rather vaguely (judged by their educational experiments) strove for; and nor, for largely the same reasons, did women achieve the Aryan-modern-educated mother synthesis.

There is little evidence to suggest that women received any kind of formal schooling in late nineteenth-century Banaras at all. The institutions where education was imparted—tols, pathshalas, vidyalayas, madrasas, and maktabs—were exclusively for boys. The three British-controlled or British-aided institutions that had been set up—Cutting Memorial, Jai Narain Ghoshal, and Sanskrit College—were all for boys. The only formal institution for girls that we have record of is a Normal School set up by the Anglican Missionary Society.

This is not to say that women were not (*i*) educated, (*ii*) trained, and (*iii*) learned. Literacy was imparted informally at home, by senior family members, sometimes to both boys and girls together, more typically separately to the girls, occasionally by semi-professional teachers such as a *panditayani* or a *maulani*. In many occupations, formal training was imperative (singing and dancing); in others, a more informal training (crafts, midwifery, housework). The former involved recognition of guru, school, length of training and level of achievement. The latter did not, but was nevertheless looked upon as systematic, rule-bound, demanding. Finally, there was a knowledge of the scriptures, mythology and the *shastras,* which most women had to a different extent, and which was acquired over many years from many sources, orally and informally.[2]

Given this, and given the absence of any girls' schools in Banaras, we can say that in the nineteenth century there was little worrying about what the new British system of education had to offer or was going to mean to girls. This attitude may be expressed negatively as a stubborn prejudice against education for girls. In 1885, 92 percent of the population of the then North Western Provinces and Oudh was quite illiterate, and one in 350 females received an education. In Banaras the number of girl students crossed the 1000 mark in 1924, and 2000 in 1932.[3]

In Banaras there was a marked resistance to British education on the whole. The testimony regarding Sanskrit College put this succinctly and brought out the contrast: the popularity of Sanskrit education demonstrated 'the maturity and strength of Hinduism' as well as 'the dense heathenism of the sacred city'.[4] Regarding girls, the government regretfully admitted that the people were unappreciative of official efforts, and 'did not want their girls to be educated.'[5] Their reasons, we may surmise, were partly the same as for boys—it was a foreign and 'meaningless' system—and partly peculiar to the status for females: the new education meant physically leaving the home; coming under the influence of unknown, mostly Christian teachers; and being socialized into norms that threatened social cohesion and the order of morality.

In the twentieth century there began, if not exactly a flurry of activity, some movement to mobilize effort for girls' education. This was typically within the *jati* structure, *jati* referring to the category not only of caste and subcaste, but of linguistic, regional and religious identity. Women—also a *jati* category—became for each such self-identified group a sign; and while the protected woman had been a sign of male superiority, she became within years the sign of male backwardness. It was the protected and also awakened, reformed and educated woman who was the new persona that had to be constructed. A similar agenda confronted men: how to remain rooted in tradition and also modernize, but there was for women a double leap to be taken since they were emphatically not regarded as the actors.[6]

The Agrawal Samaj School

The Agrawal Samaj, founded in 1896, registered in 1904, made not a sound about females at all in its first twenty-two years. It held regular annual meetings, worried about land and space, the appropriate orthodox rituals for its sons, the state of business (specially silk), space for its boys' school, and helping destitute members. Not a single resolution was passed in which women figured in any way. The exception was the noting and acceptance of a gift of Rs 12,000 by one Shrimati Jarau Kunwar, widow of Nanhe Babu, from the sale of her house. All the other donors of money for a school building, 22 in all, were men. Its membership grew from 6 to 98 in 22 years, keeping an average of 65 per year, and was, of course, strictly male.[7]

The Girls' School, Kanya Pathshala, is described as established in 1918, the twenty-second year of the Samaj. In retrospect, the history was seen in a different light:

> Fifty years ago when the English had made us their mental slaves in order to rule over us, it was laudatory for one man to get the kind of idea in his head that women's education was necessary, and that only an educated woman can bear such patriotic sons who will break the chains of slavery and construct a new nation. This pure and far-sighted goal inspired this school where today over 2000 girls receive an education and over the decades have influenced so many girls who are spread over all parts of the country, building up India.[8]

The founder was Satyanarayan Prasad Agrawal (1895-1931), and the school was merged with the society only four years later. 'With a lot of pleading, begging, and convincing, five girls got admitted to the pathshala . . . This school ran for many years with one teacher in the Harishchandra Peshwa temple at Sora Kuan [a dense lane off Chauk, the heart of the city].'[9] Damodar Das Shah was appointed in charge of the education of girls upon merger of the school with the society in 1922. With half a dozen girls, one teacher, and no building, it is not clear what he was exactly deputed to do. Whereas his name is present in each version of the Agrawal Samaj history, as is a complete list of all the secretaries in charge of girls' education from that date onwards, the first teacher who held the fort is unnamed, as seen in the reference just quoted. Apparently she was the same Jayanti Devi mentioned by Headmaster Jiwan Das in 1945 as the first headmistress.[10]

Only in 1950 was the foundation laid for the present building of the school near Town Hall by Seth Chiranji Lal Bajoria in memory of his mother, Shrimati Dakhi Devi. The building was completed in 1953. The only two ladies mentioned at all in the 'Golden Jubilee Souvenir' of the caste association are Dakhi Devi, in whose name Bajoria donated land, and Krishna Devi, the second headmistress. The latter, about whom nothing is told us but the name, was innovative and started an annual Mahila Sammelan ('women's conference') after the annual Samaj conference, but what this included or was like is also not described.

The Agrawal Samaj members are neither the first nor the last to be guilty of weighing the scales in the creation of their history—in this case in favour of the men who developed the ideas for service of their caste, those seths who lent or donated gardens or buildings (or oranges from gardens), and those who occupied various offices in managing committees. The term used is *shraddhanjali*, a tribute of holy respect, paid to forefathers. Against these, those ignored are the ones who taught, brought and returned students; organized the daily running of lessons; and, of course, permitted men to have the necessary leisure for all this public activity through management of the homes—the same management that led both males and females to claim when the question arose that women did not have 'enough time' for public work. I bring up this second point only because all the ideological literature produced by the education activists in Banaras is so saturated with identification of the woman as mother and housewife, that one cannot help but look for at least these mothers and housewives as one turns the pages of records of work done.

Some of the questions that remain unanswered today, largely because never raised in the massive records kept by the Samaj, deserve to be discussed:

(*a*) Was the Kanya Pathshala really a chance idea of Satyanarayan Prasad, or was there perhaps some demand for it from among women? Oral reports from women educated in the 1920s and 1930s suggest that it was girls who had to overcome resistance from guardians and neighbours, often through tears, vows, and hunger strikes.[11]

(*b*) Who were Jayanti Devi and Krishna Devi, the first two important teachers/headmistresses? When all those who contributed to the building up of the school are named: patrons, presidents, secretaries, departmental heads, members, assistants, donors—all hundred percent male—the names of these pioneering teachers are completely absent. Indeed, on the occasion of the Golden Jubilee celebrations, the category 'teachers' is simply not included in all the categories remembered and thanked for the school's progress![12]

(*c*) Whereas the Samaj pressed for 'education for good mothers', did not the teachers themselves, and the young students, and perhaps even some of the mothers/parents have the notion of 'education for employment'? Interviews with older educated women give us a picture of many of them, at least, conscious of education as a gateway to employment and not motherhood.[13] From the Samaj's own records we know that many of the girls were not from very

prosperous families,[14] so did they not need to work, even if they
did not wish to? The fact that education was free for certain girls
is made much of, again implying a low economic level; although
wealthy parents liked free education for their daughters too.[15]

(*d*) Was the shifting of the school from one inadequate building to
another not a reflection of the limited interest in the subject on the
part of Samaj members? Were they simply waiting for an appropriate donor to appear, even if it took thirty-two years?

When Bajoria donates land and/or money in memory of his
mother, thanks is given by the committee to Shiva, to the cooperation of the public, and to the continuous efforts of the
workers of the Samaj—but not to the woman whose qualities
must have inspired the donor (although the virtues of a mother
are always on the Samaj's mind), or the teachers and other workers who carried on the school, with 630 students by 1947, in a
temple garden, a home, a pilgrimage house, and the society office, in turn![16]

The sight of the building in Golghar today and its evident
self-importance immediately impresses with the notion that the
Agrawal Samaj has achieved great things in the field of girls'
education. And one hears echoes in the city of how 'good' girls
schools and colleges are, 'Agrasen, for example' (Agrawal
changed its name to Agrasen in 1967, after a government di-
rective to drop all caste nomenclature). But it took the Agrawal
Samaj fifty-four years after its inception to begin work on the
building, and they were the *richest* caste in Banaras. Not that
it may not have been difficult to raise funds, but one hears of
no fund-raising activity either.

What does the school being 'good' mean? Does it, or has it
ever, striven for greater freedom for girls, a better future, economic strength, professional training or outlook, career counsel-
ling, even education as to how to combine marriage with a
possible career? 'Good' in Banaras parlance signifies:

(*i*) Lack of indiscipline (*bandhs*, boycotts, protests, marches,
   demonstrations, riots) such as characterizes boys' schools;
(*ii*) An average to satisfactory pass percentage in High School
   and Intermediate;
(*iii*) A large attendance, with figures growing progressively;

(iv) A building, and, perhaps, endowment, both required for government aid and recognition.

When Agrasen received this aid in 1960 and opened its Intermediate section in 1961 (without science; that was to take thirty years more), 'people had, by that time, come to understand the necessity of girls' education'.[17] One might rather say, 'Agrawal Samaj had come to understand . . .'

(e) Linked to the question of quality is the issue of curriculum. As we shall see with greater clarity in the next section on the Arya Mahila School, the silence on this issue is perplexing with the weight given to producing/creating a certain 'type' of person. When the Kanya Pathshala started, it was a primary school with a curriculum similar to other Hindi pathshalas. Extra subjects were health education, religious education and art. English was introduced in 1931; class 6 opened in 1940, and classes 7 and 8 in 1941. Three years later we are told: 'Girls now sit for the Anglo-vernacular lower middle and Vernacular lower middle exams regularly with success.'[18]

When other subjects, such as sewing and music, were introduced, they had a chequered career; when problems with space, time or staffing arose, it was these 'extra' subjects that were dispensed with, never the government sanctioned ones. There is no information in the Samaj records about the nature of 'religious education' imparted; indeed, with the exception of the 'extra' subjects, there is no discussion whatsoever of curriculum. This is a problem that I have discussed elsewhere and that will arise again in our analysis of Durga Charan and Arya Mahila schools: however, we may evaluate the goal of these new government-model schools, the goal remained unattainable while the schools themselves marginalized what they considered 'indigenous' (subjects, rituals, physical layout) in favour of the modern and the progressive.[19]

The Agrawal ideology did not aspire to Western bourgeois notions of rights, freedom or equality; and stressed on the contrary inherited hierarchies, social bonds and mutual responsibilities (of siblings, spouses, hosts and guests, parents and children), envisioning a future where they would retain the best in these values together with an acquired veneer of Western science and knowledge. The ideological question that is of interest in this paper does not concern the strength of patriarchy and the techniques of incorporating women into this new schema of change, on which so much has been written already.[20] The ideological question of interest to us is, given that we have established that the conceptualizations of women that exist in the literature are men's conceptualizations, why do we continue to accept them, merely critiquing them, and exercising our interpretive capacities on them in various ways? A more difficult but useful exercise may consist of trying to recover alternate and dominated representations often invisible, always hidden. When the data are scarce, as is certainly the case with the women of the Agrawal School, we may simply have to develop alternate techniques of narrating or hypothesizing the past.

One interesting prejudice is that which trusts the written word above the oral one. Whereas the records of the Agrawal Samaj eulogize certain men, interviews with women activists of the past put the weight of choice, initiative, and effort on the women. An alternative narrative that may be constructed in the style of the *shraddhanjali* we have just quoted, if we were to take the oral testimonies as seriously as the written ones, would go as follows:

> And let us remember all those brave women who, as raw girls, had the courage to withstand the hateful comments and condemnation expressed by family, friends, and strangers; who often went hungry and undertook other painful penances to extract certain rights and liberties; who actually could dare to wear chappals and be stared at for doing so as they marched off to their schools. It was thanks to their steadfast efforts that the public in general and the men in the Samaj in particular slowly accepted them and developed a will to act.[21]

A related prejudice favours offices and titles above the unnamed work of those merely active but not bestowed with an office or title. In the education of girls women remain anonymous even when they are engaged in more important work than men. This is part of the larger objectification of women, where they are never directly addressed even when physically present, as they were at the school celebrations, and remain the third person, drained of any will to act. This is doubly ironic because unlike in, say, a reform movement, girls were not merely the objects of education but the very subjects—the teachers, the principals, and the inspectresses.

With this in mind, we could construct an alternative narrative with Satyanarayan Prasad Agrawal, the founder of the school, or Damodar Das Shah, the so-called manager, simply empty names or positions, and pay tribute instead to Jayanti Devi or Krishna Devi: how they sat together into the night and discussed plans, were fired with the need to act, developed ambitious ideas, and finally gave up everyday comfort and peace of mind to pursue these ideas . . .

To conclude, the history of Agrawal Samaj discloses the most obvious kinds of hegemonic activity at work, where no notice is taken of women's demands, expectations and activities, and no recognition is given to their work in building up the institution. Nor is it likely that they possessed the will or agency that we may attribute to them by simply replacing a Damodar Das as eulogized in the literature with a Jayanti Devi. Nor, given the division of labour in the family and the acceptance of it in general, was it likely that girls planned futures of autonomous work—when even for boys it was progressively clear that schools had no direct routes that led to jobs. Agrawal women were important in the reproductive process through the marriage links that united merchant communities across distances. They shared the ideology, worked within the cultural system, and did not seek to upset the overarching economic system with its formal and informal channels of socialization. Not only were they 'contaminated' by patriarchy and left the larger system unaffected in their notion of a small, private circle of autonomous action, they did not develop any perspective of planned action across time or space. But they certainly, even with their economic dependence on men, adopted many ways to act that were marginally permissible and that could lead to expanded spaces for action—such as, at the simplest level, by choosing to teach and to study.

II

Arya Mahila Vidyalaya

This school was the main project of the Sri Arya Mahila Hitkarini Mahaparishad established in 1912, itself an offshoot of the Bharat Dharma Mahamandal set up by Swami Gyananandji to combat the forces of change that were threatening 'the home of Aryan culture'.[22] The trust for women had two parts: the first, a widows' ashram with four sections: (*i*) to teach Indian music; (*ii*) to teach domestic science, crafts, religion and languages; (*iii*) to do propaganda for *varnashram dharma* and a domestic role for women; and (*iv*) to train Indian governesses who would be better than foreigners. It was against the re-marriage of widows and in reply to the question, if widows do not re-marry, how will they survive, the organization asserted that it could answer: if women want to survive, our organization has begun unparalleled work among widows with which they can happily manage. Those who want to be fallen of course cannot be helped by anyone in the world.

Then, to serve the cause of Hindi literature was started *Arya Mahila*, a quarterly, later a monthly. A series called *Vani Pustak Mala* was published to fill the vacuum of appropriate reading for women. The second part of the Mahaparishad consisted of a regular government-aided school for girls called Arya Mahila Vidyalaya.

The management of the organization was completely in the hands of *paramvidushi* and *tapasvani* (the very learned and saintly) Vidya Devi. A widow from Bihar, she came to Kashi around 1920-21, took initiation from the swami, learnt philosophy and the *shastras* plus the management of the different trusts from him. She demonstrated, according to the records, the absence of gender divisions in her activities.

Arya Mahila School was inaugurated in 1933, first as a primary school. In 1939, it was recognized as a high school by the Education Department, in 1947 as an intermediate college, and in 1958 as a degree college. By 1962 there were 1300 girls in all. What is special about the school is not its growth, but that from its records we have the most complete picture among all the schools of Banaras of the construction of a mechanism that would create a certain kind of individual. The list of problems with prevailing education was long, but revolved around the lack of realism in the curricula and the overt materialism of it. The solution of Arya Mahila School to this was to take over the existing model of the British school and re-charge it with a new spirit. We are fortunate in that Vidya Devi wrote copiously, usually in the journal *Arya Mahila*. Almost every issue of the journal saw her reiterating how much contemporary education was at fault. In contrast, the discussions of concrete schemes for action seem very feeble. Vidya Devi's technical suggestions consisted of: (*i*) the publishing of a series of books on Hinduism to be used in the classroom; (*ii*) special classes in religion; and (*iii*) 'stirring into' (their term) school life certain rituals, such as *yajna* and *puja*, religious discourses and speeches on annual functions and special occasions, as well as everyday transition rituals in the fields and classrooms.

The school journal in its articles quoted extensively from Manu and *Durgasaptshati*. It reiterated how there had been a great absence of efforts for centuries to rescue women *jati* from the great pit into which they had fallen. The kind of education given by Arya Mahila, by contrast, was appropriate for the 'true progress, welfare, pleasure and peace, and national development of a nation like India'. That nothing concretely was done is

evident from the wordy and abstract discussion on the subject in the
magazine, and the absence of any pedagogic suggestions.

The one suggestion that may be considered concrete were the classes
for religious instruction. These were arranged beyond and in addition to
the government syllabus and, as I have discussed elsewhere, would be
ineffective for that very reason.[23] All the subjects of the much criticized
government curricular were retained including the useless and despised
(as Vidya Devi rated them) algebra and geometry, and then the desired
subjects were taught as optional on top of these. All schools that were
interested in retaining religious instruction or teaching any other relevant
subject found that government regulations were such that there was no time
for extra subjects. Yet they persisted in introducing these new classes and
pretending that students could carry this double load.[24]

Apart from some rituals and the extra classes, Vidya Devi like other
educationists had no suggestions for her school. By contrast, the education minister K. L. Shrimali, talked at an annual day of the lakhs of
teachers and nurses needed by the nation. Similarly, Shri Prakash in a
1960 welcoming address, gave a speech with concrete ideas about how
education should proceed. Education for jobs was all right, said he, but
should not be such that girls run away from housework. The parents
had sacrificed the daughters' help at home and were giving them an
education. So girls should look after the home alongside. The organization they experienced in school was what they should emulate at
home, so that they became competent, and from managing the home
moved to managing the nation. Alongside, they should make efforts
towards good behaviour, civility and unity. There were many differences
in India of caste, religion, language and province . . . these must be
removed to create unity . . . 'I hope that your school will be helpful
in solving these problems'.[25]

There was not a whisper of such suggestions from the Arya Mahila
family. In 1943, even as the school was trying to get an intermediate
section, it was expressing disappointment with ever achieving any worth-
while result within the existing educational system.[26] Vidya Devi, however, was an unmatched fund-raiser. On one of her numerous trips, all
detailed in the magazine, she collected Rs 90,000 from Bombay; Rs 68,000
from Calcutta; and again Rs 76,000 from Bombay. Her donors were
typically Marwari and Sindhi seths: Khatau, Somani, Bhuwalka,
Kanaudia, Bajoria, and so on.[27] She collected the funds for the grand goal
of resurrecting the ideal of Aryan womanhood and motherhood, simultaneously preserved and expanded the institution based on the British

government model, and complained that achievement of the goal was impossible within this model.

The Arya Mahila School offers us the following conclusions about girls' education: it is the clearest case of a grand philosophy that fails for reasons of a familiar contradiction: the logistical problem of following a modern government syllabus and simultaneously breeding a new generation of Aryan mothers. The much trumpeted Indian culture to be transmitted by her school restricts itself, and that with mixed success, to art, music, dance and recitation, all described as 'optional subjects'.

In her own life, Vidya Devi preached one set of things but demonstrated the opposite: autonomous living, independence from men, free speech, self-dictated movement and action, political interests, and decision-making. In her voluminous writings, by contrast, her commitment to *varnashram dharma*, non-revision of a marriage age for women, opposition to property inheritance for them, and even a pro-sati position was very striking. Why does she, and indeed other women like her, who are seemingly active agents in their own lives, consistently promote male ideology? Because they are contaminated, as we know, by patriarchy. Because they wish to be accepted within the system, and adopt what seem to them the only permissible ways to be active. But also because of their economic dependence; even for a widow with no private ambitions, it is men who are the donors for her public work.

Arya Mahila's is the case of the most disguised patriarchical ideology in so far as its spokesman was always a woman who speaks throughout in a male voice. As with Agrawal Samaj members, she recognizes no female assistants, except one Sundari Bai who is given passing mention. She never includes, in her descriptions of the school, praise or recognition for active female co-workers like teachers, or even ever addresses her staff or students directly. Given the pattern and the weight of her fund-raising, we may question if hers is not in fact the voice of her male donors.

While emphasizing the need for the training of widows, and girls in case they become widows, there is no articulation of a need to work. Only the speeches of Shrimali and Prakash broach the issue and highlight the absence of it in Vidya Devi's many writings. Yet, it would seem that Vidya Devi was ideally placed to argue in favour of training or qualifying women to work, being the accepted and recognized independent activist that she was. Why she did not do so must have had something to do with her own philosphical proclivities, her calculations of success on her impressive fund-raising ventures, and her assessment of what was possible to assert even for an independent widow with a strong personality.

That Vidya Devi was referred to as an ascetic and eulogized for being 'other-worldly' precisely when she was busy and successful in worldly affairs is really the key to the paradox. As an ascetic she had a freedom to travel and interact that was totally denied to ordinary women. Her management of the school and the other ventures of the Trust could be explained as deriving from her dedication to the cause of her guru, Swami Gyananandji. Her orthodoxy reinforced the image of religiosity, and her strength and perseverence in building up the school could be attributed to the concentrated energies achieved by her austerities.

There are no grounds for imagining that the role of an ascetic was imposed on Vidya Devi by her male peers or that she was merely the victim of a certain discourse. On the contrary, there was a very constraining discourse of woman as *grihastini* ('homemaker') that she escaped. This totally dominating discourse specified the 'place' of women in the private, internal domain, and the role of women as mediators and transmitters, including the role as the necessary reproductive link. A woman's dharma, in this discourse, consisted of service, by which she became heir to the fruits of all those karmas that men sought through ritual, gifts and meditation. But what then of the widow who was unable to follow this single path of acquiring merit through service to her husband? On the one hand, she was inauspicious; the discourse of widowhood was a coercive weaving of knowledge and power that tied the individual to an identity in a constraining way. But on the other hand, her 'otherness' rested on an ambiguity that could get re-constituted as a space.

For the widow was available what I have called elsewhere the larger Hindu discourse of '*atma*-development'. Freed from the duty of *pati-seva* ('service to the husband'), which would have been consensually ranked as first among duties, a widow could engage in that series of actions that led to control over one's physical self, and gross energy became transformed into spiritual power. This could include learning or not learning from a guru, practise or not practise of certain rituals; but the basic components seem to have been the solitude of bereavement and a deliberately cultivated lifestyle of strict austerity. Vidya Devi, like many other educationists in Banaras who were widows, was often described with reference to her lifestyle characterized by vegetarianism, early rising and early retirement to bed, plain and coarse cotton clothes, sleeping on hard surfaces, and giving *darshan* ('sight of herself'), with difficulty. She, like other activist widows, was referred to as 'saint-like' and 'goddess-like' (of *satvik pravriti* or *devi swarup*). While the scope and impact of her public activity matched that of any male public figures in Banaras, her image was completely fashioned by this aura of 'other worldliness'.[28]

I am inclined to consider this as an instrumental technique adopted by widows like Vidya Devi rather than as a victim role imposed upon them by male normative discourse partly because it was so successful. Within Hinduism of course such 'sainthood' with its discipline is regarded as an instrumental technique that almost guarantees success in whatever goals one sets oneself. But in the public world as well, success was possible by this effective deployment of the symbols of sainthood. The 'saint' achieved a freedom of movement and expression, of interaction and opinion that totally escaped from the constraints of the prevalent gender discourse.

Of course these widows worked within existing institutions to consciously uphold the traditional bulwarks of society, and some, like Vidya Devi, championed the new orthodox anti-reformist Hindu (male donors) discourse to an extreme. It is their action we must judge them by, and the consequence of their moderate liberal action was a radical one. Institutions like Arya Mahila School were a radical departure from the kind of private schooling an older generation had received at home. By working firmly within the government model, never challenging any of the principles behind curricula or school rituals at all, trying merely to mix some more 'indigenous' practices with them, which had limited success, Arya Mahila in fact permitted girls to shake off in many cases the *grihastini* discourse and choose alternatives for themselves.

III

Durga Charan Girls' School

Little is known about the founder, Krishna Bhamini, a widow, except that she came from Calcutta not as a 'deprived' woman, that is, a child widow from an unconsummated marriage, or penniless, or friendless. She was one of those once-happy women who were 'highly charged with nationalism and independence'[29] and wanted to teach other widows, to read, for example, so that they kept fruitfully busy, by reading, say, the *Ramayana*; and to work by hand. Thus was a new school started with free education and a syllabus half-academic (English, mathematics, history) and half-vocational (weaving from rags).

This widow had company in that from the 1920s on there came to Banaras widows who did not take their widowhood as a burden to be merely lived with. Some were from Vivenakanda's Sister Nivedita

School in Calcutta; one outstanding example was Basumati Ma, who came around 1907, and was famous as the author Banga Lalana. Krishna Bhamini was also a student of this institution. In 1918, she started a school with three girls in her father-in-law's house in Ramapura. Upon her death three months later, Hemangini Guha, about whom nothing is written in school records and who is not even mentioned by the manager in 1945, continued the school in another house and called it Krishna Bhamini Girls School. In a few years it had grown to class 6. It was the first such institution where 'Bengali girls could receive proper education in their mother tongue'[30]—at a time when other communities had no arrangement for girls' education at all.[31] A nationalist, Hemaprabha Majumdar, together with Hemangini Guha, renamed the institution Vivekananda Vani Bhawan Krishna Bhamini Balika Vidyalaya and had it registered in 1924. It was recognized in 1931 as Anglo-Bengali Lower Middle Girls' School.[32]

At this point a discrepancy occurs in the school's records: 'some noble-minded gentlemen' are supposed to have worried about the poor condition of the institution and adopted the cause of education. Their association, Nari Shiksha Vidhayani Sabha, took up the school and amalgamated it with the Brojo Sundari Bayan Vidyalaya and then renamed it Vivekananda Vani Bhawan.[33] This latter version could be placed in doubt because it is the manager himself talking about noble-minded and efficient management, and because the women ignored by him are mentioned in both oral reports and in most of the contemporary write-ups.[34]

To continue with the history, the Municipal Board gave a monthly grant from February 1924 onwards, Rs 20 growing to Rs 150, till it was directly recognized in 1931. A prosperous and religious Bengali businessman, Durga Charan Rakshit, lived in Sonarpura, busy with his Shri Ghi business in Calcutta and his religious life in Banaras. He died in 1937. His son Ashok Chandra Rakshit came to Banaras; the latter's wife was equally religious, donating beds to Anandamayi's hospital, books to the library, and building a temple; and they decided to donate Rs 20,000 to the growing school. Durga Charan had apparently been very keen on education, and had had all the girls in his family educated, initially at home and then in school—and permitted them to wear chappals.[35] In October 1937 the school was renamed Durga Charan Girls' School. Of the sum donated, Rs 12,000 was used to acquire land through the Land Acquisition Dept.[36]

The ideology of Durga Charan is nowhere spelt out as precisely as of Arya Mahila or Agrasen. It is clear that its earliest founders, the widows, were motivated by a spirit of nationalism combined with self-help. The managing committee that took over, completely male, emphasized the progress of Bengali girls, and sought support from within the community of Bengalis. There are no names of Marwari, Gujarati, Marathi, or any other donors or activists in the Durga Charan annals, as there are none of Bengalis in the records of Arya Mahila or Agrasen. Of the three schools we may say that Durga Charan was the least concerned with religion, social orthodoxy or a return to the Vedas. We might further connect this to the nature of the Bengali community and their connection with the bhadralok experience in Bengal.

Two pieces in its journals give clues to the ideology of Durga Charan. In the 1988-89 annual number of the school, the principal, Archana Ghosh, begins her piece on 'Women's Education' with:

> Ma. There are so many feelings embedded in the very word. She is both the giver of *shakti* and the giver of *mukti* [power and freedom]. Mercy, pity, sympathy, and other such feelings are contained in this word. She gives *shanti* [peace] as well. So, right from ancient times women were considered a form of *shakti* and were worshipped. A Russian writer has praised the importance of women in these words: 'You give me 60 mothers, I shall give you a good nation . . .'

The article continues by describing the fall of women—'who can stop the wheel of time?' Many women are in high positions today. About Indira Gandhi it was said, 'She was the only woman in her Cabinet'. Ghosh proposes eleven solutions to give equal opportunities to women in all spheres of life so that India may be ranked with the progressive nations of the world. The first ten deal with villages. The last is an open suggestion criticizing society for thinking of women only or primarily as housewives, even when they have careers—a 'dual mentality' that must be removed. As we move towards the twenty-first century 'it is the call of the times that women should get the same freedom as men to get an education and choose an occupation according to their interest and ability'.[37] In the light of this closing suggestion, the opening lines seem as compulsory lip-service to a dominant ideology, reflecting, in feminist terms, 'the oppressor within each of us'.

In the 1972-73 number, Kamala Tonape, lecturer in Hindi, in an article called 'Indian Women's Education' goes through the usual history of Vedic greatness and decline under the Muslims, and then suggests ways of improving a defective educational system. Girls need more training as mothers and housewives, a statement supported by an anecdote about a newly married graduate who was unable to whip up delicious enough halwa for her husband's guests, because she followed the recipe from a book! Among her suggestions for curriculum reform are: one or two discussions per month should be organized by Indian history and language teachers on matters of culture. Books should be fewer and courses more concise so that students have time for other activities leading to physical and mental development. Some institutions such as Karve University, Pune, and Prayag Vidyapith Vanasthali have tried to make their curricula more relevant. But they cost a lot and ordinary people cannot go there. So it is the duty of the government to improve the system. Only in this way can the state get women's full and successful contribution.[38]

This plea, this despair, was shared as we know, by all the three institutions we have looked at. At one level, then, the ideology espoused by the institution is almost irrelevant—the grandeur of motherhood (Agrasen), Vedic glory (Arya Mahila), or regional cultural nationalism (Durga Charan)—as long as it served to increase attendance. The net result was the same: girls educated in a government-controlled system.

What the case of Durga Charan particularly brings out is the following. In the Durga Charan records, although the founders and principals are mentioned, the manager's returns of 1945 suggests an actual conflict. As in the case of the other two schools, we do not have the records kept of activism or of female consciousness. But not only do we have cracks in the data to reveal that it must have existed, we also have an obvious contradiction that gives evidence of the suppression of one perspective in favour of another. Interestingly, in an 1986 book on *Bengal and Varanasi* there is no mention of any Bengali woman except for Mallika, the paramour of Bharatendu Harishchandra, and the legendary Rani Bhawani.[39]

As we see from the contemporary extract just quoted, the bottom-line argument in favour of girls' education has throughout been: these are the future mothers of our country. It receives slightly different emphasis in each case. For Agrasen, a few words are used: a few popular quotes from Manu clinch the argument. Arya Mahila is the most stridently missionary in its revived Hinduism. It has the best propaganda machines, intellectual representation, and consistent philosophy. Durga Charan is silent on the subject as a rule, but uses no alternative discourse.

If we think of the many ways that gender hierarchies are constructed, legitimized, and maintained, it is the *varnashram* and *jati* discourse in Banaras that presumes a woman to be constituted by birth as a separate *jati*. Anyone who knows Sanskrit seems to be able to confirm this. Durga

Charan spokespeople rarely quote any Sanskrit. It is further maintained
with the ways that production is organized. Here we see that Agrawal
women play a very clear-cut role as resources for creating alliances and
reciprocity between families, and keeping linkages interact. Bengalis have
been a diverse group, mostly professional, and though preferring marriage
and a quiet domestic role for their daughters, wished to provide insurance
against their late or non-marriage. Finally, who challenges the discourse?
Those who know Sanskrit, as I have shown elsewhere, and can quote
examples of learned and free women in the 'past'. Those who are smart
enough to cite the case of *viranganas, bhakti and shakti*. And those who,
like the Durga Charan female activists, at least named, and the Agrawal
activists, totally invisible, cite nothing, but simply do.

Conclusion: In Search of Our Female Subject

Is there any such category as women? The question stands for me as an
empirical one that I have answered here only tentatively. To report on any
phase of the history of modern Banaras, including that of women, is to go
to the Marwaris, the Agrawalas, the Khatris, the Bengalis, the Yadavs, and
so on. This community-based approach that I adopt does not overrule the
possibility that just as men in Banaras have displayed a self-conceptuali-
zation of being men, both as members of *purush jati* (the *jati* of men), and
as regional and historical identity, neither of which precludes class and
caste-based institutions; so may women display a conceptualization of
themselves as 'women'. My data show that regardless of whichever
community or institution they belonged to, women worked within a
categorization that represented them through negation, repression and
opposition.

We face two important difficulties with the representation of women.
One is the empirical one of knowing what in fact they were doing or
thought they were doing when not fitting in perfectly into the suspiciously
watertight discursive structure of housewife and mother. Were they on
hunger strikes as our oral reports tell us? Pleading and begging for the new
experience of public education? Quietly resentful but unable to speak or
act? Simply indifferent?

The second difficulty lies in the discrepancy between the justification
for action by women that we have in the literature and the nature of
the action itself. Education seemingly fits into the reproduction of motherhood, and the category of 'mother' encompasses all women in the
dominant discourse. Yet most of the school founders and teachers were
not mothers, but were either widowed and childless, or unmarried, or

separated and alone. This internal differentiation within the category 'mother' is never mentioned, even obliquely, even by an institution like the Arya Mahila which had set up special services for widows. Most founders and principals who were non-mothers were relegated to, and adopted, the role of ascetics, that is, in a sense, neither male nor female, beyond gender and other worldly distinctions.

While this indicates a positive self-evaluation on the part of women, as well as politically astute handling of cultural givens, it also indicates a satisfaction with the larger hierarchy. Women as ascetics, or even simply persons of service to larger causes than families, were able to gain respect and broaden significantly their circles of autonomous action, even if the structure of patriarchy remained unchallenged. And this points to the crucial, fundamental contradiction in women's efforts to act for themselves: their actions could be radical, but the representations of them were always as merely liberal or more typically as conservative ones.

The contradictoriness of women's position was increased by the nature of schooling as it developed in the colonial situation and continued in the postcolonial one. Schools in twentieth-century Banaras were expected to create a new individual who retained the best in Indian culture while acquiring necessary Western knowledge, and girls' schools were supposed likewise to perform a similar feat of cultural engineering. The two aims, as I have maintained here, and expanded further elsewhere,[40] were incompatible in the way they were tried. They were incompatible partly because incompletely conceptualized, being based on inadequate constructions of the past. And partly because of a pedagogic problem: an expanded curriculum set by the state to be further burdened by additional subjects set by a school committee that had no comparable legitimacy. How did schools, as a result, cope with the conflicting demands of society? They did not. Which was a fortunate result for women in so far as they had not had audible voices to begin with, and after the modern schooling such as offered by Agrasen, Arya Mahila and Durga Charan, they had expanded spaces for action but still no voices.

Notes

A shorter version of this paper was presented at the faculty seminar at the Centre for Studies in Social Sciences, Calcutta, in March 1992. I would like to thank all the participants at the seminar for their comments.

1. *Sri Agrasen Kanya Vidyalaya Swarna Jayanti Smarika.* 1972 (Sri Agrasen Girls' School Golden Jubilee Souvenir). No pagination; my page number 40 (All references henceforth from this volume have my pagination.)
2. On indigenous education and nineteenth-century institutions see Nita Kumar (forthcoming) *School curricula in twentieth-century India.*
3. *Selections from the vernacular newspapers published in the Punjab, North West Provinces, Oudh, Central Provinces, Central India, and Rajputana.* 1885. vol. 18; *Annual Administrative Report* of Banaras Municipality, 1910-11.
4. Sherring 1863:. 163; 1884: 174.
5. File V/26/860/11 (India Office Library).
6. See Kumar 1991a; also Kumar in Crook, ed., *Education and transmission of knowledge* (forthcoming).
7. Sri Muraridas (headmaster), ed., 1918.
8. Rajkrishna Das 1972. In *Swarna Jayanti Smarika,* p.4.
9. Ibid., p. 13.
10. Sri Jiwandas 1945.
11. Interviews with Leela Sharma, August 1991 and February 1992.
12. *Swarna Jayanti Smarika,* p. 43.
13. Kumar 1991b.
14. *Swarna Jayanti Smarika,* p. 43.
15. File No. V/26/860/11 (India Office Library).
16. *Swarna Jayanti Smarika,* p. 41.
17. Ibid.
18. Ibid.
19. See Kumar in Nigel Crook, ed. (forthcoming) *Education and transmission of knowledge.*
20. See Uma Chakravarti, Partha Chatterjee and Lata Mani in Sangari and Vaid, eds., *Recasting women: Essays in colonial history,*1989.
21. Many ladies have told me of the radical departure from custom that wearing chappals in public constituted; it seems to have been symbolic of an assertion of freedom comparable to not covering the head. Leela Sharma, October 1990; Swati Rakshit, great niece of Durga Charan Rakshit, August 1991.
22. *Shubhabhindan patra* (An auspicious welcome address), 14 December 1986, from the members of the Arya Mahila family to Vidya Devi.
23. Kumar in Nigel Crook, ed. (forthcoming) *Education and transmission of knowledge.*
24. Ibid.

25. *Arya Mahila* 1941.
26. *Arya Mahila* 1945.
27. Ibid.
28. Kumar 1991b.
29. Interview with Amitabh Bhattacharya, social activist and journalist, August 1991.
30. A short history of the Durga Charan Girls' School, Banaras, from the Manager's Returns file, 1945.
31. *Arghya*, Durga Charan Girls' School Magazine 1985.
32. Ibid.
33. A short history of the Durga Charan School.
34. *Arghya* 1985.
35. Interview with Swati Rakshit, August 1991.
36. Manager's Returns file, 1945.
37. *Arghya* 1985.
38. *Arghya* 1972-73, p. 17.
39. Ram Dular Singh, *Bengal and Varanasi; A study in cultural synthesis and national integration*, 1986.
40. Kumar in Nigel Crook, ed. (forthcoming) *Education and the transmission of klnowledge*.

References

Arghya. 1972-73. Durga Charan School Magazine.

Arghya. 1985. Durga Charan School Magazine.

Arya Mahila. 1941. 23,10:633-37.

Arya Mahila. 1945. 26, 6-8: 39??

Banaras Municipality. 1910-11. *Annual Administrative Report*.

Chakravarti, Uma. 1989. Whatever happened to the Vedic dasi? In Kumkum Sangari and Sudesh Vaid, eds., *Recasting women: Essays in colonial history*. Delhi: Kali for Women.

Chatterjee, Partha. 1989. The national resolution of the woman question. In Kumkum Sangari and Sudesh Vaid, eds., *Recasting women: Essays in colonial history*. Delhi: Kali for Women.

Das, Rajkrishna. 1972. In *Sri agrasen kanya vidyalaya swarna jayanti smarika*, p.4. Varanasi: Srivilas Gupta.

Jiwandas, Sri. 1945. *Sri kashi agrawal samaj ka ardhashati itihas 1895 se 1945 tak* ('Five decades of history of the Kashi Agrawal Society from 1895-1945'), p. 12. Kashi: Sri Kashi Agrawal Samaj.

Kumar, Nita. 1991a.Changing education and the stubborn work concept in the Banaras silk industry, 1880-1930. *Purushartha* 14: 315-38.

—. 1991b. Widows, education and social change in twentieth-century Banaras. *Economic and Political Weekly* 26, 17:WS19-WS26.

—.(forthcoming) Ritual and religion in Indian schools. In Nigel Crook, ed., *Education and transmission of knowledge*. Delhi: Oxford University Press.

Mani, Lata.1989. Contentious traditions. In Kumkum Sangari and Sudesh Vaid, eds., *Recasting women: Essays in colonial history*. Delhi: Kali for Women.

Muraridas, Sri. 1918. *Sri kashi agrawal samaj ke pratham bayis varshon (1894-1917) ka sankshipt vivaran* ('A brief history of the Sri Kashi Agrawal Society's first twwenty-two years'). Banaras.

Selections from the vernacular newspapers published in the Punjab, the North Western Provinces, Oudh,the CentralProvinces, Central India, and Rajputana, 1885, vol. 18.

Sherring, M.A. 1863. *Benares and its antiquities*, p.163. Benares: Medical Hall Press.

—. 1884. *The history of Protestant missions in India*, p.174. London: The Religious Tract Society.

Singh, Ram Dular. 1986. Bengal and Varanasi: A study in cultural synthesis and national integration. Calcutta: Bibilographic Society of India.

Sri agrasen kanya vidyalaya swarna jayanti smarika ('Sri Agrasen Girls'School Golden Jubilee Souvenir'). 1972. Varanasi: Srivilas Gupta.

List of Contributors

Leslie A. Flemming   Department of History, University of Maine

Ann Grodzins Gold   Department of Anthropology, Cornell University

Patricia Jeffery and Roger Jeffery   Department of Sociology, University of Edinburgh

Nita Kumar   Fellow in History, Centre of Studies in Social Sciences, Calcutta

Gail Minault   Department of History, University of Texas

Gloria Goodwin Raheja   Department of Anthropology, University of Minnesota

William Sax   Department of Philosophy and Religious Studies, University of Canterbury

Index